STRESS AND EMOTIONAL HEALTH

Applications of Clinical Anthropology

JOHN A. RUSH

AUBURN HOUSE
Westport, Connecticut • London

Library of Congress Cataloging-in-Publication Data

Rush, John A.
    Stress and emotional health : applications of clinical
anthropology / John A. Rush.
        p.   cm.
    Includes bibliographical references and index.
    ISBN 0–86569–290–4 (alk. paper).—ISBN 0–86569–291–2 (pbk. :
alk. paper)
    1. Cultural psychiatry.   2. Ethnopsychology.   I. Title.
RC455.4.E8R87   1999
616.89—dc21   99–11414

British Library Cataloguing in Publication Data is available.

Library of Congress Catalog Card Number: 99–11414
ISBN: 0–86569–290–4
        0–86569–291–2 (pbk.)

First published in 1999

Auburn House, 88 Post Road West, Westport, CT 06881
An imprint of Greenwood Publishing Group, Inc.
www.greenwood.com

Printed in the United States of America

The paper used in this book complies with the
Permanent Paper Standard issued by the National
Information Standards Organization (Z39.48–1984).

10 9 8 7 6 5 4 3 2 1

Contents

Figures and Tables

FIGURES

TABLES

Preface

Stress, as experienced by living organisms, is a product of information. This information comes in many forms. It can be information intrusion, as with viruses, bullets, and unkind words; it can be information loss, such as when blood is lost or a loved one dies. It can also be information alteration, as is the case when poor nutrition leads to an alteration in hormonal functioning or when a person changes his or her job and has to adapt to new circumstances (see Rush 1996 for other informational categories). Through analogy the reader can see that bullets, bacteria, unkind words, and unsettled events all lead to stress.

This work is about the way we communicate and how our interpretation of the messages from others, life events, and health issues leads to stress reactions, or mechanisms to reduce unpleasant stress. This emotional stress, through a suppression of the immune system and a general loss of regulation of the body's physiology, is a primary factor in emotional/social and physical health because it interferes with healing in an overall sense.

In this work the reader will discover a very different way of looking at and thinking about emotional and physical stress; the approach taken is informational and anthropological. Through this approach the reader will discover numerous techniques—incantations, if you will—designed to help clients place different meanings onto messages, both historical and current, for the purpose of stress reduction and enhanced healing.

We are all counselors and therapists; we are also demons and each other's worst nightmares. This all comes about through the way we communicate. For the most part, through a process called enculturation, we learn our language. While we are learning a specific language—for example, English—we also learn the style of language use from those around us: our parents or caretakers, siblings, friends, teachers, heroes on television and in motion pictures, and pulp fiction. We communicate with one another, using our respective styles, almost automatically; we say and do things, and others experience stress. As a health practitioner, as all of us really are, you likewise use your language automatically. It is important, therefore, that the reader use the information and tools in this work to explore the way he or she communicates before using the information with others.

Keep in mind that as a clinical anthropologist you deal with the total person, which includes emotional reactions to life events—that is, the words and behaviors of others in the past as well as in the present. You are not, however, a psychiatrist, psychologist, marriage/family/child counselor (MFCC), or licensed clinical social worker (LCSW); do not present yourself this way. In fact, a recently released report from an eight-year study by the National Institute of Mental Health states that the main ingredient in effective therapy is the alliance or trust developed between the therapist and the client rather than any special type or brand of therapy (see Bower 1997: 21). Being a psychiatrist, psychologist, MFCC, or LCSW does not guarantee that you can (or even know how to) build trust or an effective alliance with clients. This work will explain and demonstrate to the reader how to build trust as an initial process in effective counseling and therapy.

You are an educator, and health education does not end with a consideration of physical symptoms, but with cause of the symptoms (information of one type or another). Moreover, emotional problems do not occur in a vacuum but involve input from significant others. At times, it will be necessary to engage a family and the family's communication style in order for individual stress to decrease and health to return.

Counseling and therapy, as represented in this work, are educational processes. There is nothing mystical about them, although they are often wrapped around mystical activities and settings, as is the case with divination procedures, tent-shaking, or sleight of hand.

There are numerous strategies for educating, all of which use the most powerful tool ever created by humankind: the symbol—words, phrases, paragraphs, stories, and the ritual that wraps all these together. Through the use of symbols, you are educating the client to experience his or her world in a different light, to appreciate the different angles to events (current and historical), and to immunize him or her against the unkind and usually unintended words and behaviors of others. You educate the client with respect to new possibilities and create an environment wherein these possibilities become real. Remember, however, you cannot help anyone, you cannot force solutions onto people. You can only give information onto which the receiver places meaning.

This work stems from a need within the anthropological, naturopathic, and holistic health communities for information and techniques to use when dealing with the emotional issues that surround illness. Emotional issues surround each and every illness and health problem encountered by the clinician. Removal or alleviation of emotional problems is a primary step for healing of any kind, physical and/or social. Knowing how to counsel and engage in therapy is an integral part of the clinician's training. Many a therapeutic setting has been destroyed because the clinician did not know how to communicate with the client, did not understand that certain types of information are high-risk for stress reactions, reactions that interfere with alliance-building and healing. In short, this work is about the power of symbols, words, phrases, and rituals, and how to use language so that others can reduce stress and promote healing.

Finally, I have chosen not to duplicate, in large measure, the information available in an earlier publication (Rush 1996). The reader is directed to that publication for details only outlined in this work.

Chapter 1

What Is Counseling?

Counseling can be defined as giving advice regarding social living. Therapy can be defined as dealing with more severe problems evolving out of social living. Both are educational; neither needs to be construed as mystical or magical, although the magical and mystical factors can be therapeutic in certain settings, in that they set up expectations of action, and thus possible success.

Both counseling and therapy are designed to impart new possibilities (framing and reframing), and in that sense, they are educational. Since counseling and therapy usually deal with the individual's relationship with others (problems in social living involve dyads and groups), interpersonal and group communication are focal points of therapy/counseling and/or education. How the individual interprets information is a key factor in personal and social stress reactions. Thus, we are dealing with information input, the meanings assigned, and the therapist's ability to educate the individual, couple, or family (message delivery and acceptance) with respect to alternatives or more comfortable interpretations. These new perceptions or meanings assigned to events are designed to allow the individual to take positive, socially approved steps to resolve conflict with self and others. The processes or methods of educating are the tools of the counselor. This work is about the processes of educating others to solve their problems in social living, and I stress the word *educational*.

In order to accomplish this, it is necessary to develop a model of how individuals are influenced by the information in their lives, then develop a set of tools for use with this model or philosophy. What the reader will not encounter is a book full of lofty intellectualism or convoluted theories without techniques. Moreover, the approach taken in this work is anthropological rather than psychological. I will be using research and findings from cultural/social anthropology, linguistics, physical/medical anthropology, and even archaeology. The approach to counseling presented in this work can best be described as holistic, in that the model and techniques come from a comparison of what goes on in other cultures in an attempt to cure the individual and society. As Bates (1996:8) states:

Holism is the philosophical view that no complex entity can be considered to be only the sum of its parts. As a principle of anthropology, it is the assumption that any given aspect of human life is to be studied with an eye to its relation to other aspects of human life. Anthropologists attempt to understand specific problems or questions of interest within a wider context.

Contemporary Western psychiatry and psychology do not, in most cases, attempt to incorporate the wider picture. Instead, these disciplines use their models and assumptions as a template for judging the worth of curing systems in other cultures. Western psychiatry and psychology, by and large, are ethnocentric and culturebound, and because the models are for the most part culturebound, they cannot be accurate renditions of the human psyche, human emotions, and human behavior. There is absolutely nothing wrong with the metaphors or explanations generated by these disciplines or the divination techniques for decision-making, but they are not truths.

Curing systems that do not match the beliefs and practices of most Western psychiatrists and psychologists are considered unscientific or superstition, and there is a reluctance to enlist the aid of indigenous curing techniques or curers. (See Harner 1982 for an example of an anthropologist's attempt to integrate shamanistic teachings and techniques into Western healing traditions.) Vyse (1997) is one of the psychologists most recently stating that life's uncertainties should be approached in an intellectual, decision-making manner learned through education, rather than relying on what is considered the illogic of superstition. One gets the impression from his work that counseling and therapy should be based on logic, as this is the only way to get to the truth of the matter. What Vyse fails to point out, in an otherwise delightful work, is that Western biomedicine, including psychiatry, is based on the magical practice of suppressing symptoms, assuming that this will cure the condition. Not only is this illogical, but it is also dangerous and, in my opinion, less than responsible (see also Blumberg 1997).

As we will see, logic does not often change behavior or thinking patterns. But what Western psychiatric and psychology approaches often do not appreciate is that there are common elements that knit all curing systems together, and these common elements have been in place for thousands of years. Much of the curing process is identical across cultures;

the differences are wrapped around the content as it is constructed within each unique cultural context.

There are numerous frames of reference for counseling and therapy that relate to Western cultural philosophy. In a general sense, they can be broken down into the following populations: individual, marriage, family, child, and group counseling and therapy. We do not engage in social curing or healing, for we do not see the individual's discomfort as a mirror of the larger system. This points not only to our cultural belief in individualism but also to the economic necessities of a market economy. As Harley (1970) comments, individual healing in Africa is actually a cleansing of society and a process of reinstituting morals that are necessary for maintaining the social beliefs and ethics.

Western therapy is preoccupied with individual psychology and functioning. This is a foreign idea among Asian and Southeast Asian populations, where the focus is the group, not the individual. Ego psychology (Freudian, neo-Freudian, psychodynamic, object relations, and so on) does not fit with the philosophies of these cultures, although there is still a belief within the psychoanalytic community (see Foster et al. 1996) that their theories are universal and thus useful when explaining the thinking and behaviors of members of these cultures. Even the insights of Roheim (1950), Bettelheim (1962), and more recently Sissa (1994) can be verified only through assumption, associations, and mythological interpretation. As fascinating as the analytical statements are, this is all feel-good speculation. Many anthropologists have abandoned such theories as universal truths, and instead see these models as connected to specific and time-related aspects of Western culture.

When the therapist does not integrate the larger society into the therapeutic process, there can be no social reintegration of the individual, and therefore no cure. Emotional problems are not singular problems; they are, instead, social phenomena. When the individual is the focus of therapy, this leads simply to more and more therapy, with the client usually becoming sicker and sicker as the therapist invents more and more "diseases." The emotional problems experienced by the individual are symptoms of a larger issue: the individual's relationships with others, and these others represent society.

WESTERN APPROACHES TO THERAPY: ART OR SCIENCE?

The approaches used with these populations (individual, marriage, etc.) have various names that include rational-emotive, psychodynamic, transactional, Gestalt, behavior modification, and so on. All of these are "cognitive," although cognitive therapy is seen as a separate approach as well. However, no two therapists use the same information, theories, or techniques in the same way. Moreover, counseling and therapy are not just techniques or the use of some school of thought. The therapist, the environment, and the dynamic patterns of interactions are also part of the process. There is a tremendous amount of information generated in the therapeutic process, and that information varies from individual to individual and from session to session. No therapist or counselor can take all of this information into consideration, and therefore selects according to his or her biases (which cannot be eliminated through psychoanalytic training, as is the belief of some analysts [see Chessick 1992:xx-xxi]—the training simply creates another bias of interpretation). And because each individual will develop his or her own unique interpretation of events, there can be nothing scientific about the process; we are dealing with an art form. Each state licenses and enforces the practice of this art form under the pretense of protecting the public. Licensing is simply legal trade restriction and the creation of legal monopolies in the marketplace. Licensing does not confer competence or credibility (see Rush 1996:206–209), but merely reflects a feature of market economies wherein free enterprise and competition are compromised under the guise of protecting the public.

Training to be a therapist (MFCC, LCSW, psychologist) differs from university to university. Each year, it would seem, a "new" therapy emerges that the public eagerly buys into, especially if it is adequately promoted. A careful examination of each such therapy shows that it oozed out of the social conditions existing at the time. In the 1960s, for example, we had transactional analysis (Berne 1961, 1964) and Gestalt therapy (Perls 1951, 1973). Perls's work was initiated in the late 1940s but had to wait for a revolution in thinking. That revolution involved interpersonal and group communication, a lack of which was seen as the downfall of the family and interpersonal relationships. By the end of the 1970s both these art forms fizzled out, the reason for which may have had something to do with the death of the originators of these approaches. Certainly there were other approaches—primal scream, Rolfing, and so on—all of which were very popular when they first hit the marketplace, but dropped out of favor as the public searched and searched for the magic bullet to heal their emotional and social problems.

In the mid-to-late-1970s the hot item was neurolinguistic programming (NLP) (Bandler and Grinder 1975b; Grinder and Bandler 1976; Dilts et al. 1980). NLP is based on Ericksonian hypnotherapeutic techniques (Bandler and Grinder 1975a; Grinder et al. 1977) and the linguistic position of Noam Chomsky (1957, 1968; see also Pinker 1994), which involves generative grammar. That is, the language/symbolic process is innate to the human mind (and perhaps other animals as well), and the specific language(s) learned represent content. The content or grammar, therefore, has unlimited possibilities. Although still in the marketplace, NLP, a mirror or analogy of computers and digital processing, does not have the popularity it once enjoyed.

In the 1980s and 1990s we have been introduced to the "little child within," *Iron John* (Bly 1990), *Women Who Run with the Wolves* (Estes 1992), and other metaphors that have a flavor of Joseph Campbell's (1988, 1990) teachings of mythology and the relevance of mythology to social and spiritual living.

All of these approaches have features in common, as the reader will understand shortly. The main point, and I cannot stress this too forcefully, is that all these approaches are art forms; they do not represent truths. They are metaphors representing the individual's connection to, or disconnection from, society. No one approach is better than another. In fact, some of the best counselors and therapists are your friends and family members, not the licensed professionals. Successful therapy is a fit between the therapeutic setting (the environment constructed by the therapist), the similarities the client feels or experiences with the therapist, beliefs the client and the therapist have about the efficacy of treatment, the therapist's techniques, the events preceding client-therapist contact, the events occurring after contact, the weather, nutritional deficiencies experienced by both client and therapist, and on and on. Most of what goes on in counseling and therapy cannot be taught. This is why all therapies are successful, but not for everyone; this is why a therapist can never be successful with all his or her clients. In our culture, successful therapy is determined by the client, for it is the client who determines the usefulness of the experience. Clients who do not benefit from the experience are often blamed, by the therapist, for "being resistant" or "not ready." Using a Freudian frame of reference, these rationalizations are designed to protect the ego of the therapist. By blaming the client, the therapist never has to take a look at his or her part in the process. In other cultures, when the desired result is not forthcoming, the blame is placed on the techniques. That is, the magic was not applied in the correct manner (see Fortune 1932; Malinowski 1948).

Because of the complex nature of human interactions, success can be related, in some measure, to the therapist's ability to control and manipulate the information presented during the counseling/therapy process. However, this information has to relate not only to events preceding therapy but also to events that will happen in the future. This future consideration is often left out of therapeutic procedures. The only way it can be accomplished is through an understanding of what happens as people talk and listen, taking into account history (prior to counseling) and building a future (what will happen when the individual reintegrates into the larger social milieu). The theory or theories that you have regarding cause and effect will to a large degree direct your understanding of the process. Standard counseling courses talk about resistance, transference, inferiority complexes, and the like. More recent counseling perspectives talk about the child within, codependency, object relations, and so on. The language and the theories are continually being altered. This opens the door to new complexes and diseases of the mind. Just as we have new styles of automobiles to sell the public, so we have new theories of cause and effect to sell clients.

There are elements or processes of counseling and therapy, however, that can be recognized in every culture. This work is about those processes and how to apply them. The one thing this work cannot do is give you the actual experiences of applying the processes. Through a consideration of your own life events, your experiences with others, you will quickly see that you already possess a great deal of therapeutic knowledge. Attending college for many years and listening to the experiences of professors does not prepare you as a therapist or counselor, nor does interning at a clinic. What you gain is a model of why people are the way they are (again, this is a metaphor and not truth), and techniques for sending and receiving information. All of this can be learned from a book and then applied to your own life experiences. Statements to justify formal education, supervision, and licensing often include not hurting, and/or protecting the client(s) from incompetent therapists and "unscientific" approaches. This is absurd, and a misrepresentation of the nature of counseling and therapy. In fact, there may be reason to believe that many of these licensed professionals do a great deal of harm by indoctrinating and forcing their own values onto clients (see Dorpat 1996).

Counseling therapy is an economically based profession dependent on clients remaining in therapy for months and sometimes years. As the reader will learn, the need for such long-term counseling/therapy is questionable at best.

THE BASIC ELEMENTS OF ALL COUNSELING/THERAPY: AN ANTHROPOLOGICAL PERSPECTIVE

The fact that all counseling works, but not with every client, should lead the therapeutic community to ask, why? When I say "works," I mean that the counselor or therapist is able to convince the client to alter thinking and/or behavior in a way that is stress-reducing. Such stress reduction has to be experienced and acknowledged by the client. The main ingredient in all this, as stated in the preface to this work, is trust. Without trust, information presented in the session will not be perceived as true, useful, or believable. So, viewing trust as the basic element in effective therapy, what types of techniques work, and why?

A way to approach this question is observing and listening to what happens when people talk and listen. This can be broken down into several components. First, you need a sender and a receiver with a shared code—

for example, English. Second, you need to understand elements of the communication process that are common to all human interactions, in this culture as well as others. Third, you need a model for tying these communication elements together so that you can establish a rationale for using the fourth consideration, techniques or tools. The remainder of this work will be an exploration of what works and why.

Senders and Receivers: Talking and Listening—Some Basic Elements

According to the First Amendment of the United States Constitution, "Congress shall make no law . . . abridging the freedom of speech, or of the press." As one reads through the ten amendments forming the Bill of Rights, in no place, in no manner of speaking, is the individual accorded the same right to listen. In the United States we are intellectually and ideologically, at least, considered to be individuals with the right to free (and, one hopes, responsible) speech. Through our ideologies and explicit freedoms, we create a reality wherein we are talkers but not necessarily listeners. In order to be a counselor or therapist, you need to know how to collect data and, more specifically, data or information that will be most useful in helping clients and systems to reduce stress, a basic goal of all counseling, therapy, or curing.

In order for human language to serve as an effective survival mechanism, there must be both sending and receiving, that is, talking and listening. I am sure, however, that the reader can appreciate the "see me" phenomena that can evolve out of an ideology of individualism, the freedom of speech, and the urban reality of being anonymous and therefore wanting attention, to have our words heard above all others. The counselor/therapist must place himself or herself second (initially, at least) in the information-sending process. In a phrase, "Shut up and listen."

Because our language, our ability to symbolize, is our basic tool for social survival, the information-sending process is redundant (see Colby 1958). In other words, we send out more information than appears to be necessary at first glance; this increases the probability that the receiver, either consciously or unconsciously, "gets the message." Redundancy is probably the reason why we can be relatively ineffective listeners and still get at least part of the message, consciously or subconsciously. If you are a counselor or therapist, this is not good enough. To add to all this, the therapist must be aware of the context within which things happen, since context will affect how individuals (and groups) send and receive information. The communication patterns in your office are very different from the communication patterns encountered during a home visit or while observing the same individual(s) in public. This is one of the great reservations I have about the conclusions drawn by psychologists for court evaluations in our culture. The psychologist, unless he or she does extended home visits, never sees the role of husband, wife, or parent, only salesperson, client, or adversary. As the reader will see (Chapters 3 and 4), the roles we assume give us a set of rules for communicating, but without observing the actual role of husband, wife, or parent, how can it be evaluated? The use of psychological testing, as "scientific" as it appears, is misleading (the reasons for this will be discussed in Chapter 2). The message to the reader is, quite simply, Do not believe, for a moment, that the people in your office are the same people that others experience at home or at work; you are experiencing the tip of the iceberg visible to you at that moment in time.

Most of our communications, because talking and listening are complicated, are automatic. In other words, we learn styles of talking and listening early in life and automatically use them in our respective social environments. In this process, we learn to look at and listen to specific cues for allowing (or not allowing) information to get past our conscious filters. What we do not appreciate is how much information enters our subconscious minds, especially when we are stressed. The subconscious mind is "hardwired" for many functions that interpret information both inside or outside of the physical body. These functions have variously been called reflexes, instincts, and autonomic responses. Every one of these reflexes can be reprogrammed, reeducated, mutated, or otherwise altered through and by the body's and mind's interpretations of information. This is one of the keys not only to successful counseling but also to successful living, that is, creating a situation wherein the mind perceives past, present, and future in a more stress-reducing manner.

In order to become an effective communicator, it is necessary to pull yourself off automatic pilot and reeducate yourself in the techniques of sending and receiving information, talking and listening. This is not easy. However, the rewards of doing so are immense. Your personal and social powers definitely reflect your communication abilities—with yourself, family, friends, and clients.

Verbal and Nonverbal Components

When we discuss the gathering of data or listening, our attention is usually directed toward the spoken word. However, this is only part of the process. Nonverbal messages are extremely important in terms of understanding—for cutting through deception, for example—and picking up symbols for feedback purposes (body movements while answering certain questions, how a person dresses, colors chosen, use of jewelry, odors, eye movements, etc.). The nonverbal aspects, at least in a general sense, should be familiar to most readers (Hall 1959).

Expanding on this, words and phrases are only representations of what goes on inside the person's head. They are connected to the social context in which they occur, and are wrapped around the person's history, or memories and earlier experiences, and future expectations. Moreover, your perceived status communicates, and can either enhance or inhibit the information-sending and -receiving process, just as the symbols that decorate your office can spell success or failure in building trust with specific clients. As an example, my office is very "busy" in the sense of the many books and decorative pieces. One of those decorative pieces is a wizard given to me by my wife many years ago. One client refused a second appointment because she was a "Christian," and connected the wizard to pagan worship.

Further, words and phrases can be considered compressed data, much as a computer will store compressed files in order to save room on a floppy disk or hard drive, or because of memory limits of a specific program. Human language is compressed data; if it were not compressed data—that is, the use of a symbol or the combination of symbols that stand for more complex ideas—language would be neither an efficient nor a useful survival mechanism. The reason for this lies in the fact we would get bound up in the details, for it is through generalizations that we are able to socialize, instruct, and cooperate efficiently. (The downside of this is that generalizations lead to stereotypes and prejudice.)

A problem immediately becomes obvious. The sender is using his or her reality in the information compression (the symbols chosen) and decompression process, while the receiver uses his or her reality to "unzip" that compressed data. We all have separate realities; we do not all run on Microsoft. This can create immense problems in understanding unless other mechanisms are available: feedback for clarification, the context within which events occur, and so on. Your reality as a sender and receiver is not the same reality of the other communicator. The problems become even greater if both are using different codes, for example, one speaks English and the other speaks Chinese. Theoretically, at least, the more time you spend with someone, the closer the realities become. This is so (in part) because the shared context in which many things happen helps add to the meanings of the messages. Cross-cultural communication is difficult because the shared code is often a secondary language, and if interpreters are used, they can distort the intended message. The context within which things happen is often foreign to each speaker. If there is no mutually perceived goal, the "us vs. them" distinction can result in mistrust and/or messages indicating compliance or agreement that might simply mean "I'll say Yes so that I don't offend you, but I really mean No," or "I need to think about it further." In these cases, a solid grasp of the culture is necessary in order to assign meaning.

Language as we know it today emerged between 100,000 and 40,000

Table 1.1
Language (Verbal and Nonverbal) as a Tool for Setting Rules

Rule Category	Relationship To
Relationship Rules (Beliefs and Behaviors Toward) →	1) In-Group 2) Out-Group 3) Superordinate Agencies
Division of Labor →	1) Male 2) Female 3) Children 4) Elders 5) Specialists, etc.
Technology →	1) Manufacture 2) Use (How, Who, When)
Rules About Rules (Metasystems) →	1) Law/Sanctions 2) Formal Teachings 3) Myth 4) Ritual 5) Art Forms

Source: Rush 1996:47.

years ago in response to some crisis or crises. (Readers desiring an interesting and informative discussion of language origins should see Bickerton 1990.) Obviously, language conferred upon humans an immense survival strategy that has to do with organizing, storing, and retrieving data, all of which leads to enhanced cooperation between individuals and groups.

For the most part, the purpose of language, both verbal and nonverbal, is (a) to create rules (which lead to conformity and expectations) and reach goals, both group and individual; (b) to explain, express, or clarify situations, intentions, behaviors, and emotions; and (c) to deceive. Deception is a normal part of human interaction; it is not necessarily pathological, and is a way to protect against discovery of one's socially inappropriate behaviors, and consequent rejection (see Rush 1996:243–248). Language also informs about temporal and spatial relationships.

Rules are an important consideration, and they fall into four general categories (those who desire an elaboration on these categories should see Table 1.1):

a. Rules about division of labor—who is to do what, where, and for how long
b. Rules of relationships—how one is to communicate with others according to each person's status, sex, power, your goal in the process, and so on
c. Rules involving use/application of technology
d. Rules about rules, or metarules (this book is essentially rules about rules).

All of the enculturation process involves learning rules and teaching rules to others. Without rules you cannot obtain conformity, which is absolutely necessary for developing expectations, cooperation, security, and social survival. In a culture that worships individuality, the idea of conformity might seem out of place. The reality is, however, that most of us conform to social expectations most of the time, and we do so because we have learned our culture's rules.

Apart from general communication rules found in all cultures (see Appendix A), the individual acquires a set of his or her personal rules for relating to the world. A personal interpretation of rules is universal to everyone, even in societies where individualism is traditionally discouraged, such as India. Some of these rules involve shyness, abrasiveness, fearfulness, and so on. Thus, one of your tasks, while collecting information from clients, is to determine his or her personal rules of social living that impede effective social interaction as defined by that society or culture.

Rules can also be seen as wrapped around ritual processes that orchestrate the flow of human interaction. We often think of religious rituals or ritual of court procedure, but rituals, in fact, are woven within and throughout the fabric of your life (see Chapters 6 and 7). Berne (1964) referred to some of these rituals as "games," which implies some sort of incrimination or "badness" on the part of the players. When transactional analysis was at its zenith, we were all accused of "playing games," accusations that blame the individual and are at high risk (as we will see in Chapter 3) for creating rather than lowering stress in most everyday encounters. Avoid directly blaming in counseling unless you think that it will alter, in a positive way, the person's beliefs and behaviors with respect to interactions with others. Indirect blaming, which can be part of the third-person approach, however, can be very useful. It will be discussed in Chapter 3.

Thus far I have discussed some of the basic elements of all counseling: (1) you need a sender and a receiver; (2) communication involves compressed data; (3) the compression/decompression process is individualized (each person does this using his or her own reality or interpretation of events, historical as well as current); (4) the necessity to collect data or observe and listen to the client's formulation of his or her problem; and (5) as the client communicates, he or she is expressing his or her rules of social living, some of which interfere with social interactions. It is precisely these rules (and rituals) that the therapist needs to uncover and, with feedback, clarify and alter. To get the privilege of uncovering these rules, the clinical anthropologist has to build and maintain trust and know when trust has been lost.

The above paragraph contains some basic elements that one can find in all therapies or curing throughout the world; I will give examples in Chapter 2. However, through a discussion of the factors that are involved in socializing (enculturation) the individual, I will uncover more specific elements.

COUNSELING/THERAPY: A MATTER OF INFORMATION-PROCESSING

As the reader will quickly appreciate, the language used in the book relates to information-processing. Essentially, we get to be the way we are, the way we think about our world, and the way we communicate with others through our genetic code and, more important, through the information (the intrusion or interpretation of the world and events) around us. Using the information presented to us over time, we construct our beliefs, attitudes, and emotional and behavioral responses. If our relationships to ourselves (who we believe we are) and others (our interpersonal communication patterns) are constructed through information input, then it is through a reconstruction (through a reinterpretation of life events) of information that we reduce (or increase) stress. On top of this, through learning new communication techniques we can apply our new perspective and reduce stress in our social interactions.

Counseling/therapy, then, is a process of reinterpreting historical events, teaching the client to translate the messages of others more usefully, and teaching useful sending and receiving techniques to add to the process already in use. The beauty of this approach is that the techniques and tools of counseling/therapy are the very tools that you teach the client. Essentially, you educate clients in life skills so that they can solve their own problems without always having to resort to the professional. Moreover, through this educational process the client is in a better position to educate others. Counseling and therapy need to return to the public domain.

Healing with Words

Western biomedicine attempts to heal with synthetic chemicals and invasive procedures, but, outside of trauma medicine, these approaches have not lived up to the billions and billions of dollars spent and promises of cures for everything from the common cold to cancer (see Fabrega 1997; Blumberg 1997; Robbins 1996). This can definitely be seen in Western psychiatry, which more and more turns to a philosophy of "bad genes" as the cause of maladaptive behavior (depression, schizophrenia, etc.) and chemical methods of therapy. In order for psychiatry to be considered medicine, and to separate it from Western psychology, it has had to assume the Western biomedical model that points to a noncultural medicine or a belief that one medical procedure fits all (see Iwu 1993:314). Healing is more than the administering of drugs and surgery; it is a holistic and social phenomenon. Once healing is removed from its social dimension, its meaning and efficacy are lost to the illusion of scientific endeavor. The physical effects of the drug or herb administered, by the shaman or the M.D., is not without a social healing component often referred to as the "placebo effect." As Bower comments (1996:123), with respect to Prozac and other antidepressants, "the placebo effect—a measure of the psychological impact of being given a medication, even if it contains no active substances—plays a dominant role in sparking favorable responses to antidepressants."

The current Western psychiatric position of blaming emotional problems on bad genes and the consequent use of psychotropic medications fits in well with the Judeo-Christian concept of nature being corrupt and in need of correction. Moreover, much of the research defending current psychiatric practices has been labeled "pseudoscientific" by many social scientists (see Ross and Pam 1995; Van Praag 1993). Fortunately, not all psychiatrists subscribe to genetic blaming and the administering of drugs. The outcome of most psychiatric practice in this country is drug dependency and addiction. The Justice Department, with its war on drugs, needs to look in its own backyard at the legalized drug-dealing, the legalized addiction, and a license to kill. With legalized drug-dealing, you avoid most of the danger and violence inherent in illegal drug-trafficking, but you still get addiction and many, many deaths. Whether someone dies from a bullet, drug overdose, or drug reaction, the outcome is the same.

Emotional problems are essentially problems in social living; this is an issue of communication or the sending and receiving of messages. As Iwu states (1993:323):

Incantation exploits the power of the spoken word, vibratory fiber of existence as denoted by rhythm, and the participatory role of designated images. The components of an incantation are word, rhythm, and imagery. The power of the spoken word gives a meaning, status, and designation to "things." . . . The word is before every other thing; in its fluid forms it constitutes the material that fills the oceans and sacred rivers and also provides the soluble base for animal erythrocytes, including those of man. As fire, it erupts in volcanoes and gives teeth to lightning and thunder. The word in its simplest conception is a force, effective and yet dormant until uttered. "Thought," no matter how ferocious, can never equal the force of the spoken word; the word is life.

Words (phrases/incantations), then, and the symbols that they embody for the individual (not necessarily the intent of the sender), are the healer's tools for approaching emotional issues, that is, for reducing individual and social stress. But it goes beyond this, for it is through words and symbols that the individual moves toward social balance, and thus physical healing, regardless of whether it is a broken leg, a laceration, kidney disorder, or AIDS/HIV.

In reverse, it is the words and symbols (information intrusion) that lead to stress and the interruption of healing and other natural biological processes. Childbirth, for example, when assisted by Western biomedicine, is, more often than not, a tremendously stressful process. As the mother is usually attended by strangers in a sterile environment, and by a physician and nurses trained to see and engage in the process in an impersonal, clinical manner outside of a social context (in which it is naturally embedded), she endures a painful and lengthy delivery (see Robbins 1996).

Unkind words from friends, the impersonal and cold nature of the government and legal system, the negative images/symbols on the daily television news programs, the violence, conflict, and sick and twisted plots of movies at the local cinema and on television, all impinge on the senses. We literally make ourselves sick with these words and symbols, these incantations.

Our words and symbols tell us who we are—not as singular individuals, as the psychologists would have it, but as members of groups, social beings in need of recognition and acceptance. We stress ourselves with messages that tell us we do not belong; we stress ourselves with the symbols that tell us we are the next possible victim of violence—rape, murder, physical assault. We distress ourselves with the lies and deceptions of our politicians, who, once in power, turn away from the public good and pursue their own agendas. We begin to distrust others and ourselves; stress increases. Our personal stress alters our chemical nature; we make ourselves sick with the interpretation of words and symbols. Our sickness, however, is a metaphor, and it mirrors the words and symbols around us; and when we cease to see ourselves as a reflection of the society within which we exist, we no longer can utilize the feedback for altering or balancing the social structure. This is where we currently stand in North American society.

In the chapters that follow, I will be exploring the therapeutic processes wrapped around words. First, however, we need some reference points, and this brings us to a closer examination of the other therapies used in our society and the metaphors embodied within them. From this, the reader will gain a clear appreciation of words and how they relate to the healing process. In Chapter 3, I offer a model that contains the elements necessary for healing with words, along with the tools or incantations.

In Chapter 4, I consider definitions of male and female, husband and wife, and the family, and offer insights and techniques for dealing with family problems. Chapter 5 reviews special issues: cross-cultural counseling, AIDS/HIV, death and dying, and conflict mediation.

Chapter 6 involves communication via more specialized techniques: hypnosis, light therapy, and therapeutic touch. Chapter 7 is a discussion of termination rituals and social integration. Chapter 8 concludes this work.

Chapter 2

The Different Schools of Counseling
and Therapy

PHILOSOPHICAL CONSIDERATIONS

Western counseling and therapy, whatever name we want to assign, operates from a philosophy that places the individual at the center of the universe. The emphasis on the individual can be traced back to many philosophical traditions, the Greeks and Celts, for example. But even within the hero myths found in cultures around the world, both ancient and modern, there is the spark of the individual acting for the benefit of the group. According to Campbell (1989, 1990) the Arthurian legends that burst forth in the Middle Ages are a prelude to the intense sense of individualism experienced in our own time. These legends represent a living out of one's own spontaneity rather than simply following social dictates, with this idea manifested today in "falling in love" and following one's heart or, more simply, love over social duty. These legends illustrate personal quests designed to find one's own path rather than following the path of others. These legends did not represent on-the-ground reality as experienced by Europeans of the Middle Ages as a whole, but instead ideals or wishful thinking emanating from the upper class. These concepts have persisted through time, and are alive and well in North American culture. The emphasis on this type of individualism is not universal at this time in history.

Sigmund Freud (1856–1939)

The development of the Freudian theory of the human psyche was not a singular effort but involved a synthesis of the work of many philosophers and physicians contemporary with Freud (see Sulloway 1979 for an overview of the other contributors). One of the primary features evolving from Freud's synthesis was psychoanalysis, which can be seen as a theory of emotional problems, a method of collecting data, and a treatment procedure. Central to Freudian theory is a subconscious mind that tends to work not only in conjunction with the conscious mind but also in spite of the conscious mind. The subconscious mind, in the Freudian sense, is concerned with self-preservation, and therefore disguises or hides information from the conscious mind; this is called repression and resistance. The subconscious mind reveals itself both in dreams and consciously, for example, during Freudian slips, verbal statements that betray an underlying emotion, wish, desire, and so on.

Freud was also strongly interested in infantile sexuality and could see within the infant, toddler, and so on, elements of the Oedipus complex, a male child's intense sexual attachment to his mother and fear/hate of his father.

Neurosis and psychosis are the products of psychic conflict, mainly between the id (the subconscious, genetic drives) and the ego, (which tends to be a buffer between instincts and the social world). Neurosis is what we all end up with, because there can never be a balance between the id and the ego; psychosis results in disturbed communication patterns and an inability to function in society.

This all sounds very scientific, and there are points that seem to ring true in our dealings with our inner selves. However, Freudian theory developed at a time in history when id, ego, superego, repression, Oedipus complex, and the like can be seen as metaphors and mirrors of social functioning in general, existing within a specific historical and cultural time frame. The id is what one would like to do but cannot. The ego is "self" articulating with society. Superego is the reality inherent in class-based society. The Oedipus complex is a reflection of Freud's dislike and fear of authority, experience of prejudice, and so on (keep in mind that Freud was Jewish and intensely discriminated against by many of his peers). In this sense it has been recognized that Freudian psychology is about Freud and his problems in social living. Freud put this model together using his own self as a basic point of comparison, as all of us have to do in order to make sense out of our worlds. Freud simply sold his view of the universe, and he sold it because the target cultures for his theories were ready for a new metaphor. This is an extremely important point—anyone who comes to you for counseling is looking for a new metaphor.

Freud's metaphor accentuates the individual, his or her mental dynamics, and how those processes articulate with the social world. Words are powerful, and Freudian incantations still ring true for many in the psychoanalytic, psychiatric, and psychological communities. As Iwu (1993: 323) comments, "The word in its simplest conception is a force, effective and yet dormant until uttered. 'Thought,' no matter how ferocious, can never equal the force of the spoken word; the word is life. Once expressed, human thought becomes a reality, effective and binding."

Thus, Freud's words became reality at a time when there was a need for new beliefs and rituals that would match what was known at that time (turn of the twentieth century) about microbes and pathogens. The corresponding metaphor is revealed in Freudian theory: there must be something "microscopic" and hidden and often elusive that leads to mental illness.

There is just one small problem with this. If Freudian theory is really true—if, indeed, it does stand as an accurate rendition of the workings of the human mind—then why doesn't psychoanalysis work as a cure for everyone in all cultures? From the analytical point of view, the answer is resistance; people resist the "truth." This type of thinking, this blaming of the patient, only serves to justify Freud's position. Resistance to acceptance, however, could mean that the metaphor simply does not fit.

Carl Jung (1875–1961)

Freud had his opponents, those who did not entirely accept his metaphor. Carl Jung, for example, could not agree with Freud's position on infantile sexuality, and saw libido not as a sexual instinct, but as a life urge connected to a collective unconscious. Jung, like Freud, was influenced by "microscopic processes" that are reflected in the concept of the collective unconscious or archetypes. The beauty of this approach, as with Freud's, is that it cannot be proved, disproved, or tested; there is no way to validate it, and it must be accepted on faith. Again, these are beautiful metaphors—incantations, if you will—for moving the individual out of one field of thought and into another. Estes's work (1992), based on Jungian archetypes, is a contemporary example.

Alfred Adler (1870–1937)

Adler was also a contemporary of Freud who added new terminology to the metaphor (see Adler 1964). This included the inferiority complex, overcompensation, and an interest in birth order, which, according to Adler, affects the child's relationship to others. Age and status are universal concepts, and partnerships evolving out of age relationships are important in most cultures.

Adler differed from Freud in that his approach to psychic processes was dynamic and socially connected rather than digital, singular, and sharply defined. Adler, moreover, was less dogmatic, which allowed input from others so that they could fill in their own details.

However, Adler's approach is still individual-oriented, with the main focus being on a redefinition and organization of a person's lifestyle, thus decreasing the individual's sense of inferiority and, at the same time, increasing social effectiveness. I was strongly influenced by the Adlerian approach. As time went on, however, I realized that his position was not explicit enough in regard to the specific social factors that lead to feelings of inferiority and the need for overcompensation. Yes, society enculturates; yes, parents influence; and yes, birth order is important. But, what are the specific factors that lead the individual to interpret his or her world in a threatening manner? What are the social incantations that lead to insecurity and feelings of inferiority? As the reader will discover, these specific factors are precisely the interpretations placed upon specific social incantations, the words and phrases ever present in our daily lives.

Milton Erickson (1901–1980)

Milton Erikson was a medical doctor but practiced as a hypnotherapist; as such, his approach to problems in social living was goal-directed. Rather than subscribing to lofty intellectual theories of mental functioning, Erikson was interested in the nature of consciousness and the use of symbols—incantations, if you will—as well as personal quests and social situations, to initiate, sustain, or even stop the reinterpretations of life events (see Erickson and Rossi 1979; Erickson 1980; Watzlawick 1978, 1990). In short, Erickson did not attempt to sell the client on any theoretical position, but instead attempted, through numerous language tools, to alter the client's perception of the world and his or her place in it. Many of the tools used by Erickson can be found in the curing techniques and rituals of many cultures (see Rush 1996:202–203).

Noam Chomsky (1928–   )

No discussion of therapeutic process can proceed without a consideration of linguistics and language, for it is through the sending and receiving of information that changes in thinking, and consequent behavior, occur. Noam Chomsky, writing in the 1950s and 1960s (Chomsky 1957, 1968), came to the conclusion that because all languages have features or general rules in common, these must be innate and part of the neural processing that naturally occurs in the mind/brain. Chomsky's significance can best be appreciated when it comes to how the individual interprets messages and why, among other things, no two people interpret information in the same way (generalizing, deleting, and distorting—discussed in Chapter 3). Perhaps more important, Chomsky opened a door for understanding how to deliver information so that it will be internalized. I do not know if Milton Erickson was aware of Chomsky's writings, at least through the 1960s, but certainly Bandler and Grinder (mentioned above) were, as they

incorporated Chomsky's concepts (as well as Erickson's) into neurolinguistic programming.

I have just scratched the surface with respect to contributors to a path
initiated, for the most part, by Freud. Abraham Maslow (1954), for example, looked at what he considered to be "healthy" people and developed his theory of self-actualization. According to his position, creativity
and positive accomplishments are achieved through the fulfillment of
needs arranged according to a hierarchy of priorities. My personal opinion,
revealed in Chapter 3, is that creativity and social success are, in fact, more
likely a product of rejection and pain, and a striving for social acceptance
and stress reduction. Yes, people can possibly reach great heights in the
manner outlined by Maslow, but my experience is that people strive and
reach greatness because some of their physical and emotional needs are
not met, they aspire to reach them, and are terrified if they do not.

There are many reviews of the various personalities involved in the
development of contemporary psychiatric/psychological theory and practice; I direct the reader to Hampden-Turner (1981) for an overview. The
point is that all these perspectives offer a metaphor (interpretation, reinterpretation, or reframing) for why we are the way we are. These metaphors are incantations; they are powerful and they all work, but not for
everyone. All these metaphors reference the individual as the therapeutic
subject, which fits with our culture's ideas of individualism and freedom
of choice. But how do other cultures engage in curing? What is the common ground between us and them?

HEALING IN OTHER CULTURAL CONTEXTS

The processes of healing in other cultures are not very different from
those in our own. The individual who is "ill" is brought to the attention
of family members, and because the illness demands attention, he or she
is brought to the attention of a specialist. Which specialist—or whether or
not a specialist is consulted—depends on the initial interpretation rendered by the individual or family. If a specialist is called, rituals are performed that lead to naming the illness; once named, the illness becomes
a disease. Illness is the individual or social expression of discomfort (symptoms), and disease is the name or classification of these symptoms. There
is a hierarchy of symptoms. For example, diabetes is a symptom of blood-
sugar imbalance (hyperglycemia). Blood-sugar imbalance is a symptom of
liver dysfunction. Liver dysfunction is a symptom of possible genetic issues, trauma, long-standing nutritional issues, alcohol abuse, and so on.
The point is that symptoms always point to multiple causes. The reason
for this is simple—any alteration of metabolic functioning will affect the
total system. Every time you think, you alter your physiology. Negative
thoughts alter your physiology one way; positive thoughts, another.

The naming of the illness and the ritual procedures are wrapped around some philosophy of cause and effect. In Western culture most of the current philosophies center on genetics and pathogens (viruses, bacteria, helminths), with genetics representing information alteration or loss and pathogens representing information intrusion (see Rush 1996:110–116 for other informational categories). As we will see, illness in non-Western systems is also attributed to information intrusion, information alteration, and so on. In short, the processes are the same but the content differs according to each culture's philosophy of cause and effect.

The Nuaulu, Seram, Eastern Indonesia

The Nuaulu (Ellen 1993) reside in south-central Seram in eastern Indonesia (see Map 1, Appendix B). Illness, as conceptualized within the Nuaula philosophy, can result from sorcery (*kau osane*). Sorcerers (*suangi*) are special people who "inflict" illness on others through spirit entities. This philosophy, as the reader will appreciate, is a mirror of society, of the stresses that are ongoing in social relationships and day-to-day environmental demands. The beliefs, then, serve to bring these stresses into the open in a metaphorical, third-person fashion.

Sorcery is divined through the manipulation of objects (*nau*) or by communing with spirits (*saruana*). Once the illness is definitely attributed to sorcery, the *saruana* may be called upon to undo the sorcery through counterspells and incantations, as well as the administration of herbal remedies. Although the victim may use countermeasures to inflict harm on the offending sorcerer, this does not always happen. Actually, there are few sorcerers known to the Nuaulu, and the accusation or potential accusation probably serves, in part, as a social control mechanism.

In any event, the Nuaulu use divination to determine the nature of illness and to name the illness, then take appropriate steps to cure or rid the individual of the intrusive information, which, in the case of the Nuaulu, is usually some spirit entity. Illness is not an individual matter but involves, at the very least, family, friends, and acquaintances (individualism, as expressed in the West, is a foreign concept). Moreover, Ellen's (1993:95) interpretation is that sorcery accusations are social interpretations of psychological/social problems—anxiety, depression, and so on—which otherwise do not have any clear means of expression. Most people withdraw from social confrontation because it disrupts society and the cosmic order. This ritual process, then, serves to reduce stress in the individual and the group. Spirit entities, curses, and the like are analogous to pathogens (viruses, bacteria, etc.), which represent information intrusion.

Curing is accomplished through an interpretation of the illness (an individual condition) and then placing it within a social context (reframing).

Through the use of symbols or incantations (ritual words, phrases, etc.) to enlist the aid of spirits, the sorcery (the cause of the illness) is removed. Doesn't the therapist or M.D. do exactly the same thing in Western culture? There is a divination of the illness (the therapist listens to the language of the client; the M.D. listens, looks, does blood work, etc.), a name is assigned to the illness (a disease is assigned or created), and then there are incantations (reframing by the therapist, incantations in the nature of a prescription, surgery is performed—surgery is a nonverbal incantation, a ritual designed to physically extract or remove the offending substance).

At this juncture, however, Western biomedicine, psychology, and psychiatry diverge from most other curing systems. As I will point out in more detail, the Western practitioner (counselor, therapist, or M.D.) usually does not signal when cure has taken place (leaving the doctor's office or hospital does not signal cure, only the end of that part of the ritual procedure), and there is no clear process of social reintegration, elements that are extremely important in healing.

The Navaho

The Navaho, indigenous to the southwestern United States, occupy the Four Corners area where Utah, Arizona, Colorado, and New Mexico converge (see Map 2, Appendix B). Much has been written about Navaho culture, which was a focal point of anthropological research in the early part of the twentieth century; the reader is directed to Ortiz (1983) for an overview.

Morgan's (1931) account of the Navaho focused on diagnostic procedures for determining causes of illness, the ceremony (rituals/incantations) for curing, and which specific shaman should perform the ceremony. Morgan distinguished between the diagnostician and the shaman, singers, or other healers. Perhaps the analogy here is with the family practitioner, who divines the cause and then refers the patient to a specialist, that is, the shaman, for cure. The training period of a diagnostician, such as the family practitioner, is shorter than that of the specialist.

There are three basic types of diagnosticians: "with motion-in-the-hand," listeners, and stargazers. One clear difference between the shaman and the diagnostician is that the shaman has to perform rituals and incantation in an exact manner; the diagnostician has more latitude in this. Moreover, the shaman does not have a ritual procedure for discovering the cause of an illness.

The diagnostic procedure does not occur in isolation from the rest of the community; friends and relatives are present. Those who diagnose "with-motion-in-the-hand" enter the hogan and discuss the illness with the patient and the others present. The diagnostician (male or female) then sits and, in a trance with arms extended, thinks about all the possible causes. Analogous to dowsing, when the correct cause comes to mind, the diviner's arms shake. He or she also uses this technique to determine which part of the body is afflicted.

Illness can be caused by dreams (sent by specific gods), witches, animal spirits, and the deceased; all represent forms of information intrusion. Rituals, with words and incantations, are always part of the process. In some cases emetics are administered as well as herbs that are used both internally and externally.

Once again we find curing wrapped around information intrusion (dreams sent by gods, animal spirits, and so on, which are mirrors of social functioning). Moreover, divination is a group phenomenon that perhaps (although Morgan does not specifically say this) helps, in a metaphorical sense, bring social antagonisms to the surface in an indirect manner. This would serve as a safety value for reducing social stress and individual stress.

Shamanism on St. Lawrence Island

Murphy's (1964) study involves the Eskimo living in a village on St. Lawrence Island (St. Lawrence Island is in the Bering Sea, approximately 120 miles from Nome, Alaska; see Map 3, Appendix B). Indigenous healers, termed shamans, are individuals who are "thin" or have telepathic perception; they are able to experience things out of the ordinary, see into the future, find lost articles, and, more specifically, cure illness. Shamans learn their trade and/or have experiences (near-death experiences and "emotional breakdowns," for example—see Eliade 1972; Rasmussen 1908) that lead them into the profession.

Illness cause (etiology) centers on soul loss, object intrusion, spirit intrusion, sorcery, and breaking social rules. For example, a person's soul can be stolen by evil spirits, which are everywhere (soul loss equals information loss—see Rush 1996). Object intrusion (information intrusion), although not as important as soul loss, is the entering into the body of foreign objects that include anything from "worms" to sticks and pebbles. The violation of social rules can likewise lead to illness, and it would seem reasonable to suggest that such beliefs as soul loss function as a social control mechanism.

Sorcery beliefs among the St. Lawrence Eskimo are quite strong and probably stem from polarity, the normal functioning of the human mind. In other words, if there are healers, then there must be their antithesis, sorcerers (*auvinak*). Moreover, if there are good people in the world, there must also be evil people. The shaman's job, then, is to use countermagic, in the form of incantations, sleight of hand, tent-shaking, and so on, to reverse the evil.

Spirit intrusion, less common as an explanation of illness, can be that of an animal, but more commonly that of a deceased relative, especially a relative who is either attempting to get back into the community of the living or whose death has somehow been caused by the patient.

Their philosophy of illness has other elements. For example, a disease cannot be in two places at the same time; it is either inside or outside the patient (Western biomedicine has a similar view). Moreover, disease is more likely to be found in some geographical locations rather than in others. This leads to placing the disease entity onto or within some expendable object, or perhaps forcing it into the air, where it is neutralized.

Determining cause through divination is usually accomplished during a seance, in which the shaman goes into a trance and learns the cause through spirits or familiars. The shaman is part of the group that employs his services. It is rarely the case in our own culture, except in perhaps pastoral counseling/therapy, that the counselor or therapist belongs to the client's group. Thus, the Eskimo shaman is well aware of social antagonisms, likes and dislikes, and often intimates such details to the patient.

Trance is not the exclusive property of the shaman, for through his behaviors, he initiates a trance state in the patient and the observers. Trance occurs when there is information-processing stress. That is, the individual cannot compute what he or she is seeing, hearing, and feeling, and his or her attention is fixated. This is accomplished with tricks, sleight of hand, beating drums and singing, and theatrics (seizures, contorted gestures, and so on). All these scripted behaviors serve to "break process" (see Chapter 3) and take the patient, and the audience, away from the ordinary flow of events and lead them to conclusions or expectations (reframing) that can result in actual physiological changes and emotional as well as physical and social cure. Through these symbolic processes the shaman is able to remove objects from the patient and/or set up a situation where information related to the cure is created (the shaman shrinks in size, voices come out of nowhere, objects appear and disappear, and so on) and accepted.

Cure is signaled by the end of the ritual/seance, and because curing is a community event, reintegration flows from community involvement.

The Italians

I have written in some detail about the illness beliefs and curing practices among the Italians (see Rush 1974, 1994, 1996). At this point I would like to point out some of the similarities with the cultures noted above.

In 1969, I began a study of a large Italian kinship network in Toronto, Canada, that lasted until 1981. During that time I made an in-depth study of curing practices and how Italian indigenous beliefs represent a mirror of social relationships and function as mechanisms of stress reduction and social control.

At the turn of the twentieth century, many immigrants from southern Italy settled in the Toronto area. With them they brought beliefs and practices that aided in explaining illness, death (especially infant mortality), and other misfortune. Canada, however, offered a different environment and culture in which infant mortality dropped and individuals who formerly had worked the land, found themselves in a less precarious economic position. Instead of abandoning their beliefs, they altered them to fit this new set of environmental and social conditions. Let it be understood that not all my informants believe or believed in witches and the evil eye. Western biomedicine, and the concepts presented during formal education, have slowly eroded these beliefs and practices, not because they are better or "true," but simply through enculturation of succeeding generations.

There are two main agents that cause illness: the witch (*strega*), an impersonal entity, and the evil eye (*malocchio*), a more personal attack through envy, amorous desires, jealousy, anger, or general ill will toward another. I might add that car headlights and evil glances from drivers (see Rush 1974:144) can likewise inflict the evil eye; thus the *malocchio* can also come from impersonal sources that, in many ways, represent the impersonal nature of the urban complex.

The indigenous curer (*fattucchiera*) is usually part of the client's close kin network, perhaps a grandmother or aunt. She is sought out when the individual has, for example, a persistent headache or stomachache, is experiencing extreme fatigue, or needs an explanation for a more serious condition—cancer, kidney failure, and so on. At the time of the study, all curers were females, and it was usually females, rather than males, who utilized their services.

The diagnostic process is initiated by the *fattucchiera*'s questions about the illness: when it was first noticed, where the patient was at the time, who she was with, and so on. Next, divination is performed to determine the cause of the complaint. This is accomplished by placing a few drops of olive oil on water and then interpreting the movement of these blobs (i.e., whether they clump together, form separate clumps, etc.). After observing many of these rituals I concluded that no definite interpretation corresponded to a specific configuration of the blobs. In other words, the curer had a more open approach, similar to the divination practiced by the Navaho diagnostician. The interpretation of the blobs, however, falls into three general categories: (1) indirect suggestions about people (often relatives) who are envious, and so on; (2) attacks by nonrelatives known to the individual; and (3) attacks by impersonal witches. No one was ever specifically accused, although the interpretations usually led to a conclusion, on the part of the patient, of who was causing the illness and why.

After the divination procedure, a secondary ritual, using silver knives held together in the shape of a cross and accompanied by incantations, signaled cure through a removal of the curse or evil eye. The cause of illness, then, can be considered as information intrusion (a *strega* putting a curse on someone) or as intrusive thoughts of others as projected by the evil eye.

These curing ceremonies are conducted in the presence of other relatives, and once the cure is signaled, reintegration is accomplished through the consumption of food and tea or coffee, accompanied by small talk about family members and friends, usually wrapped around gossip about who is doing what to whom in the kindred.

Other Studies

In the literature the reader will encounter culture after culture in which illness, both emotional and physical (many cultures do not make such a distinction), is the product of social antagonisms/social stress as mirrored in witches, sorcerers, ancestor spirits, animal spirits, and so on (see Rush 1996; Lehmann and Myers 1993; Morley and Wallis 1978; Hart 1978; Marwick 1970; Middleton 1967; Kiev 1964; Salar 1964; Epstein 1959; Evans-Pritchard 1937 for more examples).

The reader might be tempted to say that these cultures are practicing superstitious behavior that has nothing to do with modern medicine/psychology. Such a position represents an ethnocentric bias. The metaphors used by these cultures differ from Western metaphors only with respect to content. Their conceptions of illness are neither more nor less scientific than those in the West. People do not become ill simply because of the intrusion of bacteria or viruses; people become ill through a multitude of factors, including stress in social relationships, eating habits, hygiene, genetics, lifestyle, purposeful disturbances of the ecosystem (clearing land), natural alteration of the environment (earthquakes, floods, etc.), cultural contact, and so forth. And no culture, that I am aware of, can know all the causal factors. Western psychiatry's "scientific" preoccupation with genetics as the causal factor of emotional problems (schizophrenia, bipolar disorder, etc.) is about as scientific as believing in the connection between witchcraft and illness. Taking this further into Western biomedicine, to place the cause of cancer on bad genes, because we are ill equipped to deal with all the carcinogens produced by the petrochemical industry or the fractionated foods we consume day after day, is likewise less than scientific. In this case "bad genes" is analogous to witches.

Western and non-Western systems have many features in common. For example, there is the use of specialists and all the symbols that represent specialization, a philosophy of cause and effect, a set of ritual processes including divination procedures, a naming of the illness that evolves out of the divination process, and the use of incantation and/or written and visual symbols that move the system toward cure. One substantial difference between Western and non-Western systems lies in the termination of treatment, signaling when cure is complete, and social reintegration. If Western biomedicine/psychology sees its theories and procedures as non-cultural, then social reintegration becomes only a minor detail. Integrating the individual back into society, once the illness is named and appropriate rituals are performed, is, in my opinion, one of the basic features of cure.

The *Diagnostic and Statistical Manual of Mental Disorders (DSM-IV)*

There are only three general types of social behavior: normal behavior, the gray area, and abnormal beliefs and behaviors that do not fit a social norm—social norms that are invented. Just what is normal and abnormal was an easy distinction in small, conservative societies with face-to-face contact, and aberrant behavior was relatively easy to suppress; this is no longer the case. What was considered normal thirty years ago is considered abnormal today; the reverse is also true. For example, smoking was the norm when I was growing up in the 1940s and 1950s; it seemed that every-one smoked. Now it is a "disorder" and coded as such in the American Psychiatric Association's *DSM-IV* (305.10).

Coffee, once considered the "think drink," can now lead you to caffeine-induced disorders (305.90, 292.89, 292.9). Many of the codes and descriptions in the *DSM-IV* did not exist ten years ago, and others did not exist twenty years ago, although some, like schizophrenia, have been in the medical vocabulary for over 100 years. So what is the significance of the *DSM-IV*? Is it a description of "real" behaviors, or are the behaviors a creation, a naming process to fit some other agenda? The *DSM-IV* rep-resents a reality, constructed by members of the psychiatric/psychological community, to name, and thus force into existence, conditions that have no reality of their own. These conditions are then presented to the re-mainder of the medical community, and the public at large, as scientific justification for their specialty. The *DSM-IV* also contains a section on "culture-bound" syndromes (Appendix I), all of seven pages long. Outside of specific behaviors listed—*amok, pibloktoq*, and so on—one is left with the impression that all the preceding behaviors are universal, and thus "true." All of these descriptions, however, occur within a cultural setting; they cannot be extracted and dissected without reference to the social system within which they occur. The *DSM-IV* is an attempt to take these syndromes and place them squarely on the shoulders of the individual. Treatment, then, is an individual matter and noncultural, much as you would set a broken leg.

For example, there are two eating disorders listed in the *DSM-IV*, an-orexia nervosa (307.1) and bulimia nervosa (307.51); both are considered illnesses. The symptomatology of anorexia is the maintenance of body weight less than 85 percent of a medical norm, fear of gaining weight, limited intake of nourishment (restricting type) or bingeing/purging type. Bulimia symptoms include eating above and beyond what is considered normal and then purging (vomiting, use of laxatives, enemas) and/or fasting or exercising to compensate for caloric intake. Although the connection between attractiveness and being thin (a cultural attitude) is mentioned, I have never encountered any therapeutic approach that involves a direct confrontation with the fashion industry, the medical specialists who perform surgical procedures that play into this illness complex (liposuction, breast augmentation, etc.), the mass media (television, motion pictures, etc.) that represent the female body as thin and with large breasts, and so on. These representations are far from the norm but are believed to be true and necessary for acceptance by a vast majority of North American females, whether or not they are practicing anorexics or bulimics. Dieting and the dieting industry are part of this behavioral illness complex, as are the medical industry and plastic surgeons who live off those caught up in body image neurosis, although these industries are not considered part of the symptoms. The therapy centering on these eating disorders, as well as the dieting industry and plastic surgery, are big business. Whenever the medical community creates an illness, it is not without economic consequences. Therapy for anorexics and bulimics should involve a community reproach to these images and behaviors fostered by society, because they are not solely individual issues without a direct social interface.

There are also what are termed "gender identity disorders." In a society where there is no clear definition of male or female, there is no clear statement about male or female behavior. Without a clear definition of male or female, or husband or wife, and the falling away of sexual restrictions, the sticky question of same-sex marriage moves into the political arena, an issue that would have been unthinkable twenty years ago.

Moreover, the creators of the *DSM-IV* have used politically correct behavior by not using the term "homosexuality" in its index. In fact, the term does not even appear (I cannot find it) in the *DSM-IV*, although it does appear in the index of *DSM-III* and is mentioned in *DMS-I* under "sociopathic personality disturbances" as a "sexual deviation" (Bieber 1967:963–976; also see Gadpaille 1989; Bayer 1987).

The *DSM-IV*, as stated in another work (Rush 1996: 160), is the psychiatric/psychological community's attempt to emulate Western biomedicine. It is a construction by the psychiatric and psychological communities, word magic and incantations in a most elegant form. These labels are magical in another way, in that once the individual has been tagged with a "condition," that label can never be removed. Once a "schizophrenic" or "bulimic," always a "schizophrenic" or "bulimic," and so on; these words show up on medical records in the future, and will bias educational and economic opportunities.

In order to treat a condition, all shamans, witch doctors, psychiatrists, and psychologists have to engage in divination procedures and a process of naming, for without a name there is no condition to treat. Moreover, insurance companies, another facet of the ritual curing process, demand numbers or codes for payment of claims. And just as naming is the grist for applying treatment, so codifying and numbering is the grist for payment for services; no coded diagnosis, no payment.

It is important that the reader become acquainted with *DSM-IV* and *The International Classification of Diseases* (PMIC 1997), both as research tools into Western medicine/psychiatry and for filling out insurance forms. The *DSM-IV*, however, is only a description of behaviors without any clear suggestion of cause. In order to understand the cause, the clinician must attach these syndromes to some philosophical perspective; you can choose any of the philosophies discussed above (Freudian, Jungian, genetics) or invent your own. My perspective will be presented in Chapter 3.

Divination and Psychological Testing

Numerology has been practiced in many cultures over the millennia. It is based on the idea that numbers are a gateway to a hidden structure of the universe. In the Middle East, approximately 3000 B.C., there was a recognition of five planets (wanderers) in the heavens and the construction of constellations as reference points, suggesting that the experienced world was a product of cosmic laws, a never-ending cycle of events. Through the observations of the comings and goings of stars and planets, an analogy evolved that was transposed onto the existing religiopolitical structure.

One of the earliest recorded systems of numerology was the *I Ching*, the book of changes. Another ancient text is the Cabala, a Jewish rendition of numerology, in which the *Sefer Yetsirah* outlines the construction of the world, using numbers and letters. Current and popular forms of numerology include taking a person's name, assigning numbers, making a calculation, and comparing it with similar numbers connected to personality traits collected from others. This can also be done with a person's birth date, which is then compared against some assigned interpretation (see Matthews 1992:188–194 for an overview of numerology and other systems of divination).

This brings us to one of the main props used by Western psychologists, psychological testing (see Rush 1996). Numerous tests have been compiled over the years: the MMPI (Minnesota Multiphasic Personality Inventory), PAI (Personality Assessment Inventory), SEI (Self-Esteem Index), and so on, which have been designed to uncover personality problems, parenting suitability, stress, and the like (see Appendix D for a divination procedure for predicting violent/aggressive behavior). Most of these tests are set up so that the individual answers a question according to some scale, for example, a 1 for "no" and a 4 for "yes," with 2 and 3 representing gradations. Below is the Impact of Events Scale, created by Mardi Horowitz (Corcoran and Fischer 1987: 186–187).

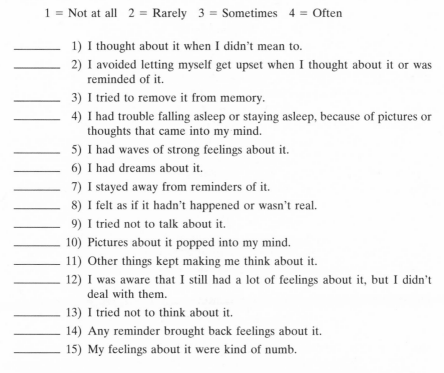

Below is a list of comments made by people about stressful life events and the context surrounding them. Read each item and decide how frequently each item was true for you during the past seven (7) days, for the event and its context . . . you are dealing with in treatment. If the item did not occur during the past seven days, choose the "Not at all" option. Indicate on the line at the left of each comment the number that best describes that item (see the four [4] options below). Please complete each item.

    1 = Not at all 2 = Rarely 3 = Sometimes 4 = Often

_____ 1) I thought about it when I didn't mean to.

_____ 2) I avoided letting myself get upset when I thought about it or was reminded of it.

_____ 3) I tried to remove it from memory.

_____ 4) I had trouble falling asleep or staying asleep, because of pictures or thoughts that came into my mind.

_____ 5) I had waves of strong feelings about it.

_____ 6) I had dreams about it.

_____ 7) I stayed away from reminders of it.

_____ 8) I felt as if it hadn't happened or wasn't real.

_____ 9) I tried not to talk about it.

_____ 10) Pictures about it popped into my mind.

_____ 11) Other things kept making me think about it.

_____ 12) I was aware that I still had a lot of feelings about it, but I didn't deal with them.

_____ 13) I tried not to think about it.

_____ 14) Any reminder brought back feelings about it.

_____ 15) My feelings about it were kind of numb.

This test is designed to measure intrusive thoughts (questions 1, 4, 5, 6, 10, 11, 14) and avoidance of ideas, feelings, and situations (2, 3, 7, 8, 9, 12, 13, 15). By adding up the score (the higher the scores, the higher the stress), the clinician can tell relative amounts of posttraumatic stress for specific life events. But is this what this test really measures?

This, like most of the psychological testing conducted by Western psychologists, is nothing more or less than a form of numerology. Most systems of numerology represent comparisons between the current test and those taken by others. The numbers are crunched and a generalization is produced. But how accurate are psychological tests? Do they really give an indication about personality, stress, and the like? Is the numerology as conducted by Western psychologists a representation of truth and all other systems, for example, the *I Ching*, false and superstition? It is highly unlikely that any of the psychological tests mean what the creators think they mean. Unfortunately, too many psychologists treat these tests as truths and often, after only brief interviews with the client, use these tests to diagnose "conditions" that often end up influencing opinions in civil and criminal court cases. Presenting such tests as truth is clearly a misrepresentation, as I have stated elsewhere (see Rush 1996). Moreover, there is no predictive value in any of these tests.

Psychological testing is a prop analogous to any type of divination procedure, such as tea-leaf reading, olive oil on water, or astrology. It is not truth, and serves to create an illusion of science wrapped around what is essentially an art form. I have had a fair amount of success in determining outcomes in marriage counseling by consulting the place mat at any Chinese restaurant. These place mats outline personality characteristics and whom one should or should not avoid! The Chinese zodiac is made up of a twelve-year cycle; each cycle is named for an animal, and each animal has specific characteristics. Personality traits, including mentality and ability to relate to others, are thought to derive from one's year of birth. For example, if you were born in the year of the ox (1949, 1961, 1973, 1985, 1997), you are considered to be "Bright, patient and inspiring to others. You can be happy by yourself, yet make an outstanding parent. Marry a Snake or Cock. The Sheep will bring trouble."

We do not think that this is scientific, although the Chinese constructed it after countless generations of observing birth dates and temperament, and have used this and similar divination procedures for over 2,500 years. This type of divination smacks of limited choices and predestination, and does not fit our model of individualism and self-responsible decision-making. But is it any more or less accurate for forming an opinion or making a decision? The word to place in large print is *DECISION*, which is the purpose of divination. That is to say, divination procedures, whether we are considering blood tests, psychological testing, or the *I Ching*, are designed to help people make decisions. They offer people wonderful metaphors for action.

The point of this is simple. Avoid psychometrics as the major form of divination in your own practice, and be cautious of any interpretations rendered by psychologists through the use of such testing, since these interpretations become self-fulfilling. Patients always have their diseases after they leave the doctor's office, not before entering, and after the name is assigned, there is an expectation that the patient will live up to the symptoms described for that disease. That is to say, there is now an expectation to live up to the behavior described for that disease; this locks the individual into the disease, especially if the symptoms are subject to litigation, as in work stress. Moreover, and with respect to psychological testing for the courts, such tests are usually interpreted in the negative— this is where artistic license comes in. By evaluating in the negative, the psychologist protects himself from misdiagnosis. In other words, he can say "I told you so" if the individual lives up to the interpretation, and if there is no new negative behavior in the future, the report is simply forgotten.

The use of psychometrics should be in reducing stress rather than labeling or accusing. Undoubtedly some readers will be called upon at some point to render an opinion, perhaps in contradiction to an opinion rendered by a psychologist. Psychological opinions are, for the most part, culturebound; they are still valid opinions, but not truths. One of the least appreciated aspects of opinions or conclusions drawn by psychiatrists and psychologists is that the conclusion drawn by the general public "without training" is similar (see Milton et al. 1987:17–18). Why is this? This is because disturbed communication patterns are a breach of social rules, rules and behaviors with which we are all familiar; such breaches cannot be ignored.

The basic point is that nothing takes the place of numerous contacts/ interviews with a client for determining and/or predicting behavior. Using any divination technique as your main source of information about emotional/social functioning is inadequate at best.

REVIEW

All curing systems around the world, whether involving emotional and/ or physical problems, contain similar elements. Each system is best appreciated within a specific cultural context and, with respect to emotional problems (as well as the vast majority of physical issues), Western biomedicine/psychiatry/psychology, in my opinion, is no more effective than the indigenous systems.

Curing is brought into action when the patient manifests or reports symptoms that diverge from the norm as defined by a particular group or culture. Specialists are brought in to divine the cause of the illness and assign a name. The naming can be seen as a framing or reframing process. By placing an interpretation on the symptoms, the doctor, shaman, or medicine man alters the patient's belief and places it within the realm of hope and cure. If the symptoms have been named, then there is experience with them, and thus a promise of cure. It is important to realize that naming the symptoms makes them tangible in a symbolic sense, and opens

Figure 2.1
The Curing Process or the Process of Life, Death, and Individual/Social
Resurrection

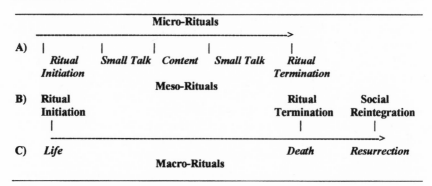

Source: Figure from *Clinical Anthropology: An Application of Anthropological Concepts Within Clinical Settings* by John A. Rush. Copyright © 1996 John A. Rush. Reproduced with permission of Greenwood Publishing Group, Inc., Westport, CT.

the door to action and stress reduction. Stress interferes with the body's natural healing abilities. Rituals are performed that include props and incantations, with cure signaled at the termination of the ritual and reintegration of the individual into his or her social group or integration into a new group. This brings the individual and the social system to a balanced state. The intrusive information is removed (the shaman removes the intrusive spirit, the M.D. removes the intrusive bacteria), or lost information (i.e., soul loss, blood, etc.) is returned, and so on, moving the system toward balance. Figure 2.1 is an outline of the curing process.

The curing process, in reality, is no different from everyday interactions (A), wherein there is a ritual greeting, then usually small talk, followed by some content or reason for the encounter, small talk again as the encounter is winding down, and then a termination ritual. This is a process encountered in all cultures, and without it social interaction cannot proceed. The content of each part differs from culture to culture.

Part B represents an extension of the everyday interaction pattern, wherein the ritual is the stereotyped display of symptoms, the small talk is the information initially sent and gathered (by shamans and M.D.s) that signals the course of content discovery (divination), other auxiliary ritual processes, and cure, followed by small talk, as the process winds down, and culminating in a completion of the interaction. The completion can signal social integration, or social integration can be a separate ritual in itself. A signal of cure and social reintegration, for the most part, is lacking in Western psychiatry and psychology; I cannot stress this too strongly. Without a signal of cure and social reintegration, Western biomedicine practices an illness maintenance rather than a health care system.

Part C, or Macro-Ritual, indicates that everyday interaction and curing are analogous to life, death, and resurrection. It is important that the clinician understand the above process, for without it you cannot clearly define what you are doing. When you understand a person's ritual (actually, this is a set of rules), you are in a position to assist the client in altering thoughts and behaviors.

All cultures have philosophies of cause and effect that are wrapped around rituals or procedures of cure. With this said, I want to introduce the reader to a philosophy in Chapter 3 that will be quite useful in understanding emotional problems and stress reactions. This philosophy is, in my opinion, a starting point to one of the quickest roads to individual and group stress reduction. Following this, the reader will be introduced to communication tools (incantations) for dealing with his or her own emotional problems and the concerns of others.

Chapter 3

A Model for Successful Counseling and Therapy

BECOMING OUR KIND

The following, with some modification, has been taken from Rush (1976, 1978, 1993a, 1996:86–101), and most of the concepts are anthropological rather than psychological. Table 3.1 is an encapsulation of the model. The separation of physical and social information is done for explanation purposes; the physical and the social cannot, in fact, be separated.

In the Beginning . . .

In a mythological tradition inherited from the Greeks, the Germanic peoples, and the Celtic peoples, each person represents a unique expression, something that has never existed before. This is contrasted with the Oriental mythologies, especially the Hindu tradition, that individualism is an illusion, that there is a cosmic order, and everything that is happening has already happened. In my opinion there is enough evidence to confirm that each individual is, indeed, unique with a different genotype (except in the case of identical twins) and phenotypic expression. Identical twins aside, human infants come into the world with unique characteristics, for example, neural wiring and brain chemistry. From a neural chemistry perspective, each person is born with different capacities for chemical production, uptake mechanisms, enzyme production for removing secreted chemicals, and so on. These differences, individually or in combination, result in each individual's having a unique interpretation of his or her world that translates into varying degrees of sensitivity and reactions to information available to the senses. When considering the genetic model of schizophrenia or manic-depressive psychosis, these differences become

Table 3.1
Humans as Information-Processing Systems

INFORMATION		
Physical		**Social**
1) "Predispositions" (the "More" or "Less" in Neurochemistry)	---->	1) Social System Survival Depends on Rules That Allow the Development of a) Conformity
2) Information-Sending -Receiving Potential Language as Genetically Programmed		b) Expectations c) Security
		2) Rules (Division of Labor and Relationship.Rules): Communicator Using "Tool Kit" Called Language
3) Grouping Mechanism: Fear of Rejection-- Rejection Equals Physical and Psychological Death		3) Roles (Ascribed and Achieved) Learned Through Enculturation
4) Dependency: Physical Survival Depends upon Immediately Being Placed in a Social System, i.e., a Family ---------->		

important considerations. However, there are many other factors to consider, with respect not only to these extremes but to "average" reactions as well. Other factors include diet, trauma, and the individual's interpretation of socially derived information as he or she matures.

As with other mammals, the human infant comes with behavioral predispositions and reflexes that are somewhat more difficult to qualify. One of the psychological beliefs of years past was that the individual enters the world as a "blank slate," but this does not seem to be the case. In fact, it is perhaps better to say that the individual arrives as an incomplete slate, with culture adding the specific graphics, language, cultural attitudes, beliefs, and behaviors.

Even in the womb, information originating outside the fetus is contributing to uniqueness. This includes hormones secreted by the mother under both positive and negative stress, drugs ingested, the metabolic changes that occur during fetal maturation, surrounding light intensity, touch, sounds and voices, heartbeat, allergic reactions, and diet.

Another physical given is a capacity to symbolize—more specifically, a language capacity (Chomsky 1957, 1968). This ability to symbolize and engage in analogous thinking may not be unique to humans, although there appear to be qualitative and quantitative differences that set humans apart from all other animals.

Humans are also group animals, and one must explain the mechanisms that keep individuals in groups and subject to social conditioning, for it is the alignment of mind/brain in the form of cooperation, and the creative constructions that issue forth, that offer us great survival potential. One such mechanism is fear, more specifically, the fear of rejection. This fear of rejection, rather than being a learned psychological mechanism, is quite old and was in place at least 3–4 million years ago with our *Australopithecine* ancestors. The purpose of fear of rejection is to keep the individual an active participant in the group.

It is generally accepted by most anthropologists that humans are small-group animals, with grouping serving as a survival mechanism. The ideal group size ranges from 25 to 125–150 individuals. Even in large urban settings we still relate, in any intimate fashion, only within small groups or urban tribes. In other words, our prehuman and human ancestry is composed of relatively weak, vulnerable individuals whose survival depended on group cooperation. In prehistoric times, and especially before 10,000 years ago, our group was our universe. In most cases there was knowledge of "strangers" in distant geographical locations; evidence and experience of others became more frequent over time (see Fagan 1995: 159–164). Such contacts, however, were often dangerous, perhaps more so for males. The point is that being outside of the group exposed the individual not only to other, possibly unfriendly humans but also to predators, accidents, and other ill fortune. Moreover, the initial dependency on the group, for at least the first twelve years of life, is not conducive to feeling very comfortable outside of the group, alone, and with nowhere to go, in later life. Being outside the group means death, physically and emotionally, and certainly, without a mate, one's unique genetic material dies.

However, the consequences of being outside of the group could be devastating to group survival because any special talent, or simply aiding in the food quest, was lost or compromised. Rejection, then, rather than being a mechanism to drive individuals away, was designed to maintain the status quo. Fear of rejection is a universal human phenomenon. Even in urban settings, where there would appear to be great latitude for defecting from one group and joining another, one might have great difficulty joining other groups. This is especially the case in caste-based societies, where entering another group is next to impossible.

In our own society, entering groups is more fluid, and with sufficient rejection we search for individuals and groups that are more accepting. But we bring with us all kinds of emotional baggage that can contribute to more problems as we attempt to solve the rejection in the previous group(s).

My position, then, is that the fear of rejection is embedded deep in our psyche and is one of the primary mechanisms, reinforced through many years of dependency, that connects us to groups. One can observe this mechanism of rejection in other mammals, for example, in the behavior of our canine companions—their survival in the wild, like ours, depends on cooperative effort.

Physical death, furthermore, is analogous to emotional death, which is the basic element in social stress reactions. Individuals who are not attached to a social group(s) are, essentially, dead, and the terror of being outside of a group and alone has been one of the two major factors of motivation in our human and prehuman heritage (the other motivating factor is positive stimulation or inspiration). Also, the conscious ability to contemplate one's own death represents an interesting, powerful, and paradoxical form of rejection. People die physically, and in that sense leave the group, but who really leaves whom? There is loss on both sides. This loss is resolved, at least partly, by inventing stories that explain, entertain, reassure, and motivate, in order to place an emotional comfort zone between your group ego and the stark terror and the realization that we are very small cogs in a large, large wheel. Out of this terrifying realization came the invention of gods who are special to us, or gods and demons who say, "Nothing personal or malicious, just the way the cosmic order works." Our current Western scientific myth assumes that the truth about life and death will be known through research methodology, and science will save us from death. Freezing people, and then thawing them once a cure is found for the condition that led to death, fits this mythological theme. This is really little different, for example, from the elaborate Egyptian beliefs and behaviors connected to life, death, and resurrection. More about the fear of emotional rejection shortly.

Human infants, compared with those of all the other primates, are born essentially helpless, leading to a long dependency period (twelve years or more). This intense dependency has ramifications at the individual and group levels, leading to structured rights and obligations between group members. Individual and group survival, then, requires that the newborn immediately be placed within a social group, for example, the family, but once he or she is in this social setting, the group members are compelled to begin a slow process of enculturating or indoctrinating the individual in terms of group rules. Such rules (e.g., when and what to eat, where and how long to sleep, clothes worn, reactions to others, etc.) serve to build a sense of conformity that leads to individual and group expectations, and a relative sense of security.

The process of enculturation is accomplished through the use of basic language tools (warning, threatening, ordering, praising, and so on) and more elaborate processes (myth and ritual). Most of the major social/relationship rules are usually in place somewhere between the ages of seven and nine; as the individual is learning the rules, he or she is also learning the tools, developing a style of tool use, and constructing a history or memory of interaction events. It is the constructed memory of traumatic events that is the target of all successful therapy. In other words, by altering the meaning of troublesome events, a natural and protective mental process, one can potentially reduce individual and social stress.

High-Risk Messages

Along with rules, tools, style, and memory, the individual acquires a set of what I call high-risk messages (HRMs). These are acquired as the individual learns the rules, for it is during the rule internalization period that the individual acquires his or her group identity, that is, his or her acceptability or unacceptability in the group. When individuals set rules, the goal is to instill or stop/alter a behavior. However, young children, and adults as well, have difficulty distinguishing between self and behavior. High-risk messages, like being called stupid, incompetent, lazy, and not good enough, are connected to social rules, or how one should behave, and the genetic fear of being outside the group. This is the guilt and shame one experiences when social rules are broken; societies can not exist without rules, guilt, and shame. Rejection and HRM formation are a natural and necessary part of group living. HRMs are part of each person's pain, and pain motivates. A world where there are no negatives, a world where everyone is positive, contented, and happy, is not a realistic state of existence. However, it is the ideal that one encounters in heaven or similar mythological realms—realms that, in part, reinforce the realities of emotional and physical pain associated with social living. (For a detailed discussion of HRM development, see Rush 1996: 86–93.)

HRMs and Stress Reactions

Stress is a condition in which the body and mind become unbalanced or conflicted. It becomes manifest in the form of various symptoms, termed illness. Symptoms can vary from depression and headaches, to aches and pains, to more serious conditions.

From an emotional/social standpoint, when stress goes up, the ability to process internal and external information decreases. Basic and universal stress-reducing mechanisms include physical and verbal fighting, withdrawal, freezing up, emotional conversion, and sexual behavior. This is illustrated in Figure 3.1. (See Rush 1996:94–101 for a more detailed discussion of these potentially stress-reducing behaviors.)

These behaviors are universal in the sense that they are utilized by all human groups, although each culture may instill a specific preference(s), and likewise can be found in the behavioral sets of other species. Further, most human behavior can be seen as flowing from or analogous to these five universals.

Figure 3.1
Stress Figure

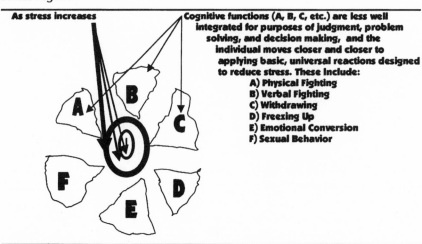

Source: Figure adapted from *Clinical Anthropology: An Application of Anthropological Concepts Within Clinical Settings* by John A. Rush. Copyright © 1996 John A. Rush. Reproduced with permission of Greenwood Publishing Group, Inc., Westport, CT.

These behaviors can also be seen as short-term and stereotypic behaviors noticeable in ourselves and acquaintances. The husband who withdraws from his noisy children, the employee who freezes up in the presence of the aggressive boss, the neighbor who yells at the neighborhood kids playing on his lawn—all are exhibiting normal reactions that individuals automatically bring into play when under stress.

High-Risk Messages, Long-Term Stress, and Psychiatric Syndromes

As mentioned, most of human behavior can be seen as flowing from the stress-reducing activities (i.e., withdrawal, verbal/physical fighting, freezing up, etc.), and many psychiatric conditions can be seen as evolving out of these general survival mechanisms over time.

As outlined in Table 3.2, there are three basic types of psychiatric syndromes: those that are directed inward, those that are directed outward, and those that seem to overlap.

Most of the *DSM-IV* listings are likewise analogues of the short-term stress-reducing behavior. However, many behaviors found in a specific and approved context are not subject to *DSM-IV* classifications (e.g., members of SWAT teams, laboratory researchers who conduct experiments on animals in the name of science, designers of munitions, CIA agents, etc.); this indicates an inconsistency or arbitrariness of application.

Table 3.2
Long-Term Effects of Continual Looping and/or Internalization of High-Risk Messages

---

Messages That Are Turned Inward

 a) Denying Reality: Psychosis
 b) Anxiety/Depression
 c) Stress-Generated Illnesses
 d) Suicide/Anger at Self/Masochism
 e) Drug Use/Abuse
 f) Eating Disorders

Messages That Are Projected Outward

 g) Verbal/Physical Violence
 h) Passive/Aggressive
 i) Vindictiveness/Sadism
 j) Theft
 k) Psychopathology

Review

The following represents, in outline form, the above model. The clinician needs some model, some metaphor of who we are, so that both the therapist and the client(s) can play ball in the same park. Therefore, it is necessary to have a story to tell your clients, one that will get their attention. It might be useful for the clinician to memorize Part B of the model below, which can be used as an incantation to reframe or reinterpret a person's total experience of life. In this model, no one is good or bad, right or wrong.

A. Primary Elements
 1. The Necessity for Time Limitations in Counseling
 2. Defining the Ritual Process
 3. Social Reintegration: A Necessary Part of Cure
B. How We Get to Be the Way We Are
 1. The Model
  a. Human Beings as Physical and Social Information Processors
  b. The Physical You
   1. Brain Chemistry: Everyone Is Unique and Perceives His/Her World Differently
   2. Innate Symbolizing System
   3. Fear of Rejection: A Grouping Mechanism That Represents
    a. Physical Death
    b. And, by Analogy, Emotional Death

    4. Dependency on Group for Survival—We Are Small-Group Animals

c. The Social You

    1. Survival Depends on the Group

    2. Group Survival Requires Socialization of Infant

       a. Must Instill Conformity

       b. Conformity Leads to Expectations

       c. Expectations Lead to a Sense of Security

       d. If the Above Are in Place, Group (and Individual) Survives

d. How Do We Instill Conformity, etc.?

    1. Caretakers/Parents Have a Tool Kit

    2. Tool Kit Is Called Language

    3. Within Language There Are Numerous Tools for Setting Rules (Language Primarily a Rule-Setting Device)

e. By the Age of Seven, Eight, Nine, Child Acquires

    1. A Set of Rules for Family Living—Everyone in North America Learns a Slightly Different Set of Rules

       a. This Creates a Problem in Marriage and Social Relationships in General

       b. This Also Leads to Creativity

    2. A Set of Tools for Setting Rules with Others

    3. A Style of Using Tools

       a. Tools One Has in His/Her Tool Kit, and Style of Use (plus Some Genetic Givens), Equals "Personality"

       b. There Is No Way to Measure Personality; It Is Simply Too Complicated

    4. A History or Memory

       a. History or Memory Is Not True; It Is True Only to the Individual Who Created the Memory

       b. Memory Is Changeable (It Is Being Renegotiated All the Time)

          1. A Natural Process

          2. Changing Memory Is a Primary Feature of All Counseling/Therapy

    5. A Cluster of High-Risk Messages (HRMs)

       a. HRMs Are Genetically Inspired (Originate from an Innate Fear of Rejection) and Socially Conditioned (Individual Develops Specific HRMs as He/She Learns the Rules of Family/Group Living Early in Life)

       b. HRMs Are Added onto and Deleted Throughout Life

          1. Many Rules Are Communicated with a Style That Represents Rejection

      2. The Meaning of a Message Is Always Determined by the Receiver

   c. HRMs Represent a Person's "Pain" or the Pain of Rejection and Being Outside the Group

      1. Pain Motivates (Pleasure and/or Stress Reduction Is Sought, to Avoid Pain)

      2. Individuals Will Hear HRMs in a Message Before Anything Else

         a. There Is Survival Value in This

         b. Negatives About Self Are More Readily Internalized Than Are Positives

      3. HRMs Represent "Loops" in the Brain, Rejection That the Individual Is Attempting to Solve and Exit from

6. When an Individual's HRMs Are Tapped into (Through, for Example, Ordering, Warning, Name-Calling, Sarcasm, Nagging, Logical Arguments, Withdrawing Love, Frowning, Invasion of Body Space, Hitting, etc.), There Are Short-Term Effects That Can Have Long-Term Consequences

   a. Stress Goes Up

   b. Communication Potential Goes Down

   c. Age Regression Is Common

   d. Information Compresses in the Mind and Leads to Six Universal Mechanisms for Reducing Stress (Mechanisms Are Used in All Cultures, Are Recognizable in Many Other Species, and Do Not Always Serve to Reduce Stress. Most of Human Behavior Flows from these Six Universals)

      1. Physical Fighting

         a. Stress-Reducing Especially When You Win

      2. Verbal Fighting (Analogous to Physical Fighting)

         a. Stress-Reducing if You Obtain Compliance

         b. Stress-Reducing if You Are Sincerely Listened to

         c. Stress-Enhancing if Other Verbally Fights Back

      3. Withdrawing: Reducing or Altering Information Input/Output

         a. Physical Withdrawal

         b. Emotional Withdrawal

         c. Use of Drugs

      4. Freezing Up

         a. By Not Doing Anything, You Limit Information Output, Reduce Risk of Detection, and Reduce Further Negative Bit Internalization

         b. Sometimes You Get "Hit by the Truck"

      5. Emotional Conversion

         a. By Converting One Emotion into Another, You Open the Door to Other Behaviors That Might Be Stress-Reducing

         b. Through Metaphor We Convert Emotions into Physical Sensation and Make Ourselves "Sick" (This Is One of the Factors in Psychosomatic Medicine)

      6. Sexual Behavior
        a. Sex Is Stress-Reducing (but Not for Everyone)
        b. Explains Why Sex Offenders Are Difficult to Deal with
      7. Long-Term Effects
        a. Analogous to Short-Term Stress Reactions
        b. Analogues of the Syndromes Listed in *DSM-IV*
C. Therapy Proceeds Through
    1. Uncovering HRMs
    2. Retranslating HRMs
    3. Uncovering Negative Implied Rules
    4. Explicit Rule-Setting
    5. Role Recognition.

HRMs, STRESS REDUCTION, AND THERAPEUTIC PROCEDURE

Explaining your model of therapy to a client accomplishes several things. First, it informs the client about your approach and helps him or her to make a decision to come back or not. In this sense, the model acts as a divination process to determine trust *and* if counseling is possible. This should be done during the first session, so that any issues of concern that would interfere with trust-building can be addressed.

Another purpose behind the model is to place everyone in the healing session in the same ball-park. One of the features of healing in traditional cultures is that all those involved in the healing enjoy the same metaphor and are playing the same game.

Third, you can use the model as a hypnotic story from which to instill more stress-reducing beliefs about people and events.

It is standard opinion that the therapist must intently listen to the client, especially during the first few sessions. It is important to get a basic idea about what the person wants from you. It is more important that both of you get on the same therapeutic wavelength as soon as possible. The client is forming an opinion of you and you of him or her. There are three beliefs that the client must have firmly in place after the first session. First, that he or she won't be judged; second, that most problems in social living are based on the sending and receiving of information; and third, that there is hope.

Your first job, then, after the client has outlined his or her problem, is to tell a story with which he or she will agree, without insulting or labeling people in negative ways. Do not let a client talk about problems too long or in too much detail, for this can retraumatize the individual. Group therapy often serves to retraumatize victims of rape and other violence through talking and emotionally revisiting the experience. Talking about problems does not necessarily mean that problems or troubled thoughts will go away. In most cases, they have to be replaced with a different meaning before they are emotionally resolved.

Building Trust

One of the first steps in therapy is building trust. This is initially done by not tapping into the individual's HRMs. If you do, however, and the relationship is important to you, you recognize the inadvertent attack and do something to reduce stress in the receiver and yourself. What to do will be discussed under data collection (listening).

During this information collection process the therapist needs to uncover the individual's HRMs, for this is the information causing the stress. HRMs can stand in the way of both emotional and physical healing. Once HRMs are uncovered, the procedure is to rapidly reframe or place a different meaning on the events/words that are distressing the client. The procedure is very simple, and to explore this you will use yourself as your first client. First, however, the reader needs to be introduced to emotional responsibility and, second, to listening and data-collecting procedures.

Emotional Responsibility

One of the reader's first exercises is to begin a systematic process of listening to how people express emotions. As you listen to others, you will often hear "He made me angry," "She pushes all my buttons," "You really piss me off," and so on. All of these statements imply that emotions are given to you by others. Think about this for a moment. If you believe that a person "gives" you an emotion, then you will act on that belief. If you believe that a person can make you angry, then you become angry, and you now have no responsibility for that emotion (it has been given to you), and consequently no responsibility for your behavior. That is why people can say "She made me angry, so I hit her. It was her fault; she shouldn't have made me angry!"

Moreover, if you believe that people make you angry, how can you listen? Being angry and being able to listen are contradictions. Being angry is a defensive emotional set, and the angry person is formulating a defense, not listening in an open manner.

Language, and the way we put words together, creates a reality for us (Sapir 1996; Whorf 1967). For example, you might say "My keys are lost." Think about this. How can your keys be lost? You may have misplaced your keys, but the only way they can be lost is if they wandered away and took a wrong turn somewhere. When we say "You make me angry," the implication is that someone else is responsible for your emotions; not only is that a terrible burden, it is simply not true. "You make me angry" is a statement of blame, and blaming is high-risk (stress will go up in the receiver). If you say "I am angry," however, you are more likely to elicit curiosity from the hearer. This is pretty old stuff, but it is a wonderful attention getter for those who have not been exposed.

A person can only give you information or create a situation to which you react, using your history (Maltz 1969; Rush 1976). Your emotions are generated in a part of your brain called the limbic system (Papez 1937; this appears to be the original source of this physiological conclusion), and seem to function in the process of storage and retrieval of information. So when someone gives you information or creates a situation, you access your history, or information that represents this event, and with that history you get an emotion previously used to tag that information. There is great survival value in this. During the enculturation process, you learn to approach certain types of information (a person, an animal, a geographical place, etc.) and avoid others. You learn to like certain types of information (soothing voice tones, friendly faces, chicken soup, etc.) and dislike others (loud voice tones, angry faces, lima beans, etc.), even though your responses are not "logical" or necessarily the responses of others. In short, we all learn to like and dislike different things. When information enters our senses and is compared with previously stored information that in some manner resembles it, we pull up those "same old feelings," to turn a phrase. This gives us the impression that emotions come from others and not from ourselves.

Let me give you a further example. Let's say you are in a restaurant having coffee with someone you really like. And this person accidentally spills a glass of water in your lap. How are you going to feel and react in this situation? In all probability you will laugh it off and make excuses for the other person. Let's say, on the other hand, that you are in the same restaurant—same waiter, same table, same water, same coffee—with someone you do not like at all. In fact, you despise this person, but you have to do some problem-solving. This person accidentally spills a glass of water in your lap. How will you feel and react? You would have to agree that your thoughts and reactions are different in these two situations.

Let me give you another example. You are trying to find a parking place at the mall; it is the weekend, and it is packed. So you are driving around and around, and finally you see a parking space. You step on the gas, and just as you are about to pull into the spot, someone beats you to it. You are angry, and without thinking, you open the door and get out of the car, quite prepared to give this person a piece of your mind. When the other driver gets out, you see that it is your best friend. What happens to your anger? It is converted into another emotion that is stored with the friendship (information) that you have for this other person. Where did the anger and this new emotion originate? Right, within you.

People get themselves in a great deal of emotional and legal trouble because they believe that people give them feelings. Such people make the best victims in the world. Selling people on the idea that their emotions are their own is quite a challenge, for using logic usually does not work. Other forms of incantations for this type of message delivery will be discussed below.

Learn to listen and really hear yourself. If you are going to be useful to others, you first have to heal yourself and neutralize your language, your negative incantations. Instead of saying "You annoy me," "He/she/they/it/someone frustrates me," say "I am frustrated, annoyed, happy," and so on. By doing this over a week, you begin to clean out a lot of information. You exit from mental conflicts and blaming because of emotional irresponsibility in the past (or even current situations). The concept of emotional responsibility, once understood, accepted, and internalized, is one of the most mind-cleansing concepts in the therapeutic field.

Generalizing, Deleting, and Distorting

The most likely purpose of emotions is for tagging information. Such tagging is necessary during the process of storage and retrieval. Let me explain further. When you bring information into your senses, you essentially do three things with it. First, you generalize it or put it into categories, some of which are culturally constructed; all of it is personalized, which accounts for the tremendous amount of creativity that surrounds us, as well as the misunderstandings. As an example of cultural categories, the Neur of central Africa (see Evans-Pritchard 1940:41–50) have many categories for cows, depending on color and horn shape. For most urban North Americans, a cow is a cow. For urban North Americans, on the other hand, there are many categories and subcategories of motor vehicles—cars, trucks, sedans, convertibles, and so on. The Neur would not have the experience or familiarity for creating such categories. We are all given culturally constructed categories, and we also construct categories that are personal or unique and might seem less than logical.

In any event, categories are the mind's process for creating some type of order or organization of people, places, things, and ideas. Without categories, it would be impossible to operate in or manage your world. This is why kinship terms are so important: they serve to organize relationships without having to redefine each relationship as it is happening.

A second thing we do with information is delete what we choose (consciously or subconsciously) not to pay attention to. There is so much information available to our senses that without deleting, we would be constantly overloaded. Some people delete visual information and do not "see" as much as others. Some people delete auditory messages and do not "hear" as well as they see; and some people delete sensations, for example, the wind against their face or the coolness on a fall evening. For those of you interested in more fully using receptor states in your counseling practice, I suggest workshops in neurolinguistic programming.

A third thing that we do with information entering our senses is distort it in some manner. For example, if you are in a good mood, you will distort in one way; your perception of that same information when you are in a bad mood will be distorted in another way.

Returning to emotions, if you believe that people give you emotions, you become the perfect victim because everyone is doing things to you; it is always someone else's fault because "they started it." Emotional irresponsibility does not allow the individual to take responsibility for the information he or she sends or receives. You cannot, in my opinion, become a responsible communicator, you cannot become a responsible parent or spouse, unless you are willing to take responsibility for the information you send and for how you interpret information. You *are* responsible for how you send and receive, and very few people are willing to take responsibility for the symbols they send and their interpretation of symbols from others.

Emotional irresponsibility comes about, in part, through realities created by the language itself. In other words, the juxtaposition of words creates meanings. For example, "Stop it! You're making me angry" has a different meaning than "Stop it! I'm getting angry!" What is the difference? Emotional responsibility also derives from the way we create our worlds through generalizing, deleting, and distorting. We generalize through the way words are put together, that is, "If you make me angry, then my emotions come from outside of me." Once we begin to think in this way, any information that contradicts it is blocked out. Any distortion, then, because this is a product of mood, is someone else's fault. With such a belief (emotional irresponsibility) coupled to generalizing, deleting, and distorting, you are free to blame everyone and everything for your predicament in life rather than realize that you are an active participant, and misery and happiness are products of your interpretation of the information available to you.

As I mentioned earlier, one of the most effective and primary therapeutic devices that you should share with clients is emotional responsibility. The problem, however, lies in the fact that most people are unwilling to take such responsibility because then they would have to take responsibility for their behavior (emotions are the triggers of behavior). Logic usually does not work, although there is a very logical method of informing others. In Chapter 4, I will come back to emotional responsibility and the method I use to deliver this concept during couples counseling.

Finally, emotional responsibility is a concept or metaphor that seems to fit best within cultures that subscribe to the metaphor of individualism and free choice. In our culture, we endeavor to create a self-responsible individual with choices that represent accountable and sensitive relations with others. Without emotional responsibility, self-responsible and sensitive behavior is difficult to achieve.

The Meaning of Compressed Data and Role-Shifting

It is next to impossible to listen if you believe that people "make you angry." So the question might arise, "Well, if I am making myself angry, how do I stop that anger? In other words, can I really choose how I feel?"

The answer to this is Yes, if you understand and have in place a number of concepts. Keep in mind that you, as a counselor or therapist, hypocritically counsel clients if you do not practice what you preach. First, you must understand what is happening as you are talking and listening. And exactly what is going on? You and the other(s), through the use of symbols and incantations, are setting rules about yourself, rules about others, and rules about rules. Yes, some of the specific rules (implied rules are discussed in Chapter 4) may not be immediately known to you, but if you keep in mind that you drift in a sea of rules, you can then start to identify these rules and alter them (if need be). Other terms for "rules" include "beliefs," "behaviors," "attitudes," and "rituals."

Second, you need to internalize the concept of emotional responsibility; without emotional responsibility you will be an ineffectual communicator. Period.

Third, you have many sense organs for perceiving incoming information; you see, hear, feel, taste, smell, and so on. Learn to use your senses, but be careful, because your creativity will increase as well as your intelligence.

The fourth concept to have in place is that the symbols with which people communicate—that is, their words, phrases, paragraphs, and stories, as mentioned in Chapter 1—represent compressed data. In short, you can never know what anyone means, and when the individual is communicating under stress, the data are further compressed, making meaning even more obscure. Under the influence of drugs, the data not only are compressed but also are uniquely distorted; people who are drunk, contrary to popular belief, do not tell the truth. So before you make yourself angry when others are communicating with you, ask yourself, "What does that person mean?" Another good question to ask is "Will anger work, and if so, how will it work?" Avoid "Why is this person communicating this way?" It is next to impossible to determine why anyone does anything, contrary to the psychoanalysts and psychologists. With patience and knowing how to listen, you can come close to meaning, keeping in mind that it is still your translation or interpretation.

The fifth concept involves role-shifting.[1] Question: How many roles do you play during the day, and what are the emotions and behaviors associated with each? For example, you perhaps play the role of a student, a sibling, a son or daughter, maybe a friend or lover, perhaps a wife or husband, maybe an employee. Now, think about this. If you are in the role of a student, and you are interacting with a professor, your mode of behavior and emotional set will be different from that of a professor's friend. Or if you are a parent, and you are acting toward your children as a lover, then you are in trouble. All emotions come with constructed behavioral sets (some culturally modeled, others uniquely molded), and all behaviors are connected to roles and emotions.

Herein lies one of the secrets to emotional responsibility, role-shifting. By shifting roles (you do this all the time), you can move from one emotional/behavioral set to another almost instantly. For example, you are growling at your children because they are doing something outrageous, "Growl, growl, growl!" And then the phone rings. So you go from Attila the Hun to happy AT&T person as you answer the phone and say "Hello" in a cheery voice. By switching roles you change your emotional set. Of course, you may return to your Attila the Hun role after you hang up the phone, but usually you are not as irate and it might take you a few moments to get back your emotional momentum. The reason for this seems to be that as you go from one role to another, there is sort of an emotional neutral gear you pass through. This certainly represents the process in a more digital, sliding-scale arrangement than is probably the case.

When you take it upon yourself to listen to others, as is absolutely necessary as a clinical anthropologist, you have to assume a role that will allow you to listen, and hold off inputting therapeutic information until sufficient information is gathered regarding problems in social living and associated high-risk messages. What should that role be? The best role to assume is that of diplomat or negotiator. In these roles, your job is to act as a go-between, a person between the individual and his or her physical and social world. You do not take sides, no matter how much some part of you says, "This person is wrong, crazy, stupid," and so on. In couples counseling, for example, taking sides and thinking that the wife is right and the husband is wrong, or vice versa, will limit your effectiveness. As you will see in Chapter 4, there can be no right or wrong, because both husband and wife created the system within which they are experiencing so much misery.

The process involved in role-shifting is to acquaint yourself thoroughly with the role of diplomat or negotiator and keep it separate from that of friend, lover, parent, spouse, and so on. Keep in mind, however, that in your private life, the role of negotiator or diplomat is extremely useful when dealing with "in-house" problems. Again, practice what you preach. Do not expect others to do what you cannot do or are unwilling to do. Now let us turn to listening.

THERAPEUTIC LISTENING

Listening Styles: General Principles

Early in the divination procedure, it is necessary to construct an environment for collecting information. Just as the fortune-teller questions and leads, so the therapist questions and leads (not always intentionally). The collected information is then mixed with other divination procedures, resulting in a decision. Implicit in the process of information-gathering is the necessity to listen. Language, however, does not represent a very efficient tool unless you can efficiently/effectively send information as well as receive it (listen). What to listen for is the flip side of what message to send in order to uncover HRMs, role confusion, and so on. In other words, don't be listening for an Oedipus complex when HRMs are the focal point. The Oedipus complex, in fact, is a metaphor that relates to HRMs.

Finally, since this is a divination procedure or tool that you teach your clients, it is not necessary to know everything about a person in order to move toward health.

We tend to have several different listening styles that are used in varying environments. For example, a person will listen differently when talked to by a judge or police officer as opposed to listening to a spouse or friend. Thus, the context, the person's stress level, being under the influence of drugs, and so on will affect how the individual interprets a message.

Below I present different techniques of listening; I will let the reader judge the relative effectiveness of each in terms of collecting quality and useful information.

Dueling

The first style of listening is what has been termed dueling (see Rush 1976). This procedure is composed of the following elements:

a. As the individual begins to communicate, the receiver processes the first few words and goes internal
b. Next, the receiver begins to formulate his/her reply, and at this point is no longer "hearing" or "seeing" the message of the sender
c. The receiver, either interrupting or waiting for the person to shut up, fires back this formulation (usually a defense of some kind).

This style of listening is very common among close friends who are second-guessing one another. It is also common when one or both are using alcohol, cocaine, or amphetamines. Husbands and wives use this style extensively, which often leads to more misunderstanding, increased stress, and loss of trust. Personnel turnover (i.e., divorce) is a frequent result.

In the clinical environment, however, where collecting quality information is important for therapeutic reasons, this procedure is not very useful. You are likely to end up "falling for the code" or accepting statements at face value. In an environment where there is little trust, you can end up with misleading information and a destruction of rapport. However, if your goal is to set up a situation of high stress and low trust, this is the listening procedure of choice.

The Apathetic Approach

This method of listening has the following elements:

a. Maintain good eye contact with the sender
b. Move your head up and down once in awhile
c. Stay internal most of the time and think about where you would really like to be
d. Try to get a license to practice humanistic psychology or psychiatry.

Listening, as you will see, is hard work, and it is easy to get tired of listening to the same old stories, problems, complaints, lies, and deceptions. However, the keys to realistic evaluation and intervention lie with the client's verbal and nonverbal language. Listening is the main therapeutic tool in much of the Rogerian, humanistic-type approaches. The client is encouraged to talk and talk while the therapist listens and listens. This approach can actually be destructive, in that it allows the client to retraumatize him or herself over and over by reviewing and inspecting traumatic events in history. You never allow the client to talk about the same traumatic event more than once without offering a reinterpretation.

The rationale behind listening, without entering the dialogue, involves the belief that the client, by talking and talking, will solve his or her own problems. This may be true. However, most problems in social living are a product of ineffectual styles of communication, and it is unlikely that the client will invent a new style by talking without feedback from the therapist.

Another rationale is that the client initially communicates presenting, not "real," problems. In other words, what the client brings to you is a "presenting problem"—not the "real problem." The belief is that only through listening for many weeks (or months or years) will the "real problem" surface. This is the old psychoanalytic position, and, although it is based on beliefs about repression and so on, it is surrounded by a sound economic principle: do not cure people too quickly. The longer the individual stays in counseling, the more payments the therapist can make on the Mercedes. However, the longer a client stays in counseling/therapy, the sicker he or she often becomes!

I used to subscribe to this "presenting problem" rationale; indeed, individuals do not often come into your office and tell you *the* problem or the total problem in the first session. Many times they do not know what the problem is. But which is the real problem? Isn't the problem also derived from the theory or model that the therapist brings to the session? Whose definition of the problem is correct? I usually bypass all this by explaining my model (presented at the beginning of this chapter), and most people agree with it. This model frames the problem in a general sense and puts the therapist and client on the same path. Solving the problem, then, means three things: dealing with HRMs, implied rules (see Chapter 4), and role confusion. In addition, you teach the client(s) more communication tools. End of therapy. Always searching for underlying problems is a brand of paranoia peculiar to Western psychiatry and psychology.

Confrontational Approach

This procedure unfolds as follows:

a. Look and act suspicious of everything the person tells you
b. Let the person know, through words and body language, that you disagree with, are suspicious of, take exception to all that is being said
c. Do not allow the speaker to finish any statements
d. Become a police officer, lawyer, or talk-show host.

The therapist often believes that he or she is more important than the client. When the therapist's status is the main focus of therapy, as is the case when the therapist has all his or her diplomas hung on the walls and desires to be referred to as "doctor," you move out of the field of therapy and into that of egotism, narcissism, and a great deal of insecurity. Assuming that you are better than the client is high-risk in this culture; we have a cultural ideal of equality. And although some clients will continue to see an egotistic therapist, they do so because they have come to believe in their own inferiority. The therapist has helped them to that place and, unfortunately, keeps them there. When nothing happens in therapy, the client is blamed for being "resistant" or "not ready." When the main focus is the therapist, there can be no cure—there is only money to be made.

Psychoanalytical Approach

The main elements are as follows:

a. Develop a belief that you can be totally objective as you listen to people
b. Develop a belief that what the person is telling you is not really what he or she wants to tell you because of repression. Accept everything the speaker says as meaning something else, especially references to you, sexual behavior, mother/father, and so on
c. Develop a belief that you know why people do what they do and say what they say, and make sure that your belief is grounded in theories that no one can prove
d. Confront the speaker's beliefs with "why" questions, but do not interrupt or imply/suggest that these questions are of particular interest to you, especially if they are sexual in nature.

The psychoanalytic approach actually has lots to offer. In fact, Freud was one of the pioneers in the development of listening techniques for uncovering unconscious motives. Having studied this approach extensively twenty-five years ago, I am still stuck with the nonprovable belief that all behavior *is* purposeful and a great deal of our behavior *is* unconsciously motivated. The psychoanalytic community, however, goes a bit too far in stating the following:

It will be repeatedly stressed that, regardless of orientation, *only the thoroughly psychoanalyzed therapist can listen properly and appropriately to the patient's material.* Any attempt to listen by an unanalyzed "therapist" will result in a collusion to disguise the basic problems and often results in a mutually destructive acting out. (Chessick 1992:xx–xxi)

This statement is absurd! The psychoanalyst has a belief system that gears him to listen to what he thinks is important and then leads the client in that direction of thinking (see Dorpat 1996). Talk about collusion! My collusion is right up front. I share my model of how I perceive that people get to be the way they are. It avoids blame and moves people toward taking responsibility in their lives through the way they communicate.

It is important to keep in mind, however, that we do influence each other with our communication—this is the point of language. Mutually destructive acting out is often what you get when you burn out, drink too much, bring your job home, develop an ulcer, and so on, after intensely working with people and their problems and not having any useful information or tools to deliver. Suicide rates among psychiatrists are statistically quite high.

The listening procedures to follow have been culled from anthropologists with whom I trained during graduate studies, as well as from the psychological and psychoanalytic literature. Keep in mind, however, that you always bring to the listening process your reality, your biases, your prejudices, and the best you can do is to stand back from a therapeutic encounter and ask the following questions:

a. What is my goal? How will I use the collected information?
b. What am I projecting into this? Was that person symbolic of my wife, mother, child, and so on?
c. Did I collect enough data?
d. What did I miss?
e. What is my intuition telling me?

Therapeutic Listening: Basic Elements, Their Process and Purpose

Therapeutic listening[2] is a process involving six parts used in an integrative manner (when possible) while collecting data. It is designed to appeal to all types of information processors (to be discussed shortly): visual (V), auditory (A), and kinesthetic (K). Further, it is important (in most situations) to avoid initially making judgments, interrupting, offering analysis, giving advice, or asking questions; these can derail the sender and move him or her down often unproductive paths. The individual parts are the following.

Passive listening, which involves up-and-down shaking of your head (intermittently), along with a vocalized "Uh huh." The up-and-down shaking of your head, done sporadically, appeals to the visual person and the vocalization appeals to the auditory person. This listening form is engaged in when the person will not stop talking long enough to use the other processes, and represents a message of "I'm paying attention" to the speaker with the least amount of risk of sending negative bits. Negative bits (Rush 1976, 1996), as mentioned, are messages that the receiver internalizes and that activate HRMs, resulting in stress reactions and loss of trust.

However, if the speaker is discussing physical violence or suicide, or projecting blame onto someone, DO NOT USE THIS TOOL; it might suggest that you agree with the person. Although listening to someone does not necessarily mean agreement, this message can come across. If the person continues to talk, instead of shaking your head up and down, "poker face" is the tool of choice, although there are suitable questions to ask at the appropriate time.

Echoing involves feeding back to the speaker his or her last words, word for word. This process is used when there is adequate pause between sentences or paragraphs, and creates a situation wherein the individual will usually continue to talk about what was last said. This procedure avoids asking questions, which sometimes can terminate communication. However, too much echoing is like having a parrot on your shoulder, and the receiver can turn off. Use this technique sparingly!

Paraphrasing involves feeding back to the sender his or her last words, in your own words. If you can do this accurately, the message is that you really understand. If you are off the mark, the speaker will (usually) simply correct you and keep going. However, in the clinical environment "too much" misinterpretation can lead to mistrust. Your ability to paraphrase is an excellent indicator that you are listening and have understood.

Sustaining dialogue takes two general forms:

1. Statements designed to keep the ball rolling, for example, "Let's talk," "Tell me more," "Describe that to me," "Let's get a better handle on this," and so on. Notice that each of the above relates to seeing, hearing, or feeling.
2. Varieties of open- and closed-ended questions; these will be discussed in more detail in chapter 3.

Active listening is the original Rogerian process (developed by Carl Rogers, a humanistic psychologist, in the late 1940s) of feeding back to the individual how you think he or she feels, for example, "You seem upset," "You appear tense," "You sound annoyed," "You look puzzled," "You feel frustrated," "You are confused," and the like. Again, each of these is designed to appeal to a specific receptor state or preference for information (visual, auditory, kinesthetic). Active listening is not for everyone; some people turn off with it because it was often used on situation comedies in the 1970s and 1980s, and people think you are "techniquing" them.

Psychopaths (antisocial personality disorder), especially, do not like this approach, because if you are right on the money, they feel vulnerable (psychopaths do not like that) and you are likely to receive an angry retort. (Contrary to some psychiatric views, psychopaths are not devoid of feelings.) In fact, active listening is often a useful tool for uncovering psychopathic-type individuals. When dealing with suspected psychopaths, stay with the other four techniques above and the one that follows.

Nonverbal pacing is a process of imitating the body language of the speaker. Such imitation, in increasing order of being detected, is as follows:

1. eye blinks (low risk of detection);
2. breathing rate (low risk of detection);
3. finger movements (low risk of detection);
4. arm movements (medium risk);

5. leg movements (medium risk);
6. head movements (medium risk); and
7. whole body movements (medium/high risk).

The goal of nonverbal pacing is to synchronize with the sender. Research conducted some years ago (see Byrne et al. 1971; Newcomb 1978) illustrated that people feel more comfortable with others who appear to be like them. By matching the individual's movements, you create that appearance at the subconscious level. Avoid large, jerky movements. If the individual is doing a lot of gesticulation, you can, by analogy, move your fingers a little. This is usually enough for the subconscious mind (minimal cues) to pick up the similarity.

The purpose of nonverbal pacing is twofold. First, it aids in building trust through an appearance of similarity. Second, it can act as a barometer indicating when trust has been built. This second part is accomplished in the following manner. Nonverbally pace the client for several minutes (do not interrupt, ask questions, etc.). Then shift in your chair, cross your legs, or make any movement that is contrary to the client, and see if he or she will follow you. If the client follows you, it is an indicator that trust (certainly not total trust) and a level of comfort have been reached. With trust, you are in a better position to influence through logic, suggestions, and so on. If you lose trust through the use of your statements, you will notice the client making movements that are out of sync with yours.

Let me explain what you are really accomplishing with these listening techniques. You are creating an illusion of understanding. Contrary to popular psychological thinking, there is no way that you can understand another human being. You can develop enough understanding to be an effective counselor or therapist, but never believe that you totally understand the person(s) in front of you. With such a belief, you become locked into assumptions that do not allow an open approach to your client and his or her problems.

It is important to practice listening in low-risk situations, that is, with friends, spouse, children, and so on. If you can secure cooperation from another person, have him or her tell you a story so that you can use the above techniques. Explain that he or she should pause on occasion so that you can practice different techniques. This is called role-playing.

Or, when you are out with your friends, start listening to them rather than talking about yourself. You can become the "best conversationalist in the world" simply by listening to others. Another way to practice listening is by watching and listening to soap operas, and pretending that you are listening to the players. In any event, effective listening, using the above process, will take many hours to master. It is important to overlearn the process much as you overlearn the process of driving a car, so that listening becomes automatic and natural.

It is also important that you listen and observe exactly how others talk and listen. Observe what people do and how they do it. Jump out of the fish bowl in which you live and pay attention to the way people communicate. Once you begin to understand what is happening as people talk and listen (friends, workmates, spouse, children, and so on), you begin to understand more fully the concept of high-risk messages and the emotional problems and social stress that evolve when HRMs are activated.

FRAMES OF REFERENCE FOR DATA COLLECTION

There are several frames of reference to pay attention to when listening, depending on your goal. In day-to-day situations, we tend to automatically change our frames of reference. For example, when listening to a friend, you are not listening for lies and denial. If you are, then the person is moving out of the friend role in your mind. If you *are* listening for lies and information distortion, and you still consider the person a friend, then you are exhibiting signs of paranoia.

While listening to clients, you are often attempting to tune into situations with which they distress themselves, family dynamics, or even denial (a protective device) if drugs or sex is involved. Remember, all human communication is subject to interpretation; what a person says and really means may not be what you receive or interpret from the message—the meaning of a message is always determined by the receiver. There are a number of things to keep in mind when you are listening. First, listen to the emotional content of messages. Second, listen for your client's rules, that is, rules for conducting his or her life. These rules involve stress reactions or how the individual has learned to reduce stress (verbal/physical fighting, withdrawing, etc.). Third, and connected to the second, listen for the individual's high-risk messages (these are also rules, rules for reacting), for it is the person's HRMs, and the people and events that surround them, that are the prime target for reinterpretation.

Emotional Content

The emotional content of a message is the safest frame to consider in terms of assumption about meaning. Since the purpose of emotions seems to involve storage and retrieval of information, they are always connected, directly or indirectly, to the information presented by the speaker. Someone expressing a great deal of anger about being stuck in traffic might also be angry about having to go to work and deal with an uncaring boss, or having to go home and deal with a less than interested spouse. Humans have an intense ability to employ analogous thinking where one thing stands for another thing, which stands for another thing, and so on. This is why being angry with the boss could mean being angry at a parent or angry at one's spouse because, in some symbolic manner, this person represents the other person. Do not look too deeply for "why" there is a connection or for logic in these symbolic associations. On the upside, a great deal of creative thinking arises from seemingly illogical connections.

Thus, when people communicate, there is always an emotional component. Even the schizophrenic exhibiting flat affect is still having an emotion; it is called emotional neutral, and it has meaning. Flat affect is a protective device, as is "poker face" in a card game; revealing emotions can be dangerous.

You can never really know how someone feels; you can only assume. This is why saying "I know how you feel" to someone is likely to result in "No, you don't know how I feel!" In short, you know only how *you* feel, and you can only guess at the feelings of others. However, the more you pay attention by listening and observing others, the closer you move to a sense of understanding emotional content.

The meaning wrapped around the emotional content is difficult to determine, for it is up to the individual to reveal meaning—this is why you listen. Listening also serves to create a safe environment, an environment of trust, where the individual's stress level will drop as listening proceeds. By listening, you include the sender in your group, and this is why stress usually decreases when you listen.

When stress is high, meaning, outside of the emotion expressed, is next to impossible to ascertain. For example, someone says to you in a loud, agitated voice, "Go to hell!" Does this mean that you should start looking for the next bus? No, you would not do that. If someone says to you in a loud, agitated voice, "You don't know what you are talking about," does this mean that you are stupid and incompetent? No, it does not. When someone says, "You are full of excrement," does this mean you *are* full of excrement or constipated? No, it does not. When the sender is under stress, always assume that his or her message is highly compressed and that you do not know what he or she means, except that he or she is having an emotion. You would certainly be far from the mark if you accepted the above statements, made in anger, literally! Emotional content, then, is the thread that knits the sender and receiver together within a context. It may be the only meaning that you can agree upon. Rule: Always listen/look for emotional content. This is true of all cultures. However, in diverse cultures one needs to understand the culturally appropriate emotions connected to specific cultural content.

Emotions are transmitted in two forms, verbal and nonverbal. The closer the congruency between the verbal and the nonverbal, the clearer the message becomes to the receiver. By "congruency" I mean that someone sounding angry looks *and* acts angry. The person smiling while professing anger is incongruous. Incongruity still has meaning: (1) confusion on the part of the sender; (2) sarcasm on the part of the sender; and/or

(3) deception on the part of the sender. As a therapist, the best posture to take is to listen; low-risk confrontation, while apologizing for your confusion, is useful in some situations. If the person is confused, and you confront in a gentle manner, the sender will usually start to cry. Always listen to crying; do not attempt to shut off these emotions, regardless of how uncomfortable you feel. Consoling through holding or hugging during counseling sessions should be avoided because it can be misinterpreted. In short, emotions can tell the listener a great deal about the nature and intensity of the sender's HRMs.

There are four ways of feeding back emotional content to the individual, three of which are designed to build trust:

1. The direct expression of the emotion you think the person is experiencing, that is, "You seem upset." This is stated with the intonation dropping on the word "upset," so that it does not come across as a question (this is the active listening technique mentioned earlier)

2. The nonverbal display of empathy, through facial gestures or nodding your head

3. Through nonverbal pacing. In this indirect method, by nonverbally synchronizing with the person (in a minimal way—do not grit your teeth, start crying, and the like, in imitation of the other), you subconsciously communicate understanding of the emotional content of the message

4. The fourth method of emotional feedback is designed to alter a person's internal state by changing an element of his or her memory associated with an event. This is part of the retranslation of HRMs that I employ every day in my private practice; it might have more restricted use with your clients, depending on your goal. I will return to the process of retranslation shortly. At this point, let's turn to some specifics of HRMs in therapy.

Listening for Rules

It is important to uncover specific rules that the individual has constructed as a map for living. There are rules of relating (to males, females, sexual partners, parents, spouses, children), or how the client communicates with others to reach goals, and whether or not these goals are reached in mutually acceptable ways.

Added to this are the rules of how the person thinks/feels that he or she is treated by others—a victim, with disrespect, and so on—which also includes assumption rules, or how people ought to behave toward you but do not. Parents, for example, should be kind and loving. In reality, this may not be the case. Assumption rules can also be called expectation rules, and when a parent does not live up to the child's expectation rules, this can lead to a great deal of stress along with stress-reducing behavior (acting out, avoidance, regression, etc.). These expectation rules are really rules about rules or rules within rules—the expectation is the rule and the real behavior is a rule about the rule. These rules within rules are likewise a focal point for therapy because they are connected to HRMs and represent contradictions on which the individual is looping. Most of the important rules, again, are relationship rules, for it is within the social arena that most personal stress is generated.

High-Risk Messages

A third thing to listen for is the individual's high-risk messages, or the types of information with which the individual distresses himself or herself (see Rush 1996: 132–138 for other categories of HRMs). Keep in mind that human communication occurs within a context, with different people, and within different time frames (day, month, year). Communication can occur without feedback (a news program) or at least without immediate feedback (letters, E-mail, etc.).

So, there is a dynamic aspect to HRMs, in that they involve words and glances, as well as the person sending the messages, as well as the context (public as opposed to private). With this said, let us explore (see Table 3.3) some of the types of message-sending (processes) that are potentially high-risk for communicating negative bits and activating HRMs. All of these devices are rule-setting strategies and are the connection between emotions, rules, and HRMs. These devices are neither right nor wrong, good nor bad. They have their place, and most are potentially high-risk. All of us learn our peculiar HRMs as we learn the rules early in life, although we can certainly add to our cluster of HRMs as we go through life.

HRMs are easy to uncover; just ask the client, "What are your high-risk messages?" The client will often reply, "What?" Then you ask the question in a different manner: "What might someone say or do and your stress will go up?" This process is sometimes easier with couples. What is quickly apparent is that many people distress themselves and are not aware of the exact message content. Help them by being specific, that is, ask about loud voice tones, facial expressions, and who might have used these strategies to set rules early in life or more recently.

One point that is absolutely necessary to convey to the client is that having HRMs is normal; everyone on the face of the Earth has his or her cluster of HRMs. HRMs are our pain, and they motivate us. Once the client has been told that HRMs are normal, he or she is more likely to cooperate in uncovering his or her specific types of HRMs. Too often in counseling the client learns that a behavior is abnormal or bad, evil, rotten, or nasty. It is no wonder that the psychologist or psychiatrist encounters resistance, for resistance is neither more nor less than the individual attempting to protect himself or herself from further rejection (HRMs). Drug use or abuse is not bad or evil. It is simply that person's method of

Table 3.3
Messages That Are High-Risk for Communicating Negative Bits and
Tapping into High-Risk Messages

Rule-Setting Strategy	Negative Bit
A) Ordering	Inferior, Bad, Incompetent
B) Warning	Inferior, Bad
C) Threatening	Inferior, Bad
D) Name-calling	Bad, Incompetent
E) Sarcasm	Inferior, Incompetent
F) Nagging	Incompetent, Lazy
G) Logical Argument	Stupid, Incompetent
H) Analysis	Stupid, Lack Insights
I) Withdrawing	Unlikable, Unlovable, Not Worth the Effort
J) Ignoring	Unworthy, Don't Count, a Non-person
K) Giving Unsolicited Solutions	Stupid, Incompetent
L) Criticizing	Stupid, Bad, Not Good Enough
M) Prevarication	Lack of Trust, Stupid, Used
N) Questioning	Lack of Trust
O) Probing	Lack of Trust
P) Moralizing	Bad, Stupid
Q) Interrupting	Person Doesn't Count
R) Ridiculing/Insulting	Bad, Unworthy, Not Part of the Group
S) Blaming	Bad, Thoughtless, Inferior
T) Judging	Bad, Incompetent
U) Just/Only	Statements That Minimize

V) Various Types of Character Assassinations: Never; Always; Anyone; Everyone; Of Course; Obviously. "If you *really* cared," "Even *you* should know better," "Why don't you *ever* do as you are supposed to," "*Everyone* understands why you," "*Some* people would," "Don't you *even* care," "Don't you *ever* think," "Don't you *ever* consider anyone but yourself," "Don't you even know that," etc.

W) Voice Tone	Inferior, Lacking Power
X) Facial Gestures	Inferior, Bad, Incompetent
Y) Violation of Body Space	Inferior

All of the above are modulated in face-to-face contact by:

1) Whether male or female
2) Eye contact
3) Context of interaction (one-on-one or in a group, while drinking, etc.)
4) Perceived status of sender

reducing stress or attempting to solve a problem. You want to tell the person that it is a wonderful, protective strategy, "But, as you know, Mr. Smith, it isn't as protective anymore. In fact, your behavior is really an attempt to come up with another strategy that's just as good. And that is marvelously adaptive of you." The above is reframing with analysis and future pacing, techniques that I will return to shortly.

The point is that using logic is rarely enough to motivate someone to abandon behaviors that interfere with relationships with others. The main reason for this is that most behaviors for which people seek counseling are adaptive and represent an attempt to protect the individual from further rejection. (These are symptoms and are analogous to the symptoms of any illness that the person presents to the health practitioner.) Many of these behaviors are learned from parents, friends, and the mass media, and have been in place for many years. Logic conveys a judgment, and judgments can imply that the person is bad and incompetent.

High-risk messages, and the events that surround them, are the target for reframing/reinterpretation; the process for accomplishing this will be discussed shortly.

There are other frames of reference in the listening process, and each is designed to aid in detecting HRMs that are less obvious.

Ego vs. Other Referential Statements

There is another type of divination that I find very useful, mainly because the divination elements or markers are found in very basic aspects of our language and are easy to detect; most people detect them automatically. The procedure works like this: The way we relate to ourselves and others is relayed in the pronouns, adjectives, conjunctions, and so on. Such referential statements have to fit within some close boundary, close to either side of which we begin to feel increasingly uneasy. Our rules of proper reference have been breached, sort of an intraculture shock.

We live in an egocentric society, and how often the individual refers to self and others can indicate a great deal about the individual and his or her ability to relate to others, probable compliance, primary group(s) of reference and influence, social isolation, and so on. The exclusive use of "I" indicates self-preoccupation, and it is usually very difficult to directly critique or give direction to this person, although he or she will tell you a great deal about himself or herself. Too few references to "I," on the contrary, suggest avoidance of commitment or intimacy; there needs to be a balance in all things.

The use of "we" can indicate the inclusion of "I" with others, for example, "we" when referring to family, class members, peers, and so on. It can also be used in an impersonal way, such as "We put her on the moon," indicating an impersonal connection to something. But this impersonal reference is also encountered when a person is referred to as a "we" rather than a "you." This is the case, for example, when one person says to another, "We are really having a bad day, aren't we," where the "we" does not really include the speaker. Although this could be interpreted as sarcasm, it also represents detachment. When there is a high frequency of "we" and a low frequency of "I," it indicates an avoidance of intimacy and commitment, especially if there is a high incidence of the impersonal "we."

The pronoun "me" is more intimate than "I," and is often used with passive verbs, for example, "They're going to get me for this." A high percentage of "me" (along with "my") references can be a signal of depression and impulsiveness when combined with the pronoun "I" and high incidences of evaluatory statements (discussed below).

Evaluators are continually making judgments about the goodness or badness, rightness or wrongness, correctness or incorrectness, of the behaviors of others. This admonishing approach to assessing others is common among those who think putting others down raises their own position. Being criticized is usually high-risk in these cases.

Negatives, like "not," "never," "no way," "nothing," and so on, can indicate stubbornness and also, in the extreme, a tendency to be in denial. Reality testing is a threat to group worth. I use the term "group worth" because how you feel about yourself is dependent on how you think others feel about you. Self-worth or self-esteem derives from a Western psychological perspective that places the individual at the center of the universe. Yes, we are individual biological units, but we are parts of groups. It is the group (for example, a family) that socializes the individual; individuals do not socialize themselves.

The continual use of negatives can likewise indicate that the individual has created a negative future for himself or herself, but it can also mean that he or she wants to be reassured. The overall context of these words must be considered.

Qualifiers indicate a hedging on commitment or waffling. Statements such as "The family meeting was kind of okay," "I think I'll be able to stay off the booze," "I'll try to stay on the diet," and the like, weaken the conviction in a belief or behavior, and can signal anxiety about decisions or commitments. For these individuals, being judged is high-risk.

Retractors include conjunctions like "but," "however," and "although," and tend to cancel preceding statements or a conviction in those statements when used frequently. For example, "I love my wife, but she just hasn't learned to keep a clean house"; "I think that you do good work, but you need to improve in this area," and so on. "But," in these cases, literally cancels the preceding statement.

Direct references to people, places, or circumstances, such as "Thank you for seeing me today," "I wish we could have met somewhere more comfortable," and "I'm really pressed for time" can indicate a connectedness and sensitivity to "now" events. However, this should not imply truthfulness, just awareness. On the other hand, it is through direct references that one can most obviously detect disturbed communication patterns of the schizophrenic variety (see "Disturbed Communication Patterns," below). A lack of direct reference can indicate shyness, a rule of relating.

Adverbial enhancers, such as "She is really crazy and always overreacts"; "Every time he comes over, he is abusive"; "I'll never, never, ever raise taxes"; "It was the worst accident I ever saw," when used frequently, indicate "polarity" or "black or white" thinkers; they represent statements of exaggeration. Under stress, individuals are likely to utilize adverbial enhancers. This being the case, adverbial enhancers (as well as all polarity statements) represent good examples of highly compressed data; they deserve to be listened to and dissected.

Nonpersonal references indicate that the person avoids responsibility and perhaps intimacy. For example, "Everyone knows that it is true" and "One has to be careful around such people" are nonpersonal statements. An example of a personal statement would be "I have to stay away from such people; I lose control."

Disturbed Communication Patterns

Disturbed communication patterns have been defined by Jurgen Ruesch (1972:41) as follows:

> Too much,
> Too little,
> Too early,
> Too late,
> At the wrong place,
> Is the disturbed message's fate.

Expanding on this, the following represent the elements we encounter when exposed to the communication patterns of those with thought disorders.

Excessive output, in which the speaker goes on and on, rambling and disconnected from the original question or objective; pauses are infrequent or nonexistent. The receiver feels a need to interrupt often in order to clarify. Disconnection from other statements is most important, and indicates a great deal of confusion and disorder. The meaning that I usually attach to excessive output is that the individual is attempting to solve some problem.

Deficient output is most commonly represented in depression. Depression is usually a product of emotional conversion, for example, when frustration is converted into depression, which represents an internal looping state. Depression is likewise a form of withdrawal. People who are internal processors are not necessarily depressed; on the contrary, they simply spend a lot of time with their own thoughts. Those who are too internal are certainly not gregarious. Depression, however, comes with a set of nonverbal characteristics: a downcast look, shoulders slumped, and so on.

Incessant interrupting implies excessive self-interest, an intense need to tell a story or express a need. It also indicates a great deal of loneliness and disconnectedness from others.

Delayed output occurs when the sender mentions something or responds to something after a prolonged delay and at a time when the context of the conversation has moved to other concepts or topics. It is as if the person's sense of time is out of sync with the other communicators.

Out of context refers to statements made during a conversation that have nothing to do with the topic under discussion. For example, you might ask someone, "How long have you lived in that neighborhood?" The reply is "Where is the nearest gas station? I'm almost out." Individuals who are feigning mental illness most commonly use this technique, since it helps to avoid questions or communication in general, and gives the impression of personal disconnection from social reality.

Word salad is most common in schizophrenics and involves seemingly random phrases that are usually meaningless to the receiver. Such statements are meaningful to the sender in that they disrupt the communication process and the sender avoids the social communicative process (socializing is dangerous because it opens the door to further rejection). On the other hand, psychiatric theory states that the random phrases often represent symbols that are meaningless to the sender, although I'm at a loss to understand how this is determined. Another term for word salad is "paraphrasis."

RECEPTOR STATES

It is impossible to pay attention to all the information surrounding you at any one time; there are limits to your processing abilities. Essentially we generalize, delete, and distort, as mentioned earlier, and how we do this becomes part of our communication style of pulling information into our senses—everyone is different. There is another element involved in our processing ability, called Miller's Number (Miller 1956). Briefly stated, we are able to handle seven, plus or minus two, chunks of information at any one time. A chunk of information is perhaps best defined as an "over-learned set" of behaviors or ideas that are generalized to be one unit in the mind. When stress is low, we are able to pay attention to seven to nine chunks; when stress is high, that number drops to five or less.

It is like starting a new job. As a new employee, your stress is probably high to begin with, because you do not know exactly what to expect. The supervisor, who takes you around and acquaints you with your duties, has, through time, overlearned many of the procedures and utilizes them automatically. He or she has to break down procedures to their smallest unit, communicate this information to you, and then go on to the next "learning station." Since each thing is new, by the time you have been presented with five or six things or processes, your stress begins to increase, and it is difficult to remember the procedures. So maybe you begin asking the supervisor to repeat the procedure, or you start to jot things down. By the time the supervisor runs you through all your responsibilities, you are discouraged and the supervisor thinks you are stupid. After being on the job for a few weeks, you superchunk certain procedures, which become a chunk, and you settle in. This happens to children on their first day of school—no wonder their stress is so high—as well as to freshmen in high school and college. Migrants have to learn a whole new culture, and it is expected that they will do this immediately. It is also the reason that educational television may not be the greatest learning tool; the viewer is hit with too much new information with inadequate repetition.

Computer programs present the same problem. An individual purchases a word processor and starts to read the manual. By the end of the second page, his or her head is swimming in procedures, and he or she wonders if going back to paper and pencil would be a better idea.

It becomes obvious that although as modern-day humans we have to live within the limits of our information-processing abilities, we lose sight of this when it comes to considering the problems presented to our ancestors. What seems commonplace to us was novel and complex to them, and if they could not solve problems and create order in their worlds, they died.

Keeping in mind the limits of information-processing, each person with whom you communicate falls into one of several general information-processing categories. What I will present is a very useful divination procedure that was developed in the 1970s and 1980s (Bandler and Grinder 1975b; Grinder and Bandler 1976; Dilts et al. 1980, for more details). By observing Milton Erickson, a medical doctor, and his approach to hypnosis, the authors mentioned above constructed a divination process that is very useful in making decisions regarding what information to deliver to your clients and how to deliver it. This procedure is not truth. The thinking and techniques were well worked out prior to Grinder and Bandler's works. (Observe the movie *Soldier of Fortune*, with Clarke Gable, where Gene Barry is being interrogated by the Chinese officer—the basics of what follows are all there. The movie was released in 1955.)

Visual (V). Visual processors prefer what they see over what they hear and feel. It is not that they do not hear and feel, they simply pay more attention to the visual. As you listen to a visual person's language, it will reflect this preference. You will hear more words and phrases that contain visual frames of reference than the other two categories.

See	Dream	That brightens up my day
Look	Mirage	It all seems so hazy
Visual	Seems to me	To see the light

Figure 3.2
Visual Accessing

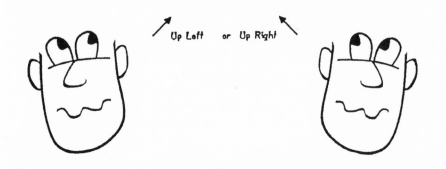

Envision	Sight	More than meets the eye
Visualize	Oversight	Get the picture
Appear	Clarify	That was a bad scene
View	Focus	What's the point
Review	Fuzzy	To eyeball something
Watch	Bright	When you frame it that way
Observe	Dim	Life is so drab

That throws a little more light on it   etc.

Visual processors likewise tend to be high breathers, that is, when they take in air, movement is usually high in the chest area. Also, when visual people are accessing information internally, their first eye movement is either up left or up right (see Figure 3.2). However, some people's eyes will not move, but the pupils will dilate as they access visual information.

Auditory (A). Auditory processors prefer what they hear over what they see or feel. Auditory processors represent that preference by using the following types of words or phrases.

Hear	Talk	Tell
Clamored	Mouth off	Listen to me
Noisy	Rustled around	All he does is whine
It all came to a screeching halt		It's too offbeat
She screamed at me with her looks		He gives me too much static

Figure 3.3
Auditory Accessing

I don't like the sound of that

Sounds good to me   etc.

There is too much discord around here

With auditory breathers you will notice center movement. Also, auditory processors, as a first movement, look over to the left or right (see Figure 3.3).

Kinesthetic (K). Kinesthetic processors access their feelings or bodily sensations simultaneously with visual and/or auditory information, and tend to use more emotion-laden or body-language words and phrases. Under stress, it should be noted, our language tends to compress more and more in the kinesthetic direction with reference to more emotion, body language, body parts, and body activities. The word "kinesthetic" is partly derived from the Greek word *kine*, which refers to movement (see Birdwhistle 1970) but is here used to denote body language, body sensations, and emotions. Words and phrases that represent kinesthetic processors include the following:

Lost your head	Heads up	Sorehead
Catch your eye	Starry-eyed	My eye
Eyebrow-lifting	Sweat of your brow	Raised brow
Nose out of joint	Nosy	Nose to the grindstone
Hardnose	Save face	Two-faced
Face up	Bend your ear	Ear to the ground
Mouth off	Tight jaws	Big mouth
Cheeky	Spill the beans	Choke up

Turn the other cheek	Stiff upper lip	Chin up
Get in your hair	Hair-raising	Hair-splitting
Can't stomach it	Butterflies in your stomach	
Grit your teeth	Skin of your teeth	Give your eyeteeth
Bare your teeth	Sink your teeth into	Bleeding heart
Broken heart	Heart in your throat	Bloodcurdling
Kiss off	Sucker	Bite your lip
Thin-skinned	Get under your skin	Itching to do it
Heartless	Pain in the neck	Get it off your chest
Shrug it off	Shoulder a burden	Shoulder to the wheel
Yellow-bellied	Lily-livered	No guts
Vent your spleen	Lot of gall	To get my hands on
Tight-fisted	Put the finger on	Palm off on someone
Lay on hands	Twist your arm	Open arms
Magic touch	Backhanded	Give him a hand
Keep in touch	Can't handle it	Knuckle down
Knuckle under	Get out of hand	Elbow your way
Get off my back	No backbone	My aching back
Spine-tingling	Get a leg up	Watery knees
Get a kick out of it	Toe in the water	Stand on your own two feet
Pissed off	Pain in the ass	Tight ass
No balls	You have a nerve	etc.

Kinesthetic breathers breathe low. Also, kinesthetic processors access feelings, as a first move, either down left or down right (see Figure 3.4). Down left or right can also mean that the individual is deep in thought, another auditory mode. You have to pay careful attention to words and movements in order to determine which "down side" is kinesthetic accessing, and which is auditory, for each person you interview.

Keep in mind that the above receptor states are generalizations. Moreover, I have presented this material in a digital fashion; the human mind has a tendency to work digitally as well as in an analog fashion.

The purpose of determining a person's receptor states, or preference

Figure 3.4
Kinesthetic Accessing

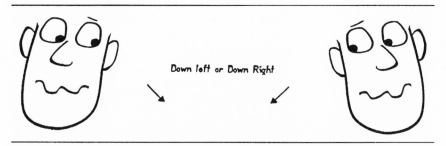

Down left or Down Right

for information, is that it gives you a primary channel with which to deliver information. If you are dealing with a visual person, he or she is more likely to "see" your meaning if you use a visual language. This is especially true when the person trusts you and is low-stress. A rule of thumb is to avoid tapping into someone's HRMs and to use a language that matches the person's receptor state. This is not to say that using an auditory language with a visual person will be ineffective. In fact, depending on your goal, message delivery to other than the individual's preference, if approached in an indirect manner, is less likely to be censored by the conscious mind. I recommend that the reader attend some workshops in neurolinguistic programming and learn the details.

As a therapist, you are an educator. Your goal is to use receptor states to build trust. Using a visual language with a visual person, as long as you are not tapping into HRMs, will aid in building trust. Once trust is built, your purpose is to educate. That is to say, to educate the client with reference to HRMs and alternative interpretations of life events, to educate the client in terms of communication processes (compressed data and its nature under stress, Miller's Number and information overload, emotional responsibility, and so on), and to teach social skills (to be discussed shortly and in Chapter 4). Some people will come to you wanting analysis; give them analysis that educates them with respect to other possibilities. Some clients will come to you because they want to blame all those around them for their predicament. Agree with them, and then teach them how not to be a victim. "You became a victim, Bob, because you were unaware of the other possibilities; you were simply trying to solve some problem and survive, and that is normal [analysis]. Now, you don't like seeing yourself as a victim, is that correct? And if you had information that would stop you from being a victim, that would erase that image as a victim, is that correct? And if you had the information, you would use that information, is that correct? Then I'll show you that information" (this is a "yes set," to be explained shortly).

Bring the client to realize that he or she needs to understand what is happening when interacting with others. Bring the client to realize that having more tools in his or her tool kit will give the client power. "You would agree that having power would be good, is that correct? And if you understood what was happening as you communicated with others, you could begin to acquire that power, right? Acquiring social power will take a few weeks, and you are willing to work, is that correct?" (This is future pacing combined with a "yes set," which I will discuss shortly.)

You demonstrate the tools. Demonstrate that people have to move their eyes when accessing complex information. Ask questions and let clients feel their own eyes move; give them homework—have them observe the eye movements of others. The questions that are asked are important because they have to be somewhat complex, and they cannot be of the "yes" or "no" variety. For example, you can ask, "How many windows are there in your home?" "Can you remember one of the first songs that you thought was really special? Where were you the first time you heard it?" "Remember the last time you walked on a beach/walked in the woods/in the park. What time of the year was it?"

Time and Spatial Orientation

The next tool is another form of divination that can be very helpful in your practice. Language (verbal and nonverbal) can indicate a great deal about how a person perceives time (past, present, and future) and how the client sees or experiences himself or herself in relation to others and the environment in general (see Andreas and Andreas 1987).

Individuals who have the past as their primary orientation are usually locked into the scenes, incantations of others, and behaviors/strategies enacted in the past, which are then carried into the future. The future is known only by the past; for those locked into the past, the future is frozen or preordained. These individuals often do not see a future and do not see a possibility of change of beliefs and behaviors. A past orientation is represented by a great deal of looping and expression of detail about past hurts and injustices (or even past accomplishments that will never be repeated, e.g., high school football star, war experiences, etc.). Individuals with a past orientation often see/hear/feel themselves as victims and continually place themselves in that role, through the relationships they establish, because they cannot imagine otherwise in the future. When they are asked to picture the future, it is usually gray, fuzzy, or a jumble of unclear images. They just can't see it. Sounds are loud and unclear, a cacophony. A year seems thousands of miles away when they are asked to place a distance on it; a day may be imagined as many blocks away.

People in the "now," a popular expression of the 1960s and early 1970s, live from moment to moment, and often do not contemplate the conse-

Figure 3.5
Time Orientation

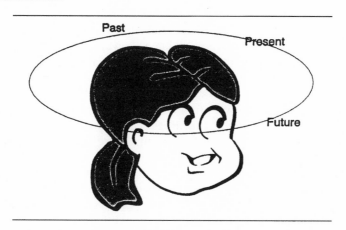

quences of their behavior. They refuse to imagine a future, "It is too far away," and the past "is gone; you can't live in the past." With such an orientation the individual has difficulty learning from past mistakes and cannot plan anything past a day at a time. Alcoholics Anonymous sets people into a "one day at a time" orientation. When you combine this with the belief that alcoholism is a disease, you remove the individual from behavioral responsibility and a future where such responsibility could happen. This may be one of the reasons that AA has such high recidivism rates.

On the other hand, those who have a future that is set and inflexible are setting themselves up for disappointment or failure. The drug addict, for example, who sees himself or herself being liked by everyone, with a high-paying job, with a detailed set of possessions, a trouble-free education, and so on, is setting himself or herself up for lack of compromise when obstacles are in the way—this individual does not have alternatives.

We all have a past, a present, and a future, and how we conceptualize these time frames can mean the difference between success and failure in terms of goals. To determine how your client experiences time, have him or her imagine a circle or space surrounding his or her head (see Figure 3.5).

Then ask the client where he or she would place the past relative to his or her head: in the back, in the front, on the side, and so on. Do this by having him or her imagine a common activity that he or she did a few weeks ago, perhaps taking a shower. Have the person tell you what type of soap was used, the color of the towel, and the nature of the shower: if there is a bath mat, a sliding glass door, and so on. Make note of where he or she sees this activity in terms of space around the head.

Next, have the client imagine the same activity, perhaps the shower/ bath he or she took today: what soap was used, the color of the towel, and so on. Note where he or she would put this image. It is important to have the individual access as much detail as possible.

Then have him or her envision taking a shower a couple of weeks from now: the type of soap, towel, and so on, and then ask where he or she would place this in terms of the space around the head.

Individuals who are able to create a future will have a time line very different from those who are grounded in the past or the now. You will find that many people addicted to drugs see the past, present, and future all clumped together in the back or front. These individuals cannot see the future through the past. Figure 3.5 shows a typical time line that allows a clear distinction between past, present, and future.

Here is where you can get creative, especially for individuals who clump past, present, and future together. Tell the person that he or she can move the times around in his or her imagination, and that doing so will, in some way, make it possible to see the world differently (this is an example of future pacing or the self-fulfilling prophecy). Then have him or her imagine moving the times, separating one from the other, and ask what was experienced.

This technique is designed to go along with other incantations, and since the reader is creative, by the end of this book you will have many tools that can be used in many combinations. Moreover, you will be able to invent new tools. The reader should keep in mind at this point that I am presenting a series of concepts and tools. What follows will be less effective if the client (or the reader) does not understand high-risk messages and have a new understanding of the communication process. The first concepts and tools you teach clients are (1) HRMs, as well as beginning a process of retranslating them; (2) emotional responsibility and role-shifting; and (3) how to listen. Also keep in mind that not all clients want to learn tools. Many will simply desire a new perspective (retranslation of life events) so that they can reduce stress and enhance physical healing. Many times simply listening to the client for twenty or thirty minutes is enough to enhance physical healing; many times people just need to ventilate their feelings about situations they can do very little about. All you have to do is listen, but do not listen to the same story twice without engaging in reframing techniques.

Digital vs. Holistic

There are two other processing styles that need to be addressed: digital and holistic. There is a great deal of literature available that discusses right brain left brain activities; I suggest the reader begin with Springer and Deustch (1989). My interest here is in how individuals solve problems in specific environments. Right now I am engaged in a rather digital, linear process of typing on a word processor. The technology and the program force me to go from point A to point B. I am comfortable with this process in many situations. For example, if you give me directions to some location, I will want to know how far away it is, the street before where I have to turn, the exact address, what lane I should be in, and so on. I need to generate a map in my head. I am also very conscious of time; I need to know what time it is so that I can be on time for appointments. When people ask me questions, I tend to give them a great amount of detail, which is just fine for another digital person. I like to start a job, do the job, finish the job, and clean up after the job; if I am interrupted, my stress goes up. When I am interrupted, order in my universe collapses. As a general statement, digital people pay attention to details; are very conscious of time; want to know who, what, when, and how; and do not like interruptions. Digital people often become CPAs, computer programmers, and drill instructors in the military.

Holistic people are different. They are not interested in detail, and they get frustrated when you do not generalize. Time is less important; they are usually late (or early) for appointments. Holistic people make good parents because they do not mind being interrupted. They also tend to be messy housekeepers and usually have many projects going, none of which are ever completed. Remember all those time management programs in the marketplace? I can guarantee you that very few holistic people gain much from the workshops unless they perceive a gain above and beyond managing time. They manage time through generalization and intuition (they guess at the time and engage in a type of celestial bookkeeping when it comes to keeping check registers). Holistic people like to think up projects and let others fill in the details regarding execution.

No one is either digital *or* holistic. For example, when it comes to correcting spelling or grammatical construction, I will run off a chapter so that I can have the whole to look at. Someone could be quite digital at work and come home and become quite holistic (my wife is a good example of this).

So what is the point? The point is compatibility. You will have clients who are in jobs that require that they be digital when they are holistic. You will meet husbands who simply cannot understand why their wife is never on time or why the house is a mess. Explaining digital and holistic to individuals and couples, educating them as to the behaviors wrapped around the two styles, will often take a large amount of stress out of the system. Why? Well, you have engaged in a form of "naming of the disease," and because now the individuals know what it is and that it is normal, they are in a position to understand how certain styles work best in certain situations. This also opens up a discussion of value clashes, to be considered in Chapter 4.

Internal vs. External Processing

Internal processing involves the thoughts, pictures, emotions, sensation, and such that go on inside your head with the reference mainly to stored information. Dreaming or daydreaming is an example of almost total internal processing. In external processing you are taking in information external to you, and of course, in order to make sense of it, you are in a continual pattern of external-internal-external-internal processing. When high-risk messages are activated through our interpretation of external information, we tend to go internal and loop, with a consequent increase in stress. Certainly, we can distress ourselves with our own stored information.

Internal processors, those who spend the majority of their time with their own thoughts, are not in contact with their surroundings; many are depressed. In the extreme, when they are speaking to you, it is as if information is leaking out of the internal state and they are not really aware of your existence. Individuals heavily into marijuana, LSD, DMT, and other hallucinogens tend to be internal processors; those on amphetamines and cocaine tend to be more external. Those using alcohol can go either way.

Internal processors have great difficulty in school, for much of their understanding will come from listening to the teacher/instructor (external-to-internal processing) or reading books (also external-to-internal processing). They are often considered learning disabled, which is not the case. The teacher usually does not know how (or perhaps does not care or have the time) to get their attention. Moreover, many of the children who are internal processors in the school environment are reflecting on events at home or wondering how they can prove themselves to their friends and be accepted. Internal processors are not sick, nor do they have a syndrome. The vast majority are trying, like the rest of us, to deal with rejection and acceptance. Teachers who imply through actions and words that these children are stupid or that something is wrong with them only add to the problem.

Counseling or teaching internal processors involves the use of more attention-getting and indirect techniques. Once again, the main goal of therapy is to educate, and a person has to be open and external in order to receive direct, logically constructed information. Some internal processors, especially those who are depressed and/or experiencing thought disorders, have to feel safe with the external information. As a counselor, it is necessary for you to build trust. This is done through initially listening and, if the individual is unwilling to talk, through storytelling (see "Fables" and "Metaphors" in this chapter).

In order to get through to clients, in order to educate, it is necessary to know about receptor states, digital and holistic problem-solving styles, and whether the individual is internal or external at the time of message delivery. The only way you can determine receptor states, and so on, is by becoming external yourself, and by paying attention to people. This is not easy in an ego-bound culture.

Discussion and Exercises

From what has been said, what are *your* HRMs (check the list in Figure 3.3)? What types of information coming from what people do you distress *yourself* with? Might it be the voice tone of a boyfriend, girlfriend, or spouse, or his or her facial expressions? Perhaps people invading your space? Maybe you do not like sarcasm, especially when you hear it from a parent, or messages that suggest that you are not good enough. How about taking exams, is that high-risk? Make a list. Throughout the day, you will have plenty of opportunity to detect your HRMs. It is imperative that you know what your HRMs are before delving into those of others.

As you deal with people in your personal life, you will notice that your emotions are on a roller-coaster ride. When your stress goes up, this is an indicator that you have activated an HRM. What was the message? What were the words, what was the context, what did you think was meant, and who said it? Write it all down. By doing so, you jump out of the fish bowl and become an observer rather than a participant (participant-observation is a basic anthropological process for collecting and analyzing data). Your goal is to look and to talk about all the possible translations of these negative incantations of the past (and present). Get creative; ask your friends if they have any suggestions. What did your father really mean when he implied that you were stupid? Was this simply his style of communicating? Was he frustrated? Was he saying this in the hope that you would become smart? Was he having a bad day? Was he under stress? Who taught him to be a parent? Do you really think he understood what he was saying and the impact of his words? Are you *really* stupid? Name all the areas in which you are stupid. Does everyone think you are stupid? How do you know this? What does "stupid" mean? What image comes to mind? How can you alter that image so that you look even more stupid? Now go in the other direction and make that picture look intelligent. Remember, because you do not know what anyone means, your interpretations are almost endless.

Some of you might say, "Well, isn't this denial? Isn't this rationalizing?" The answer to this is simple and in two parts: (1) there is no way of knowing what anyone means, so you cannot really be sure that you placed the right interpretation on events in the first place; and (2) your mind/brain/nervous system wants to go toward stress reduction, and once you find a translation that is comfortable, believable, and possibly true, your mind will go in that direction.

Are you primarily a digital or a holistic person? If you are digital and your client is holistic, you may give too much information. If you are holistic and your client is digital, he or she will require more information in order to get the point.

Are you primarily an internal or an external processor? Do you spend a lot of time with your own thoughts? How does this help or hinder you? Remember, internal processors, like external processors, are attempting to solve problems. As a counselor, your job is to help the client move in a direction of problem-solving and stress reduction through education.

A client who came to me a short time ago was depressed. Her family physician suggested that she go on Prozac. Since she was an internal processor, I asked her if I could read to her about Prozac so that she could learn some things that her family physician did not tell her. She said yes, so I read to her sections of the *Physician's Desk Reference* regarding the side effects of this very powerful and dangerous drug. She did not hear a word I said. During our small-talk phase, she revealed that she had several cats, so I told her the story about the cat that ate some snail bait and got very, very sick. She heard that and decided not to take the Prozac. Yet, she was depressed.

I noticed that she was an auditory/kinesthetic person, and I used the following language to represent her informational preferences. "Let me *tell* you that your *behavior is adaptive* in some way, and that the depression is actually helping you to *think* about your life and is *pushing* you toward problem-solving [reframing the meaning of depression]."

The physician's suggestion to take a drug was a suggestion that depression was bad, and because she was experiencing it, it must be a failing on her part.

I asked her, "*Tell* me when you first had this *experience* of depression." (I used the word "experience" rather than "feeling" because I wanted her to search for an experience in history—she was already having the feeling.)

She remembered that as a teenager, it seemed that she could not do anything right for her father. Her grades were not high enough, she was a bit overweight, and the school psychologist labeled her an "underachiever" (an example of professional name-calling, designed to display the intelligence and perceptive abilities of the psychologist, and very damaging to the client). She remarked, "I guess that it's been since my teens that I've had this off-and-on depression."

I asked her, "*Recall* for me a specific incident of your father *telling* you about your grades or your weight." She recalled that he used to tell her, "Well, at least if there is a famine, you'll survive!"

I then asked her what he meant by that. She answered, "That I was ugly and fat." Although she did not take her father literally, she did accept the message that her weight was not appropriate, and she interpreted this as "I am ugly and fat." Again, the father did not really say this; this was her interpretation. Her translation of the message was analogous to her father's message in the sense that his message was a judgment of her, as is her judgment of herself. What you want to move toward, then, is a retranslation of the original message, a retranslation that is 180 degrees away from the original. This is a secret to emotional healing that enhances physical healing.

I then asked her what else he might have meant. She said, "No one will desire me." Her message was analogous to her first interpretation of her father's message. I then asked if her father used sarcasm with her mother and others in the family. "Oh, yes," she replied. "He used to say a lot of unkind things to my mother, or at least I thought they were unkind, about her always being on the phone, and that it was my father who was keeping Pacific Bell from going bankrupt."

Then I suggested that her father had a sarcastic style, his way of being funny, and therefore it wasn't personal, "although I can certainly understand why anyone would take it as personal." She then agreed that it was "just the way he was." Now she was starting to move away from the analogous interpretations of her father's message.

Next, I wondered who taught him to be a parent. "Well, probably his parents." With this I commented that he did not receive any real training in parenting outside of what his parents did, so that he might not have understood how she would have taken his remark. She responded, "Well, he *should* have known; *I* don't talk to my children that way."

Her last statement left a very important opening for reframing. The father—not by design, of course—had taught her to be sensitive to her own children. So I asked if she would have been as sensitive had her father been gentle and kind. Obviously, she could not answer this question, so I told her the story about the young man who grew up in a wonderful family, with wonderfully concerned parents, who took him and his brothers and sisters camping, and looked after his every need—talked to him and listened and showed a great deal of concern. Well, one day the young man ran away and was picked up by the police after stealing food from a supermarket, and he was referred to me for therapy. What the young man revealed was that he felt controlled, that his parents were too concerned. "This man learned to rebel," I commented, "but *you* learned to be sensitive to your children. Isn't it wonderful what parents teach us once we talk about and experience a bigger picture?" With the word "picture" I attempted to tap into another receptor state.

She agreed, and commented that she had not thought about her parents in this way. She then asked a wonderful question: "What else have they taught me that I haven't yet appreciated?"

The process of reframing is a simple one of moving from analogous interpretations of the remarks of others to interpretations that are very different, what I term the 180 degree difference.

Warning: Always combine reframing with a positive future. As you can recall from the time line above, it is important to tell people that retranslating HRMs causes them to be different. You can also use "will be different," but the word "causes" has more immediacy about it. Ask them how they will look, sound, and feel. Again, this is future pacing (discussed below). Why is this necessary? Your reality is constructed. It is something that you create in your mind, and you are continuously constructing and reconstructing. By reframing, you are suggesting other possibilities both for history (the incantations of others) and for the future. The human brain works on a polarity principle: if there is an up, there has to be a down; if there is a good, there is also a bad; if there is an ending, then there is also a beginning; if there is a past, there has to be a future or at least the possibility of a future. With reframing, you are changing history, creating a new "now" and a new future.

It is not necessary to retranslate every message sent by a parent or significant other. The goal is to isolate specific categories (sarcasm, voice tone, etc.) and retranslate one or two. Once the individual gets the point that what people say and do is not necessarily what they mean, the subconscious mind will do much of the work for you.

Finally, I have no idea what constitutes a 100 percent cure; never go for 100 percent. Simply let people know that if they see things 10 percent more positive, or feel 15.5 percent better about their relations with others, that would be useful. There is no way that you can ever rid a person of all his or her HRMs, for these are connected to social rules. HRMs are necessary—they motivate. Guilt and shame are necessary parts of social living. Without HRMs we would truly be psychopathic. The goal is to retranslate those HRMs that get in the way of success (as defined by the client). Show the client the process, and suggest that he or she can retranslate messages, and that he or she is the doctor.

Listening for Physical Illness/Nutritional Deficiencies: More Divination Procedures

Our verbal and nonverbal language can indicate a great deal about physical health, which can have an effect on attitudes and behavior. Under stress, individuals often make kinesthetic reference to body positions or bodily discomfort; this fits under the category of emotional conversion. Such body-part references often end up being the target of illness (see Rush 1996). For example:

I can't handle it.
My back is against the wall.

I can't stand it anymore.

She is a pain in the neck.

It was a gut-wrenching experience.

I can't stomach this anymore.

I'm fed up.

He wears me out.

I've had it up to here.

She is a pain in the ass.

This is a big headache.

I bring this metaphorical targeting of body parts to awareness so that the client is at least conscious of the possibilities. The next step is to inquire about the specifics of what the person cannot handle. Can this information be retranslated? Is it necessary to give the individual some communication strategies or tools for dealing with the unacceptable behaviors of others? Some possible tools will be discussed shortly.

Not only do we target organs in our body; our diet has a great deal to do with emotional states. Any psychiatrist or medical doctor who prescribes drugs without assessing nutritional issues is incompetent at best, and a danger to the patient he or she treats. It is important to have a grasp of nutritional elements that can accentuate emotional problems. There are four basic nutritional issues about which you need to collect information. First, what does the person eat? Is it mainly fractionated foods (most wheat products), which are devoid of nutrients (B vitamins) necessary for the production of neurochemicals? Is there enough variety of foods consumed—especially fruits and vegetables? Most people are deficient in specific monosaccharides necessary for bringing nutrients into cells and removing toxins. This can have a profound effect on mental functioning.

Second, is the person constipated? By constipation, I mean not having a large bowel movement that floats every day. There are four general ways toxins are removed from your body: excretion via kidneys, bowel movements, skin, and lungs. If sufficient toxins are not removed, they stay in the body and can disrupt neural as well as all organ functioning.

Third, you can not adequately digest proteins (steak, chicken, fish, eggs, etc.) when they are consumed at the same times as carbohydrates (the carbohydrates interfere with HCL production and stomach pH, leading to putrefaction of the protein under the influence of bacteria that should not be in the stomach). If you eat according to the USDA pyramid, you will die of malnutrition. Malnutrition comes with some interesting neurological problems. Moreover, eating the "balanced diet" leads to digestive problems—just look at all the ads on television for antacids. We have an epidemic of nutritional problems in this country, problems that are correctable, problems that lead to physical as well as emotional problems.

And fourth, it is necessary to consume sufficient liquids/pure water each day. Many people are dehydrated, which can lead to physical conditions including seizures, depression, lethargy, and so on. I will have much more to say about nutrition in a future work.

QUESTIONING: PURPOSE AND PROCESS

No divination procedure of this type would be complete without questions that help steer the individual in a direction that is facilitated ultimately by both (or all) participants. Earlier in this chapter I used the term "sustaining dialogue" and presented examples of basic statements designed to continue the information output. However, this would certainly be inadequate to collect specific data. Just listening is appropriate in some situations, such as when people are confronted with death and dying, or in situations where there is really nothing one can do immediately about the situation (failing an exam, problems with a seemingly controlling parent, etc.).

Before asking questions of others, it is appropriate to ask yourself why you want this information: What is your goal? I have outlined certain types of information a person might want to collect: HRMs and specifics in history, how the individual deals with stress, nutrition, and so on. Keep in mind that the clinical anthropologist or holistic health practitioner is likewise collecting information about physical issues, and in some cases, dwelling on the emotional is inappropriate. The following types of questions are designed to let the client tell you the nature of the symptoms rather than your putting words in his or her mouth.

There are four general types of questions one can ask:

Objective, Closed-Ended. "Did you think about the consequences of driving under the influence?" "Do you have regular menstrual cycles?" "Do you get a lot of canker sores?" "Do you experience ringing in your ears?" These require simple "yes," "no," or "sometimes" responses.

Objective, Open-Ended. "What do you usually have for breakfast?" "What usually happens just before you and your husband have a fight?" "Tell me about how your mother and father argued." "What does the future look like to you?" "How do you experience time?" "How often do you have bowel movements, and do they sink or float?" With these questions, the individual has to construct a metaphor or story about an experience. In short, they require more than a "yes," "no," or "sometimes" answer, and require, instead, an assessment and elaboration of events through time. Your interpretation of these responses are a little more complicated than the closed-ended responses.

Subjective, Closed-Ended. "Did you feel concerned about the child's welfare?" "Describe your father in one word." "Do you often feel like you are losing control?" "When out in public, do you think strangers are talking about you?" Subjective questions elicit feelings about events rather than a description of the events. One problem with this is that some people are not willing to share that information. Another problem with this type of questioning is that it is now a cliché—"Tell me how you feel about that," and so on. These questions have to be especially sincere when delivered. If you cannot be sincere, or the person will not open up, use a wording that is direct but in the other direction. For example, you could say, "I bet you felt pretty bad about that" or "Yes, I imagine there were a lot of angry feelings jumping around inside of you." It is all right to tell a person how he or she feels. Just do not be so naive that you think you are right.

Subjective, Open-Ended. "Tell me what emotions you were feeling as you saw your son hit your daughter.""Who are you more like, your mother or father, and in what way?" "Describe for me the anger you feel toward others." The therapist can run into problems similar to those with the subjective, closed-ended. Do not insist that a client is having a specific feeling. Let the client tell you, but always keep in mind that a retranslation of traumatic events means bringing that meaning to a positive emotional connection. Do not lock clients into their emotions about events. For example, you could comment, "You know, Mr. Smith, being angry in those circumstances is understandable. A couple of people have told me they were frustrated before they got angry. They didn't just start off with anger. What emotion is more useful to you, Mr. Smith, anger or frustration?" Whatever emotion the individual chooses, it is part of his or her survival mechanism in the past, and it was a wonderful strategy. "But is it still useful, Mr. Smith?" Emotions can be reframed.

Relevant vs. Interesting Information-Collecting

Information on sex might be interesting, but it also might be irrelevant. On the other hand, when people are talking about suicide or violence, it is useful and important to gently ask questions about past thoughts/behaviors, how the individual engaged in these behaviors, what purpose they served, what was the outcome, and so on. If people are talking about violence toward others, are they speaking metaphorically or are they contemplating action? If the latter is the case, you might be required by law to inform the police. Remember the following.

When you begin to ask questions, you run the risk of losing trust. When someone has come to you for physical health reasons, questioning is expected because most people have bought into the mind/body split. My reference is to questions of a personal/emotional nature. In either case, make sure that you spend sufficient time listening, especially during the first session; avoid interrupting.

Observe and listen for loss of trust. If you lose trust, and you want to get it back, use the therapeutic listening procedure outlined earlier, and avoid the following:

1. *Do not defend yourself* if a client gets angry with your questions or comments; shut up and listen.
2. *Do not act uneasy* if verbally attacked; shut up and listen. Cut down on information output to decrease tapping into HRMs.
3. *If the person stops talking, do not try and get the ball rolling again* with more questions like "What's the matter?" It is best to go silent for a while and then tell a story. The old psychiatric practice (also the salesperson's practice) of not talking until the other person resumes is not always the best policy. Further, if you ignore the signals that the person's stress has increased or he or she has turned off—fidgeting in the chair, looking off into space, and so on—and continue to ask questions, you will lose more and more trust.
4. *Defensive reactions* from a client indicate that you have tapped into a high-risk message, an issue that needs attention (reframing), perhaps at a later time.

The types of answers you receive will, in large measure, depend upon the trust established by you, the listener. Many therapists are preoccupied with whether or not the individual is revealing all or, instead, deceiving (see Gediman and Lieberman 1996). This is most important to you if there is a lawsuit pending. It is important to know if the physical/emotional issue is part of a larger problem called litigation. If it is, then use your own judgment as to whether you feel competent to get involved (see Rush 1996:207–209).

For the most part, deception is not really that important when it comes to counseling (see Rush 1996:243–248 for a discussion of why deception in human interaction is normal). The client will reveal to you what he or she can trust you with. The client knows the "truth," as he or she has constructed it, and it is not really important that the therapist be informed. Many clients are relieved when you tell them that they do not have to tell you everything. Simply say that you will show them how to do "anonymous therapy," and then teach them reframing techniques.

THE THERAPEUTIC TOOLS OF REFRAMING: FROM DIVINATION TO CURE

Reframing tools are essentially incantations. Like the chants used by the Navaho or the prayers used by the Italians (Rush 1974), your words should be considered incantations designed and crafted to alter how a person sees, hears, and feels about information with which he or she is distressed (analogues of all the tools listed below can be found in numerous cultures and are briefly referenced in Rush 1996: 202–204). This is, in simple terms, a process of educating the mind. You already know many of the following techniques, but you may not be familiar with the terms that apply to them. There is nothing mystical about these techniques. Psychoanalysis, and most analytic techniques, are reframing techniques. The difference lies in the fact that the analyst or psychologist believes in the metaphor, believes that he or she is being unbiased and neutral (see Dorpat 1996), and that his or her theories are correct and true. You, the reader, must come to appreciate that you do not know the truth, that any analysis or reinterpretation that you offer is not truth, that you do bias the therapeutic setting, and that you are never neutral. You are trying to influence the individual. You are manipulating the individual to experience his or her world in a less stressful manner.

There are many concepts in both clinical and pop psychology that are not true but are useful in terms of understanding one's world from a different perspective. And there are some concepts, like codependency and power in relationships, and types of analytic statements (negative incantations), that increase stress in relationships and, in my opinion, are of limited use. Some of these will be revealed in Chapter 4 with respect to couples and marriage counseling, as well as parenting and stepparenting. Much of psychology and marriage counseling, intentionally or unintentionally, is in the blame mode. This is because of our preoccupation with morality, individualism, and freedom of choice, along with a rather paranoid outlook regarding the purposeful nastiness of people. This is not to say that blaming is out of place in counseling, but it has to be done judiciously.

The following techniques can be learned only through practice. When to use which technique or cluster of techniques comes with practice and experience. Remember, all counseling/therapy is goal-oriented and time-limited, and it is not unusual to do most of your basic reframing during the very first session. For example, I usually share with the individual or couple the model I presented earlier, that is, how we get to be the way we are. This removes a great deal of blame from the system and moves the client to action. In other words: "These are HRMs, here is how you acquired them, and here is what you can do to feel less stress." I wrap this around a language that fits the individual's receptor preference, I use numerous examples (storytelling), and I get the person to agree with what I am saying. Instead of thinking that he or she is experiencing some syndrome, instead of thinking that he or she is crazy, instead of being a victim, he or she is now a normal student.

Direct Techniques

There are two general types of techniques used in therapy, direct and indirect. Each has its place. Some of the tools require cooperation between therapist and client, while others do not.

Listening

Listening is your first direct technique for reframing and reducing stress. It is reframing in the sense that, for many people, you are the first person who has ever listened without making judgments. That, in and of itself, puts a new slant on the human condition: "There *are* people who will listen to me."

The second thing that listening does is to create a situation where stress is reduced simply through the act of allowing a person to speak his mind. It is a fact that as people are allowed to talk, their stress will come down. Just why this is so has to do with the fact that listening validates the person as being part of (rather than separate from) others, that group animal business I mentioned in Chapter 1. I do not mean that it validates the person as an individual; this is one of our social myths. It validates the person as belonging or as part of a social unit.

Requesting a Behavioral Change

As simple as it may sound, some people want to be told what to do. They come to you requesting a solution to a problem; you simply give them a solution. In fact, this is perhaps one of the more common techniques used in counseling. Telling someone who is depressed to go for a walk each day "and get some sun on your body" is a simple request that may be followed, and if the individual will follow one request, he or she might follow another.

There is a danger in this, however. If you suggest that a person do something, and it does not work out, the client may blame you—be careful what you ask people to do! The best solutions are those that the client suggests, and a method of accomplishing this is to indicate that the client actually mentioned this in an earlier session (see "Profound Intellectual Insight" in Chapter 3).

At any rate, I like to suggest that clients go on quests for things or knowledge, and usually combine this with some future pacing (see "Future Pacing" in this chapter). For example, a man came to me, quite distraught over the death of his sister, with whom he had not spoken for several years. I told him that he should go home and look around his kitchen, and he would find "something" that would give him some relief. I did not have the slightest idea what item or items of symbolic significance he would find, if anything, and I was not sure what meaning he would place on the word "something." Upon going home and looking around his kitchen, he noticed a little teapot, given to him by his sister some years earlier, with the words "Love Always" written on it. He called me several hours later, told me that his sister had made this in a ceramics class some years before, and "I always kept it on that shelf." To this day, I do not really know what meaning he attributed to the teapot, but it seemed to lessen his misery (this is a form of fortune-telling).

Over the years I have requested that individuals go and look for "something," and usually they will find "something" that has meaning in relation to the problem(s) they are attempting to solve.

Future Pacing or the Self-Fulfilling Prophecy

By stating that an event will happen in the future, you increase the probability of that event's actually taking place, especially if you have built sufficient rapport with the client. Remember, we create our realities, our worlds. You are suggesting that the individual make this event part of his or her world, using simple statements like "You will feel less depressed tomorrow because you have talked about this today" and "Right now there is confusion and lack of goals. But in a few weeks you will set some appropriate goals."

This can be combined with other statements that establish an expectation for behavior. For example, "Tonight, tomorrow night, at least within three nights you will have a dream in which you will exit from that event in history. I'm not sure why this happens, but it does." You can also add bizarre statements: "It probably won't be this week, but probably in nine days, twelve hours, and fourteen and a half or maybe fourteen and three-quarters minutes—I can never be sure of the fractions—your stress will come down significantly." It is important to sound sincere when you make these statements.

Reframing Past Information, Using Sounds and Images

Have the client imagine that he or she is observing himself or herself sitting in a movie theater. This is a purposeful process of disassociation, making it easier to alter images in the frame (by watching yourself, you "step outside" and enlist in a process called disassociation). Up on the screen is a frozen frame of an event that he or she has been looping on, perhaps a father yelling at a child. Make sure the individual is actually seeing the image by reporting detail (e.g., clothes worn, color of the clothes, etc.).

Next, have the client alter bits and pieces of the image, that is, put a smile on the father's face, make the image of the child bigger than the father, have the father's clothes change to those of a clown, and so on. Once changes have been made, have the person close down the image. If the client is looping more on the sounds, feelings, or smells in the frame, alter those and then close down the image. This technique is successful (not all the time) because all the information in your mind is a construction—you made it all up as you interpreted your world. The mind/body desires to go toward stress reduction, not stress enhancement, and any alteration of images, sounds, and feelings can potentially stop looping behavior. If we did not have the innate capability of altering our interpretations of the world and placing sounds, sights, and feelings in a more comfortable frame, we would all be basket cases early in life.

Running Situations in Reverse

I have found this especially useful for EMTs, paramedics, police, firefighters, and trauma nurses and physicians who have witnessed, and are unable to exit from, critical incidents. (Keep in mind that the longer the time between experiencing a traumatic event and conformable retranslation, the more convoluted the symbols that become attached to it through analogous thinking.) The procedure is to make ten to fifteen boxes on a piece of paper. Have the client describe ten to fifteen frames that represent a sequence of events from prior to the event, then first contact, and then ending of the event and going on to the next life experience. Obtain reasonable detail and note this in each of the boxes. Once the process is completed, have the client recall the event, beginning with the last frame first. Do as little coaching as possible; let him or her reexperience the event in reverse. This literally changes everything in a manner similar to running a movie in reverse. Once the client does this, do not discuss the event further during that session.

An employee at a hardware and building supply store was sent to me by a local ambulance company. The previous day he had been driving a forklift carrying some very heavy pieces of lumber to be placed in the back of a delivery truck. The man in the delivery truck decided to get out of the cab, and just as he did, the load of lumber came crashing down, killing him instantly. Needless to say, although the accident was not his fault, the employee was unable to exit from the experience. He kept going over and over it, attempting to determine if he could or should have done something different. Other than not being at work that day, he could find nothing, as he relived the experience, that helped to answer the question and break the loop.

In my office, I had him imagine the events while I constructed about fifteen boxes, which included events just prior to the tragedy, the incident, and events after the fact. Once this was constructed, I had him review the events in reverse. When he finished, I immediately asked him about his diet and began to discuss fiber and vitamins, which brought us to the end of the session. As he was leaving the office, I asked him to call me in the morning, and we would talk further. When he called the next day, he told me that he had slept better and that he was not as focused on the event, although he did not feel that he could return to work for a few days.

Exactly what happened in his mind by running the event backward, I do not know. However, simply talking about traumatic events usually ends up retraumatizing the individual. The individual is in emotional trauma because he or she cannot exit from the sights, sounds, and so on, and reliving them usually does not help to alter their meaning. This is often the case in group therapy for rape victims; the more they review the event(s), the more traumatized they become, their status as victim is reinforced, and men become evil monsters.

Replacing Images

This is a variation on reframing past information. Have the client imagine that he or she is sitting in a comfortable easy chair in a movie theater. On each arm of the chair is a lever that pushes forward and back. Have the client imagine that the movie screen is a split screen on which there can be an image on the left and an image on the right.

Next, have the client build an image of the event that he or she is looping on—this could involve an interaction with a parent or boss, an eating problem, or what have you. Have the individual describe as much detail as possible; write this down on your notepad and ascertain on which side of the screen this image was placed.

Next, have the client build, on the other half-screen, an image that would be more pleasing, that perhaps represents the antithesis of the first screen. Write down all the detail. Explain to the client that the levers on the arms of the chairs are for pushing the image away or bringing the image close.

Finally, review the images for the client, including as much detail as possible, and on the count of three, have him or her pull the lever bringing the pleasing image closer and push the lever moving the other image away, shooting the negative image far away until it becomes a dot. Then close out the image and ask the client about his or her experience while engaging in the task.

Disentangling Images

In our culture we have two gender images, male and female (although we are slowly allowing other gender possibilities). Everyone you meet falls into one of these general male/female images, with the result of possible confusion. For example, all women symbolically represent mothers, and all men symbolically represent fathers. A wife is also a mother if she has children. All men are potentially husbands and fathers. It is not uncommon for a woman to get her husband confused with her father, or a man to confuse his wife with his mother or an ex-wife or a girlfriend. The reason for this has to do with analogous thinking, which can lead to a great deal of creativity as well as confusion.

For example, a wife is having problems confusing her husband (who has not been abusive) with her father and other men who *have* been abusive to her. Instruct the client to put her hands together and visualize a composite image of her husband, her father, and every male she has ever met. Have her describe the image while you write it down. Then have her choose one hand to represent her husband and the other hand to represent men in general.

Next, review the composite image in as much detail as possible, instructing the client that, on the count of three, she will pull her hands apart and allow the husband to stand separately from the composite image. Once the task is completed, ask her about her experience when separating the images. Avoid the topic of abusive males during the remainder of the session.

Polarizing Images

A procedure similar to the one above involves creating two opposite images, one on each hand, and then bringing the hands together to create a third image. This is especially useful for relieving headaches (anywhere from 30 to 50 percent of the time clients come to your office with headaches).

Have the client choose a hand that represents his or her headache. As the person shakes that hand up and down, have him or her describe what he or she looks like, feels like, and sounds like with a headache (the headache will probably get worse). Write this down.

Next, with the other hand, have him or her describe what he or she looks like, sounds like, and feels like when life is just great. Write this down. Then have the client close his or her eyes, and lead him or her through the earlier descriptions (look, sound, and feel), first with a headache, and then when feeling fine. Go back and forth at least three times but no more than five. After finishing with the hand representing the client without a headache, have him or her place his or her hands together and hold them there. While the hands are together in a "praying posture," have him or her discuss the experience. (Usually the client will not know if he or she has a headache or not.) Have the client move the hands apart as you gracefully change the subject.

Conjoining Statements

The concept of conjoining statements comes from politics. When bills are put together, there are usually parts that the president does not like; these are called riders. But in order to get the bill passed, the president has to accept the riders. The brain tends to work in a similar fashion if you use the appropriate incantations (words). For example, "*Just* thinking about the exam on Monday *causes* you to feel good about it." The short formula is "A *causes* B."

The second statement is more easily accepted if the first statement is grounded in something that the individual can agree with. For example, "Just sitting in the chair *causes* you to relax." There is nothing especially logical about the statement, but it can have a large impact. You can increase the impact by modulating your voice slightly to emphasize the second statement. This could be done by lowering your voice tone or slowing your rate of speech. This is also an example of combining techniques, which means you have to experiment.

Attention-Getters

Attention-getters are magic words to which people will usually pay attention. The ultimate word magic involves the "four letter" words, although through overuse, especially in the mass media, their impact has decreased. My opinion is that such language should not be used in counseling (at least *you* should not use such words) because there is still an expectation that professionals do not talk like that.

Magic words that are quite useful, and with which you are most familiar, are "secret," "rumor," "curious," "surprise," "wonder," and so on. For example, "Have you heard the latest rumor? You will solve the problem." "It is always a big surprise as you get along better with your parents." "Have you heard the latest secret? Your mind can heal any part of your body."

There are other types of attention-getters in the form of changes in voice tone and pauses. For example, you might begin by saying, "You will be surprised by a solution to the problem . . . (pause) . . . in a few days."

Incongruent Attention-Getters

This type of attention-getter represents a juxtaposition of words that are somewhat contradictory. For example, "The real *problem* is that you're really a nice, honest person." "The *dilemma* is that I trust your judgments; it's hard to explain." "The *tragedy* is that all of this will make sense to you in a couple of weeks."

The question posed by the client, through the aligning of such words, is "Why is it a problem/dilemma/tragedy?" At the same time the second message (your intended message) is not questioned.

Attribution of Profound Intellectual Insight

This particular tool was referred to earlier with respect to giving solutions. Solutions are often rejected because, by giving a solution, you are suggesting that the receiver is stupid, that he or she cannot figure things out. However, by telling the person that *he* or *she* suggested the belief, ability, insight, answer, solution, or behavior, you avoid that possibility. For example, "You know, the other day when we were talking, you said that people do grow up and become responsible for themselves and others." Or "You mentioned to me that you needed to change the way you listen to your children, and I agree." Most people are unlikely to disagree with you, but if they do, simply attribute the insight to someone else. Remember, the best solution is the one that the individual comes up with. Do not be too anxious to take credit for what you do in counseling; it is important to attribute the changes, insights, and curing to the client, for in reality it is the client who changes—you do not change the client. This technique can be used only after a first session.

Clearly, this is manipulation, but that is the purpose of communication in general: to influence the receiver. Your motive, however, is to offer other possibilities to the client.

Confusion Technique

This technique contains two contradictory or unlike statements and is designed to get someone's attention through confusion. The intended message may be one or both of the parts, or, as in breaking process, to get the brain to "jam up" so that a third message can be inserted. I will review breaking process shortly.

An example of the confusion technique could be "I like to see your smile, and I know that you understand the need for patience and understanding." Or "In the springtime, the weather changes, and that's why cooperation is so important." It is imperative, with confusion techniques, to move quickly to other topics and not allow a discussion of what you said.

The One Chunk at a Time Approach

This technique is designed to keep the person curious and listening so that you can deliver a punch line. This is accomplished by first saying something that, although nonthreatening, demands clarification. For example, you say to the client (spouse, child, etc.), "I have a need." "Need" becomes an attention-getter because the "need" is not specified and the person usually gets curious. Once you have the person's attention, you continue, "I have a need to talk." The word "talk" is not specific to any particular topic, and the individual usually remains in the curious mode, responding, "Talk about what?" The person is now curious, so you can deliver your punch line, which must be short and to the point. "I need to talk about personal hygiene."

After you drop your punch line, it is important to stop talking and listen to possible defenses. It is not necessary to defend your position at this point because you have delivered your message and it has been received.

"Yes" Sets

"Yes" sets are an old sales technique wherein you create a situation in which the individual continually answers "Yes," and then you add the punch line, or some thought or behavior that you want the person to follow. Essentially, you are creating an instant mind-set. Example: "You would agree that you're not a stupid person, right? And because you are not stupid, you are capable of learning, right? And since you are capable of learning, you are capable of changing, just like changing your shirt, right?" Once the punch line is dropped you can listen, walk away, and so forth.

"Yes" sets can also be constructed in the following manner: "You would agree that it is summer (spring, fall, winter), right? And you would agree that it is daytime (evening, etc.), right? And you would likewise agree that I'm talking. So I'm sure you would also agree to give up smoking/exercise more/etc."

Double Binds

Double binds can be positive or negative, both of which can be therapeutic. Negative double binds usually lead to a great deal of confusion, and it is always necessary to "let the person out." (I will not go into the use of negative double binds in this work because it requires a great deal of experience.) Some years ago Bateson et al. (1972) put together the double bind theory of schizophrenia, which involves messages or instructions (rules) that no matter what the person does, he or she cannot win. From my experience, such messages are very common in families that, although loving, are very controlling. For example, let us pretend that you are my daughter. I dress you up in white and say, "Now, go out and play, but don't get dirty!" Under these conditions, you cannot play without getting dirty, but then you are not following instructions because you cannot play.

Many males in North American society, as will be explored in Chapter 4, are in a double bind with respect to openly discussing feelings. In the late 1960s and early 1970s, women wanted their men to be open and talk about their feelings but men were then presented with a bind: "Be open about your feelings, but we don't want to hear it." Or "Be open about your feelings, but we are afraid of your feelings." Or "Be open about your feelings; tell me what is on your mind, but I will probably use it against you for the rest of your life!" The reluctance to talk about feelings, then, is not a biological issue, nor is it an individual problem that the male has to work on. If women want men to share their feelings, they have to be open to listening.

With positive double binds, you are essentially making two statements so that, no matter what the person does, it will be the "right thing." For example, I made this statement to a young man who determined that he needed to smoke because some of his friends did. "Unless you are able to see your actions differently, you will not be able to resist doing what I say." (There is a bit of the confusion technique in this as well.)

This young man was experiencing peer pressure, a very normal feature of social living. We consider some types of peer pressure as bad (smoking and other drug use), and other types as good or at least neutral (e.g., watching a particular television program, wearing certain types of clothing, etc.). Although this young man was, like all of us, susceptible to peer pressure, he also wanted to think for himself. So I gave him the following message: "I realize that you have problems going along with authority figures like me, so that's why you can stop going along with Bob's [a friend and "bad influence"/peer authority figure] authority."

In many situations, you want the individual to follow instructions and there is an unwillingness to do so. In some of these cases (this particular technique can backfire with some people) you can instruct the person to be uncooperative (by continuing to be uncooperative, the individual is following your instructions). For example, "I don't want you to cooperate with your parents until I tell you to do so, is that clear?" For a really stubborn person (and stubbornness is a potentially useful posture) this does not set well. The individual is likely *not* to follow your instruction, but by not following your directives, he has to follow those of his parents (he cannot both follow and not follow his parents' instructions).

I have often used the following double bind for drug abuse problems: "Denial that you have a drug problem is the first step to solving the problem. Now, I want you to deny the problem." If the individual denies the problem, he or she has taken the first step; if there is an admission to a problem, he or she has taken the first step. Either way, he or she wins. (Keep in mind, however, that what constitutes drug abuse is an invention of our culture. I am not sure what drug abuse really is. Taking prescription antidepressants every day, to my way of thinking, is drug abuse that has been legitimized by the powers that be.)

The following is a double bind for securing cooperation: "I know you will not follow my instructions, and that's why I don't want you to go into hypnosis." (I will discuss hypnosis in Chapter 6.) This statement has an element of confusion to it similar to breaking process (discussed below).

Third Person

This is a process of talking to one person while the intended receiver is standing close by. Or you can refer to something you read in a book, or talk to someone on the phone, explaining a procedure that you want the client in your office to follow.

This approach is useful when you want to avoid giving solutions. Many people will not accept solutions offered by others; solutions tend to be high-risk because they imply incompetence or stupidity. Often clients will come in asking for solutions, you give them one, and they say, "Nah, I've tried that; it won't work." Here are some examples for using the third person and avoiding such reactions.

A young woman called me to inquire about weight loss and the kind of program I offered. She told me that she had tried "everything." I asked her to give me a list. She mentioned medications her doctor had suggested, she mentioned Weight Watchers and different health food store formulas (ephedra, *Garcinia cambogia*, etc.). Her list had the ring of someone looking for instant weight loss, and prognosis for her success with my program was highly problematical. So I mentioned to her that I had read an article in one of the medical journals that stated quite definitely that weight loss programs that combine raw fruits and vegetables with exercise were the most cost-effective, safest, and most successful. Had I tried to explain and sell her on my program without reference to a "third person" (the medical journal), she would have never accepted the logic.

A man called me to set up an appointment for himself and his wife. They were having a number of marital problems, one of which was the wife's personal hygiene. The husband told me that he had not discussed this with his wife because he was embarrassed to bring it up. I set the appointment and told the husband that personal hygiene would be dealt with indirectly because, understanding his embarrassment, I did not want his wife to be embarrassed. At the hour of the appointment, and when I could see the couple coming down the walkway to my office, I picked up the phone and was having an imaginary conversation with a client when they entered, instructing her on particulars of personal hygiene. I took my time and went into detail as the couple sat in my office. Two days after our first session, the husband called and told me that his wife heard the conversation and was acting on the instructions I delivered to this imaginary "third person."

Illusion of Choice

Freedom of choice is one of our cultural dictates; we have the freedom to choose from a wide variety of foods, clothing styles, car types, religions, beers, and so on. When giving directives to individuals in our culture, creating an illusion of choice often helps to obtain the desired result. I say "illusion" because it only appears that the person has a choice. For example, "You can sit in this chair and we can talk, sit in that chair and we can discuss this, or you can stand while we share some possibilities; take your choice." Or "It will take you a while to settle in here. Some people take a week, some two, but within three" (this combines a bit of future pacing as well as illusion of choice).

Indirect Approaches

Some of the above approaches contain indirect elements. The following are directed more at the subconscious and are therefore more specifically "indirect," designed to get past resistance.

Bridging Experience

This process is similar to the "yes" set mentioned above. It begins by building a problem common to most people and ends with a punch line that represents the common problem *as well as* the problem specific to the individual. For example:

Have you ever bought a hamburger, and you put lots of ketchup, mustard, relish on it—whatever you like? And when you bring it up to your mouth, it's too fat? And when you bite down, the ketchup squirts out on your shirt, or shoes, or the floor—can you picture that? It's like life; sometimes we make a mess of things and we need a towel to clean it up. I'm offering you a towel.

Directly saying to someone, "Let me help you," or "You need help," sometimes falls on deaf ears because it is a statement that the individual cannot help himself or herself. Individuals, for the most part, do not want to admit they have problems. Here is another example:

Do you remember the first time you were learning to tie your shoes? And you would try and imitate what you saw someone else do? And you would put this lace over that lace and try to magically tie it around? But when you let go, it all came unraveled? Well, we've got a bunch of loose ends we need to tie off, and if you don't, you'll be tripping on those loose ends and falling on your face.

Talking to the Less Dominant Eye

If a person is right-handed, he or she is probably right eye-dominant. The right eye and right hand are controlled by the left hemisphere of the brain. We exhibit many types of dominances—thumb dominance, foot dominance, and so on. To prove that there is such a thing as eye dominance, use the following process. Make a circle with your index finger and thumb. Now, holding your hand at arm's length and with both eyes open, position an object, at some distance from you, in the center of the circle created by your thumb and index finger. Without moving either your head or your arm, close your left eye. If the object is still in the center of the circle made by your index finger and thumb, you are right eye-dominant. If, on the other hand, the object goes out of view when you close your left eye, you are left eye-dominant. Your dominant eye is the one that focuses on the speaker's eyes, face, and lips during the communication process. To determine someone's eye dominance, pay attention to the individual's eyes. You will notice, in most cases, that one eye will be focused on you and the other eye will be looking slightly away. This is called strabismus (there are various forms of this) and can be detected in most people simply by noticing which eye is looking at you straight on.

Let us say that you determine that the individual with whom you are conversing is right eye-dominant (that is the eye focused on you), and you are delivering one of the bridging experience statements mentioned above. When you get to the punch line, move your eyes (look at the less dominant eye), and deliver the punch line. Your message will take on a different dimension to that person and is less likely to be rejected.

Analysis

Analysis can be an effective method of educating a person regarding other possibilities of behavior. I usually deliver analysis in a third-person fashion; this then amounts to a form of storytelling and is less likely to activate defenses. I avoid the "You're doing that because" type analysis, which is often designed to illustrate the intelligence of the therapist and is explained as fact rather than metaphor or possibilities of behavioral choices. Never believe your analysis; there is no way of knowing why anyone does anything, except to say that people act on their best choices at the time.

The analyses that I usually use are from my experiences in counseling over the past twenty-five years. Let me give you some examples of my offering analysis in order to alter behavior. A woman came to see me and, for the first five minutes, sat motionless on the couch, weeping silently. I asked her how I could help, and she said that she was married to an alcoholic who beat her. I paraphrased her by saying, "A pretty bad relationship." She responded, "That's not the half of it. My *former* husband was also an alcoholic who beat me."

Because she used the word "former" and not "first," I assumed correctly that there might have been one or two other husbands as well. As it turned out, by age thirty-five, she had been married five times; each time she had found an alcoholic who beat her.

I finally asked her about her mother and father. "Oh," she said, "My father was a drunk, and he used to beat my mother." With that I broke in and said, "Ah, now I understand why you hate your mother." She stopped crying, looked at me, and said, "How did you know that I don't get along with my mother?" I replied, "Well, if you can find yourself a drunk who will beat you, and you fix this person, you can prove to your mother that she could have fixed your father, and all of you could have lived happily ever after."

Angrily she stood up and said, "Am I doing that?" I cautioned that I really did not know, and she replied, "Well, I'll put a stop to this!" She stormed out of the office. But that was not the end of it.

About six months later I received a phone call from this woman. She asked if I remembered her; I said that I did. She stated that she had solved the problem with the fifth husband by divorcing him, but now she had another problem. She had found another man—this time, not in a bar—and he was a kind, loving person. But she did not know how to relate to his kind, loving behavior, although she knew how to relate to a violent drunk. *She* was being verbally abusive, and did not understand what was going on. I suggested to her that she knew how to relate to a drunk but had limited experience with men who treated her with respect. I suggested that she come in with her new boyfriend and learn some new tools. She agreed, and they are now living quite happily. I have no idea if my analysis of the situation was correct, but it did get results.

When I tell this story to clients, I often do not know what meaning(s) they attach. For some, it is that we perhaps are trying to solve the wrong problem; for others, it is that we can often define a problem but that, in itself, does not solve it. For still others, it is an example of polarity (for example, when one person stops being a victimizer, he or she may become a victim). The beauty of this type of analytical storytelling is that the client will attach to the symbols the meanings that are important to her (or him).

Another example of analysis is the following. It is common for couples to come in and immediately get into a fight with lots of growling and sarcasm. I let it go on for a short time and then say, "It is interesting that your husband (or wife) trusts you enough to insult you." With that I usually get a double take and remarks like, "What do you mean, *trusts* me?" I explain, "Well, who else does he have to growl at? If he growls at work, he'll get fired; if he growls at his friends, he won't have any friends. Now, this is not to say that this is good for the relationship—quite the contrary— but it does indicate that he trusts that *you won't hurt him*."

This type of analysis is clearly a reframing of the meaning of the husband's verbal abuse. One thing that is to be avoided in marital and family counseling, as we will see in Chapter 4, is blaming; whatever is going on, blame has to be removed from the equation. The dynamics have to be explained in ways that avoid high-risk communication. High-risk statements decrease the probability that they will return to counseling, and you lose an opportunity to be useful.

One final issue. A mother brought her ten-year-old son in because he had thrown a rock through a neighbor's window. She did not understand his behavior and demanded that I find out why he had done it. I then turned to the young man and asked, "Why did you throw the rock through the neighbor's window?" He looked at me and said, "I don't know."

The mother cut in and said, "There, you see? He doesn't want to admit to things." I asked the young man to step outside the office for a moment while I spoke to his mother. After he left, I asked the mother if it was more important to know *why* he did what he did or to make sure that the behavior never happened again. She had trouble answering this! She was in a bind because of a psychological mentality that seeks to know why even when it does not make any difference. (Will knowing "why" change the result or the future behavior?) This young man *did not* have an answer to the question.

So I said to the woman, "The only reason that you will accept is that he is a bad person, is that correct?" She replied, "No. I want the truth!" Finally, I used a "yes" set and had her agree that it was more important to make sure that the behavior never happened again.

I brought the young man back into the office. After he sat down, I looked him straight in the eye and said, in a low growling voice, "Don't you ever, ever do that again." With that, he started to cry; he got the message. I also instructed the mother, who was now feeling very sorry for her son, that she should never, ever bring up the incident again. She agreed. This incident took place ten years ago, and the behavior was never repeated.

The moral of this is simple: Analysis does not change behavior, but it can open a door to other possibilities. And many times knowing the "why" of a behavior is less important than altering that behavior (I'm sure the behavioral psychologists will thank me for that one).

Analogies

Analogies are short statements that associate one idea with another. Usually the first statement represents something common to the person's experience, and the second statement represents the instruction you desire the individual to internalize. For example, "Your behavior is like a banana. Once you eat it, what do you do with the peel?" What, exactly, does this analogy mean? Like some of my analysis stories, I'm not always sure, but it does instruct on consequences of behavior.

Moreover, sometimes people actually answer the analogy. I made this statement to a young man who had been arrested for shoplifting and was brought to my office by his mother. When I made the above statement, he said, "You throw it away." I then said, "How will you throw away being arrested?" He did not have an answer to this, but he did say, several weeks later, that every time he ate or even looked at a banana, it reminded him of his behavior. To my knowledge, he never shoplifted again. Here is a good example of how powerful incantations can be; this visual connection of a banana to his behavior was an unintended, but positive, result.

Other examples: "This situation is like the wind; you always know that it will stop." (This incorporates an expectation of a future behavior—future pacing.) "Not considering what you are doing is like throwing a nail in the road. You never know who will end up with a flat—maybe you." "Trust is like a sock in a washing machine; it's easy to lose."

Your mind is capable of instant, spontaneous, and analogous representations, and you have to be aware and prepared to mirror these to the client. What I call "immediate metaphors," those that a person can tie to currently generated images, sounds, and other sensations, are powerful opportunities for spanning the conscious filters and allowing information reception, consideration, and, often, acceptance.

For example, I had a client diagnosed as having psoriasis; she no longer wanted to use the cortisone cream because of the long-term side effects. On her first visit she noticed and commented on the fish in my aquarium, set in a bookshelf near where she was sitting. She admired the fish and we talked a bit about fish, and more about fish, and each time I saw her, more about fish. Fish were somehow important to her. I had been seeing her about once a month to check the progress of eliminating the condition. One of the things that I had expressly told her to do was to stay away from white bread or anything with enriched flour in it. When she was following the cleansing procedure and staying away from enriched wheat products, her condition improved almost to the point of clear, healthy skin all over her body. But just as soon as she consumed enriched wheat products, the condition slowly returned. Each month I would give her the same logic, and tell her stories to keep her motivated. She would follow instructions for a week or so, the condition would improve, and back to enriched flour she would go.

One day she came in, and began to stare at the now empty fish tank. She looked at me in amazement; there were always fish in the tank. Here was an opportunity to enhance her motivation. "Where are the fish?" she asked. "Well," I started, "remember that rain we had last week and the power went out?"

"Oh, no, did they get hypothermia?" I answered, "Yes." Then I followed it with an analogy: "Yes, yes. It was only two or perhaps three, but no more than four, degrees away from where they like to be, their normal body range. And their poor little bodies couldn't take the change, and these little bodies began to behave in strange ways. Esther, just a few degrees away from your normal body range, you're like the fish, in a sense."

I then changed the subject to the koi pond in our herb garden. She knew just how to deal with koi to keep them healthy. More important, she no longer eats products made with enriched flour, continues to follow a specific eating pattern, and no longer has psoriasis.

Fables

Fables are short, one paragraph stories similar to those by Aesop, with which most of us are familiar. In fact, I suggest to my students that they purchase their own copy of Aesop's *Fables*, read them through, and memorize several for future use. Keep in mind that fables, like analogies, are to be "dropped" on someone, and not explained. If someone asks for a meaning, simply say, "It's just a story."

Recently I was invited to sit in on a high school English class by a teacher who needed some advice regarding student behavior. The class was set up in a two-hour block with a ten-minute break between the first and second hour. Before the class started, I noticed a young man being very disrespectful to the young woman in front of him (I was sitting beside him), touching her inappropriately, and saying some pretty rude things to her; her objections to his behavior were ignored. This young man was the main disruptive force; his behavior got the attention of everyone in class.

At break, I got his attention. He asked who I was, and I said that I was observing the class. I then asked if he had ever heard the story about the Lion and the Gnat, to which he replied, "No." I then told him the following fable by Aesop.

Once upon a time there was a Lion, lying beside the road, not bothering anyone, just taking in the sun and relaxing, minding his own business. Out of nowhere appears a little itty-bitty, tiny gnat who boldly flew up to the Lion and said, "I hear that you are the king of the beasts."

The Lion replied, "Yes, I've heard that, too, but today I'm just relaxing."

To this the gnat retorted, "Well, I'm going to show you that you aren't the king of the beasts—you aren't the king of anything. I'm going to make your life so miserable that you're going to wish you were never born!"

The Lion said, "Hey, man, I don't want any trouble; I'm just resting here, minding my own business."

"Well," said the gnat, "You need to be put in your place."

Suddenly, the gnat began chewing on the Lion's ears, flying up his nose—that gnat was just all over the Lion. The Lion did his best to fend off the attack, but the gnat was too quick, and the poor Lion was getting worn to a frazzle.

Finally, the gnat tired of this adventure, flew off, got caught in a spider's web, and was eaten by a spider.

After telling this story, I got up and left the classroom. The young man went outside to be with his friends. Later that day the teacher approached me, curious about what I had said to the young man because he was a perfect gentleman the rest of the day. I have no idea what the story meant, but it had an obvious and immediate effect. Such stories do not always have immediate impact, and sometimes they have no impact at all. However, they are low-risk because they do not invite defensive reactions.

Metaphors

Every time you speak to someone, you speak in metaphor. In other words, you are telling stories—stories about yourself, others, the world. And, as mentioned earlier, all of these stories, all of your metaphors, are wrapped around rules. Some metaphors are risky because they are direct, and often communicate rules about how a person (or group) ought to be or should be. These incantations invite defensive reactions. If defensive reactions are your goal, now you're getting the picture.

The metaphors with which I am concerned are indirect and appear to be, on first glance, separate from the individual to whom they are addressed, "just a story." Grimm's *Fairy Tales*, and tales from all cultures, however, are much more than stories. They deliver messages to the listener regarding values, morals, and how to solve problems. Metaphors are likewise useful for reinterpreting events in a person's life.

Metaphors are more elaborate than fables, and contain many levels of meaning. Storytelling and listening to stories are part of the reality of all juveniles and adults, and because stories are difficult not to pay attention to, they become very effective methods of delivering instructions. Never explain your metaphors (see Lakoff and Johnson 1980 for a discussion of the significance of metaphors in structuring reality; Fernandez 1991 for numerous anthropological views of metaphor in the construction of social/ cultural reality; and Gordon 1978; Hammond 1990; Havens and Walters 1989; Mills and Crowley 1986; and Wallas 1985, 1991 for examples and therapeutic uses of metaphor).

The following is an example of a metaphor I constructed some time ago for a young man in his twenties who was depressed, living at home with his mother, and seeking direction in life. I never explained its meaning, but it seemed to start a process of exploring some of the possibilities in his world. I titled this metaphor "The Boots."

Once upon a time, there was a young prince who lived in a castle nestled within the hills of a faraway land. He was wealthy and educated, having traveled far and wide, but there were few people with whom to share his adventures. Oh, yes, there were the village people, the common townsfolk, but none of them could share his experiences, for they were wrapped up in the mundane affairs of day-to-day living. And they were suspicious and envious of the Prince.

He was alone. Oh, the King and Queen were always nearby and willing to share his thoughts and stories. And there was the court jester, but he had outgrown his antics. In days gone by, they would fool together and make light of the townsfolk, and the world in general, but that was in the past now. The Prince was feeling very much alone, day after day and night after night.

But the Prince realized that he could not simply wait for people to come into his life, that he would have to journey in search of people and things to put meaning in his life. So one morning, bright and early, the Prince saddled his mount, filled his saddlebags with provisions, said good-bye to the King and Queen, and set off on a journey, wondering what lay ahead.

As he rode into the dark forest, to the north, on a path seldom traveled, he came upon a cabin nestled between a pond and a garden. As he looked about, he noticed that there was something peculiar about the plants in the garden. These were not the usual corn or squash or beans, but plants and trees with unusual fruits. Deciding to explore, he cautiously approached the cabin. And, because he was well trained in the use of sword and knife, he fearlessly knocked on the door. "Who's there?" a voice came from within. "Don't be shy; knock louder."

And so the Prince knocked louder, and the voice within replied, "Good, you have an honest, strong knock. Now you can enter."

Puzzled by the request to knock louder, the Prince entered the cabin to find a strangely lighted room, with a hearth and all kinds of unusual objects hanging from the ceiling. And in the corner was an old man, dressed in a black robe and pointed hat, seated at a table, seemingly preoccupied with some type of apothecary mixture. Without lifting his eyes, the old man spoke. "You are the lonely one from the castle, searching and searching, always searching, yet not finding, not finding." Then the old man was silent. Assuming that the old man knew him, the Prince felt a little easier and began to engage the old man in conversation.

"Old man, how do you know of me?"

"How do you know I am old? I know of you by your boots, by your boots."

"What do you mean, you know me by my boots?"

"You had those boots specially made at the cobbler's several months ago."

"How do you know this, old man?"

"How I know isn't as important as the fact that they brought you here." Now that was a really curious thing for the old man to say, that the boots brought him there.

"What do you mean, 'the boots brought you here'?"

The old man chuckled to himself and motioned for the Prince to come closer. As he approached, the old man stood up, turned, walked toward a door at the back of the cabin, opened the door, and went into the garden, motioning the Prince to follow. Once outside, the Prince could see that indeed this was not an ordinary garden, but the garden of a master magician. But the only magician that the Prince knew was Margon the Magnificent, the court magician, who was noted for his ability to predict the future and cure the ailments of the king. But this magician was unknown to him. "What is your name, magician?"

"How do you know that I am a magician?"

"By the way you are dressed and all the curious things in the garden, and that statement about the boots. Only a magician would say that."

The magician then picked several leaves from a curious vine and motioned for the Prince to join him inside the cabin. Once inside, the magician sat down and motioned for the Prince to sit across from him.

"I have been working on this potion for several days, so that it would be just right. This potion will help you see and give you confidence in a different way, confidence in a different way."

"But how did you know that I would come to your cabin?"

"The boots, the boots. But you are here, and that is all that matters. Here, take this potion, which will cure all your ills. Your problem is that you don't know how to see and know what you want. This will allow you to see what you want more clearly; this will allow you to find that which will quench that loneliness."

The Prince was cautious. "Why should I do this at your command? Why should I trust you?"

"Very good," replied the old man. "Very good. And do those boots fit comfortably? And are they not a beautiful pair of boots, without equal in the countryside? They don't squeak when you walk, they are waterproof, and they don't scuff as easily as the other boots you have had. You trusted the cobbler to make you boots to protect your feet, YOUR SOUL. Now would the cobbler betray the rest of you?"

Finally it dawned on the Prince. "You were the strange man, the strange old man in the cobbler shop that day the cobbler took my order. Now I understand the strange remark 'The boots that wear the man.' That's what he said, 'the boots that wear the man.' "

Still a bit puzzled, the Prince took the potion. Looking down at his boots, he could see the love and craftsmanship, and felt the quality and care. Then the old man spoke.

"In the next few weeks of your travels, you will have a wondrous experience. I don't exactly know what it will be, but you will have a wondrous and unusual but comfortable experience. It is difficult for me to predict exactly when it will be, but be prepared for it, be prepared for it."

After those words the old man guided the Prince to the door and rather impolitely, but gently, pushed him out to his steed and sent him on his way, pointing to a trail, not traveled by many, going north. Off he went. The Prince rode day and night, not encountering anyone or anything. Finally, after what seemed like days and days, he found himself on the outskirts of a small town. There was a sign that pointed the way. As he rode into town, he began to feel as if he had been there before, sometime in the past, and he could see smiling faces, and people greeted him. In other villages, the townspeople greeted him with suspicion and envy, or so he thought. But here everyone seemed friendly. Even those people who looked less friendly were more friendly than he could imagine, and he felt good and warm inside.

And he spied a beautiful maiden, with soft, brown hair and a pretty face. She smiled back, and at that instant he realized his future. As he dismounted, the boots seemed to know exactly what to do. He approached the maiden, and hand in hand, they walked down the street of life.

The young man for whom I constructed this metaphor found a direction in life, and is currently in his fourth year at a local university. Again, it is difficult to know how anyone will take such a story, but I think that you would agree that my directly telling this young man to get off his duff and find his place in the world would have had little or no effect.

Breaking Process

Breaking process is a step above the confusion technique mentioned earlier, and is rightly described as an indirect approach. When a person's information-processing abilities are disrupted—for example, when frightened—that person is likely to welcome any message that will allow his or her stress to go down or help to reorganize for problem-solving. In short, the person, once his or her processing abilities are momentarily halted, will likely act on your next message if it is nonthreatening or has a stress-reducing quality—and yet not consciously hear it.

One procedure for breaking process is to create an ambiguous set of signals that are followed by the punch line, which is usually delivered with a lowered voice tone (nonverbal signals can also be utilized). For example, you might say, "Is it farther to San Diego, or by bus; get calm and relaxed." When delivering the "get calm and relaxed," lower your voice tone and/or your hand, as an analogous visual signal, at the same time you lower your voice tone.

Another example: "Although I didn't get any mail today, it did rain; positive change can happen." The same procedure would be used with "positive change can happen."

Another procedure is to present a statement with a conclusion that can be generated only in the mind of the receiver. For example, "Many people ask what's going to happen when they break the rules, but you know and I know, and that's all right to change."

A third procedure combines the illusion of choice. For example, "It is all right to resist, and then make the changes necessary, or you can not resist and just go along with it." Or "Wanting to change and not wanting to change are just part of the same thing. There is always some part of the problem that you want to change, there are other parts that you are not sure about, and still others that it is all right to keep. You have to make the decision on what to change."

Many of these types of messages lead a person into hypnosis, which is a very effective medium for reframing information. I will discuss hypnosis in Chapter 6.

Embedded Messages

This is the process of making statements within a statement, and can be accomplished by using the following techniques.

1. Tonal shifts and pauses— "It looks like the weather is going to . . . CHANGE TODAY, Bob." This is a very effective process and can easily be added to fables and metaphors. In other words, you can pause in the middle of the story, make a short statement, then continue with the story.

2. Using homonyms—Make a list of words that have the same sound but different meanings, and that could be used in the context of delivering useful messages. For example, "This is the end of an era for making errors in your life."

The secret with these types of indirect approaches is that you never pause after making the statement. Instead, you move right on to something else.

OVERVIEW

Engaging in counseling/therapy requires that you understand a few things about yourself and that you are equipped with a variety of communication tools. You also need to practice what you preach, as is the case when educating others in health procedures.

First, remember that rejection is the key to stress reactions, that stress reactions are the product of how you and others interpret the world, and that the key to lowering stress is through the use of symbols (through language).

Second, you are responsible for the information you send and receive. If you unintentionally set up a situation where the receiver activates his or her HRMs, do not defend yourself—shut up, and listen. Moreover, you are responsible for how you interpret the incantations of others. Most people, contrary to popular opinion, are not malicious, rotten, and nasty; instead, they know not what they do. Remember the concept of compressed data; there is no way of knowing what anyone means.

Third, put emotional responsibility into effect. Realize that your emotions come from within you and from how you interpreted similar messages in history; do not blame others for how you feel. You are ultimately the cause of your own misery, but most of us do not live in a vacuum, and it takes at least two people to create a problem in social living.

Fourth, begin a process of HRM immunization. Make a list of your own HRMs, find some examples of specific messages in history that you distress yourself with (from parents, siblings, teachers, etc.), and write down as many meanings as possible. Find an acceptable message that is 180 degrees from your original.

Fifth, learn how to listen, using the therapeutic listening procedure outlined earlier, and practice, practice, practice.

Sixth, understand and consciously practice role-shifting. Write down the roles that you play during the day, along with their basic behavioral and emotional components. Become aware of moving from one role to the next.

Seventh, practice, practice, and practice the tools presented above. Make them an automatic part of your tool kit. Guess what will happen. You will start to generate all kinds of combinations of these tools, and even new tools that others are not aware of.

Now that you are on the road to becoming a therapeutic communicator, we can move on to working with families and other special situations.

NOTES

1. Role-shifting occurs in all societies, including India and other cultures east of Iran. The difference between the East and West lies in the holistic consideration of one's role, persona, or dharma (support or duty). You do your duty (what society expects and demands for your station in life, which involves many roles from a Western perspective), a cat does its duty, as do the cow, the bird, and the tree in the forest. In the West, on the other hand, we digitalize our roles to correspond to our preoccupation with individualism and individual worth. If you are

an individual, than you have to act as such in ways that are readily identified. To paraphrase, the world is a stage, and we all play our parts.

2. Therapeutic listening is a term coined and described by the author in 1973 (see Rush 1976), and denotes a process that can be used in therapeutic/clinical settings as well as in all data-collecting.

Chapter 4

Family Dynamics: Rules, Roles, and the "Dysfunctional" Family

Family dynamics are more than interesting; families offer us a mirror of the larger society of which they are a part. The family has been the anthropologists' basic unit of study for over 150 years. In fact, much of what we really understand about the family comes from the comparative data amassed over the years by anthropologists.

The prehistorical origins of the family are wonderful stories and include everything from evolutionary perspectives (see McLennan 1865) and Freud's speculations mirrored in his Oedipus complex (see Freud 1948), to Knight's (1991) more recent Marxian position. However, social organization, which centers on a family unit, is more easily understood when seen within a complex of mental maturation and behaviors that has fallen into place over a period of several million years (see Rush 1996 for a more complete discussion). This complex includes a mental development that involves a special type of consciousness (see Rush 1996 for definitions), a consciousness wherein the individual can see himself as part of and, at the same time, as apart from an environmental system, and as having the ability to manipulate that system. This manipulation includes the generation of symbols in the brain that represent aspects of the environment, which are then put into action (e.g., stone tools that are symbolic of the power of predators). In short, we produce symbols and ideas, then press them into and onto the environment.

Connected to the development of symbols is the concept of analogous thinking, wherein one thing stands for another. The result of this is a great deal of interconnection of things or, simply put, creativity in terms of manipulating the environment for the general purpose of survival.

Further, this complex included a physiology (e.g., a large brain) which demands that infants are born premature, thus necessitating cooperation in the birthing process (see Rosenberg and Trevathan 1995/1996 and the concept of "altruistic midwifery") as well as group cooperation after birth. This complex also embodies the concept of implied rules, or that aspect which "automatically" organizes the system. In a word, implied rules allow social systems to self-assemble (Rush 1996). Later in this chapter, I will discuss implied rules as a major factor in marital failure.

MALES AND FEMALES

Are there contrasts between males and females outside of the obvious physical, sexual differences? To be politically correct the answer should be "No." This, however, is far from the truth. The problem in current society, and probably for the past 10,000 years, is that many cultures have seen the differences in absolute rather than relative terms. In absolute terms, men are bigger and stronger (this is called sexual dimorphism), and have, under stress while in conflict with other groups—and in order to protect their genetic heritage—fit nicely into the role (usually) of warriors or military leaders. Read your history, created by men and about men. Men became one of the first special-interest groups, and I am sure that men (rather than women) as warriors and military rulers has some justification at the genetic level.

Moreover, men are expendable; you put them on the front lines. Women are less expendable. As time goes on, you build a tradition wherein it *appears* that men create society, whereas women become taken over by nature. The problem is that although this is true on the surface (women *are* taken over by nature), there is information spillover from nature to society and vice versa. Society or culture, in effect, is a mirror of nature—culture is an extension of our nature and of both men and women, and is intimately involved in the building of culture.

The fact remains that men and women *are* different in relative terms, and each group has a different agenda in bringing new genetic prototypes into the world. Some have suggested (Hamilton, Axelrod, and Tanese 1990) that a reason for having two sexes, male and female, is a hedge against parasites. New genetic combinations more rapidly create genotypes that might survive parasitic attack. Regardless of the reasons for the existence of two sexes, their general and basic purpose is clear—sexual reproduction and survival of the offspring. Thus, the genetic agenda of males and females is sex and reproduction. However, each has his or her own part to play in the process. Culture is a mirror of those individual parts, and different cultures are simply analogies of one another. All cultures are engaged in the same processes of survival, and each culture is defined by a different content. Period.

Metaphorically speaking, it has been only a heartbeat since our kind has gone from small bands to our current large urban complexes with undreamed-of technology. This has happened without the benefit of complementary physical, emotional, and mental evolutionary changes.

So how did relationships, with rights and duties, become established between men and women? How did these relationships eventually evolve into what we now know as the family? And what does this tell us about the family today?

THE DEVELOPMENT OF THE FAMILY UNIT: A CREATION MYTH

The following is not true; it is a story. This story is not my invention, but was culled from the anthropological literature. The psychologists do not have one single story that helps to explain the origin of the family in a way that increases our understanding of relationships between men and women. Yes, they have Freud and some of his contemporaries. However, I reject their stories because they are grounded on assumptions common to a different time period. The new evolutionary psychology holds some promise, but the information is mainly from anthropologists (see Wright 1994; Fessler 1996). The story below is a synthesis of beliefs and assumptions (not truths) from the field of anthropology.

Once upon a time, perhaps 1.5 to 1.8 million years ago, there existed in Africa, and spreading into southern Europe and Asia, an ancestor of ours named *Homo erectus* (or *Homo ergaster*, see Larick and Ciochon 1996). This ancient ancestor had a larger brain than the *Australopithecines*, who existed in Africa (between 5 and 2.2 million years ago) prior to *Homo*. But our ancient *Homo* ancestors had other characteristics besides larger brains. For example, we know that the australopithecines spent considerable time in trees (see Stanley 1996) and had a birth canal that allowed the infant to be born without assistance. *Australopithecine* infants, then, were able to cling to their mothers and hold their heads up, indicating that their nervous systems were more highly developed at birth than those of the later genus, *Homo*.

By the time of *Homo ergaster/erectus*, we see numerous changes in anatomy, including finger bones (phalanges) that apparently are not as curved as those of the australopithecines, and changes in the shoulder socket making the shoulders more rigid indicating a design for locomotion on the ground rather than climbing trees. This indicates that *Homo ergaster/erectus* was not spending as much time in the trees.

Another significant anatomical change is in the pelvis. Although no complete pelvic openings have been found, what is available indicates "that the increases in cranial capacity above the average of 900cc reached in Homo 1–1.5 mya became possible only when a rotational mechanism of birth had evolved. This would mean that secondary altriciality evolved in humans some time after 1.5 mya" (Rosenberg and Trevathan 1995/1996:

167). This translates into a birthing process for our *Homo* ancestors that usually requires assistance, and the birth of infants who are totally dependent on their mothers or others for survival. It takes little contemplation, then, to realize that if the early *Homo* groups were to survive, a different pattern of social organization had to fall into place. Let us combine a few more elements.

We know that our *Homo* ancestors of approximately 1.8–1.5 million years ago were producing tools (Acheulean hand axes) that indicate a new way of thinking about themselves in relation to their environment. That is, they were more active participants in nature rather than passive recipients, and they were equipped with analogous thinking wherein one thing can stand for another (see Rush 1996). Coupled with all this was (in all probability) what Bickerton (1990) has called "protolanguage." Bickerton compares protolanguage with the symbolizing that occurs when two individuals, one male and one female, speaking two dissimilar languages, meet and have to cooperate with one another over time. Any offspring from this relationship will develop a synthesis (a creole language) of the parents' protolanguage that would be recognizable as a true language as defined by current linguistic standards.

Early human groups had to have in place three other factors if culture was to serve as a survival mechanism: (1) sharing food, (2) sexual restrictions, and (3) a home base. Without sharing food you create internal strife; without sexual restrictions you create competition between males for females, and thus internal stress; and without a home base you do not have a territory with which all identify and to which all return not only in order to share food and obtain a sense of security against predators but also to socialize.

What is lacking in the above complex of thoughts and behaviors is a mechanism that will allow for the development of relationship rules for knitting this complex together. A society is a system, just as a family is a system, and both of these levels are defined by rules. But did our ancient ancestors sit down and explicitly negotiate or set down rules? No, they did not; this came much later in human development. Cultural development proceeded through the establishment of what I call implied rules (see Rush 1996).

So that the reader can see implied rules in operation, and also to tell the story of the origin of the family, let us consider one of our *Homo erectus* females, living almost 2 million years ago, and how she inadvertently creates some rules that spawn more rules leading to sharing of food, sexual restrictions, and the concept of the family.

To begin, our female—I'll call her Pris (for Pristine)—is nursing a newborn infant. By doing so (and keeping in mind what I said earlier about analogous thinking and consciousness), she is creating a rule, "I will give you food." This is not explicitly stated; it is just happening out of the

biology of the species. She is likewise creating a rule of potential obligation. As the infant matures and begins to take solid foods—some pre-
masticated by the mother and some eaten through imitation—the child
can begin a process (through analogy) of feeding his mother. In other
words, the child begins to collect food and gives some to his mother, an
analogy of her giving to him. If the child does not do so, the mother can
reject the child in some way (tap into high-risk messages), to force the
rule of giving in return; this makes the rule more explicit.

As the child matures, he, once again through analogy, can give food to
others besides his mother, thus acting on a set of implied instructions for
give-and-take. Speaking in economic terms, mother's milk becomes the
first medium of exchange for the individual. Mother's milk, through analogy, can then represent any other type of food, as well as love, kindness,
and even life or death. (You see this in many, many mythologies.)

Because the human female (and in all probability our *Homo ergaster/
erectus* relatives as well) menstruates and ovulates at two different times
of the month, nature has provided her with a mechanism that allows her
to choose the mate who will impregnate her (outside of rape, at least—
for those of you interested in a possible interpretation of rape in human
societies, see Morgan 1990). That mechanism is that the males do not
know when the female is receptive to impregnation, and thus she can
inform the male of her choice. How does she know? Her biology informs
her. But whom will she inform? What characteristics will she select?

There are basically three attributes: (1) gentleness toward herself and
insiders, with a willingness to share; (2) absolute viciousness toward outsiders; and (3) health (the condition of the skin, etc.). But how would
males and females be brought together so that she can make an informed
choice? First, the birthing process and the dependency of the infant after
birth demanded a new social structure that encouraged more male partic-
ipation. Second, those males who caught on to the concept of reciprocity
with their mother would, through analogy, undertake a process of giving
to a female(s) of choice. What would be the medium of exchange? Right,
food.

So, our male *Homo erectus* brings food to a female, and what is it that
he wants in return? Right, immortality. And how does he move toward
immortality? Right again, sex. His basic motive is the survival of his genetic material, and the only way he can accomplish this is to combine his
genetic material with the genetic material of a female. He can likewise
ensure his survival if his sisters and brothers reproduce.

In this story, then, the male learns to share from his mother and then
uses this strategy to obtain a mate. One last thing. How does the female
keep the male around? Right, through sending positives that include sex.
Some people do not like this model and compare it to prostitution. This,
however, is far from prostitution. In prostitution, the goal for the female

(or her pimp) is to reproduce wealth, not one's self, although there is an interesting metaphor here.

By initially sharing food, and assuming analogous thinking, you begin to accumulate implied rules that individuals, for the most part, automatically follow. Through sharing food you also create sexual restrictions and a home base (this is where food is shared, initially at the mother's breast— the first home base). Food is also analogous to thoughts and ideas ("food for thought"), and thus home base becomes more than a place to share food; it is also a geographical place in which to share ideas and to socialize. The ideas that individuals share, and socialization in general—through storytelling, demonstration of technology, and so on—represent that group's rules of organization and purpose, and serve to define that group. Behaviors that are stress-reducing will likely stay around. This scenario, or something similar, had to happen. Moreover, whatever that scenario was, it had to be simple and duplicable or rediscoverable because groups die out, and with them they take any survival strategies accumulated through time.

The sharing of food, sexual restrictions, and home base also define, in large measure, a family unit. Every family that I have ever studied or read about has these three basic features, and it is precisely when there is a distortion in these three factors that we speak of a "dysfunctional" family.

At a very basic level, then, relationships between males and females center on sharing food and on procreation. The males and females have different agendas, although there are certainly aspects in common. Both use specific (but different) mechanisms for attracting the other sex. Both share in the food quest, although there may be an assigning of different types of food (and other behaviors, analogous and otherwise) to each, and both are involved in the raising of the children, which may differ in quality and quantity over time.

We also know, through sexual dimorphism (mentioned earlier), that one of the male's ascribed statuses is that of warrior or protector of the group, not necessarily just his mate and/or offspring. This is because, as a small-group animal, his survival depended (I use this in the past tense because, with our technology, this does not necessarily apply today) on the survival of the group, irrespective of selfish genes. Survival of the fittest means nothing if you are the only one who survives, and thus cannot pass on your genetic material.

MALE AND FEMALE SEXUAL AGENDAS

There is an old saying, "Men need sex, women like sex." What is being suggested here is that males have a different attitude toward sex than do women. This attitude is reflected in what is genetically useful for males and females. Let me explain.

It is in a male's best interest, genetically speaking, to have sex with any female who crosses his path. His investment is in his genetic immortality, and the more females with whom he has sex, the greater the probability that some will become impregnated. Moreover, because the male's investment in reproduction is small, he can afford to "hit and run," so to speak. I suspect that rape (not adultery) of in-group females was a rare occurrence for our early ancestors because of sexual restrictions and the conflict that would issue from the behavior. Rape of out-group members, on the other hand, was and is common, especially when we add in the "date rape" so common in the press (see Harris 1989 and Morgan 1990 for their thinking about rape). From a genetic standpoint, sex or rape of females outside one's group allows new genetic material to enter the male's immortality agenda.

At any rate, it is not adaptive for a female to have sex with every male who crosses her path, unless men are in short supply or she can induce the man (or men) to help her raise or contribute to the raising of current and future children. However, she cannot count on this even in societies, like our own, where there are child support laws. Sex can lead to pregnancy and large expenditures of energy to raise the offspring, unless abortion is performed. Pregnancy can also lead to death. So there are both biological and social restraints on the female.

Social morals regarding sexual behavior, which include the double standard we see in many cultures (including our own), are reflections of these biological and early social agendas. In Mediterranean cultures, for example, males gain considerable personal status (to a point) by seducing women. On the other hand, women who have premarital sex (or extramarital sex) shame the family. The reason for this, at least in my opinion, lies in the prospect of the woman's becoming pregnant and of the newborn's being a burden on the family—there is no new adult male to contribute to this drain on resources.

Women becoming pregnant outside marriage, and thus shaming the family, does not hold true in all societies. For the Iu Mien of Laos, infants are considered a gift, and the female is not ostracized. But the economics are clearly evident in this. Moore-Howard (1989:48) comments:

Marriage among the Iu Mien is a business transaction involving transfer of important amounts of wealth and is fundamental to the individual's success in life. A Iu Mien girl is very expensive to marry (thousands of baht or many pigs are given to her parents), so a young man may not wish to marry because of the very free customs of premarital sex relations. An eligible young woman must keep two beds, one for herself and one for her suitors, or her parents might be embarrassed that their child lacked training in etiquette. Should a young woman become pregnant and the young man refuse to marry her, the incident is not regretted, and the child is gratefully received by the girl's parents. The young man must pay a token fine and is properly and quickly excused. Intermarriage with other tribes is very rare, despite carefree attitudes in many Iu Mien circles concerning courtship and marriage.

A young man who wants to marry must pay much more than if he got a girl pregnant and refused marriage. The influence of the parents has much to do with the final decision on how much to pay, and the young man would probably pay less if he lives in the same village.

The economics and alignment of people are very much in evidence in Moore-Howard's observations. I have yet to study a culture wherein the sexual/economic/social agendas are the same for men and women. The double standard, then, goes much deeper than a simple cultural attitude.

In current Western culture we are witnessing an evolving (or devolving) away from social attitudes regarding sexual behavior, that is, the controlling and directing of sexual behavior (the sexual restrictions mentioned above). The reasons for this are many, including the breakdown of the extended family because of mobility and economic attitudes that accentuate individualism, a breakdown of the nuclear family fostered by a legal system that profits from conflict between husbands and wives, the mass media's exploitation of our biological agendas through explicit and permissive attitudes toward sex (and violence), and so on—this is complicated stuff. We do not have, and we could not have, a research base regarding the rise and fall of our North American society. We do not know where this culture is heading because we have little to compare it with. However, we can still speculate.

Currently, in our culture, the main relationship between males and females is sexual and not political and economic. We are dealing with "cats" in heat rather than a relationship based on political alignment, economics, or even simple companionship. To prove my point, let me ask a few questions. What is a male? What is a female? What is a husband? What is a wife? What is a marriage? What is a family? These are all relationship and/or kinship terms. If the reader does not have clear definitions of these terms, definitions that are explicitly designed to tell people how to behave toward one another, then it is no wonder there are so many problems between males and females (witness all the sexual harassment suits, homosexuality, etc.), including the intense marital problems in our society. At this point in history, your chances of getting divorced within seven years after marriage are over 50 percent. Without definitions, the male-female relationship is based on sex.

DEFINITIONS OF MALE AND FEMALE

What, exactly, is a male in most of North American culture? What do males do? How do they behave? Where do they get their instructions to behave in this way?

In order to understand current family dynamics in North American culture, we must understand what it means to be a male or female. With respect to the male, the image and instructions are in front of you each and every time you watch your favorite football game (or major sports event), not only in the game itself but also in the accompanying commercials. Males are warriors who fight other tribes, and the viewer vicariously identifies with his tribesmen or warriors in these ritualized events. Violence is controlled by the rules of the game; there are always rules connected to warfare.

Turning to the commercials, one sees men as beer drinkers who pursue women for sex (not to have families and cooperate in the raising of children), and who probably drive a pickup truck. On top of this, males obtain their status in relation to other men; money equals status, and it allows you to buy the pickup truck, chase women, and drink beer.

The image of the male is also right in front of you in action films. Males are heroes who avenge their tribe, save women, and then have sex with them. In these hero films the real man does not show much feeling while saving society and women; the only feeling he is allowed to show is sexual in nature. Then, of course, the psychological community turns around and blames males for not showing feelings. Why are males blamed? Because one of our social myths is that the male is to be a self-responsible individual who will make informed or commonsense choices. It is up to the individual, then, in this myth of individualism and free choice, to make the right choice and become a responsible, sentient being, one who will, without instruction, become a loving husband and parent by choice.

If we do not have a definition for males that can easily carry over into marriage, what is our definition of a husband? When I ask the question of married couples, I usually hear that the man is the provider who helps with the kids, and so on. But, of course, you do not have to be a husband to be a provider, nor do you have to be a husband to help with the kids. So, what is a husband? I will come back to this shortly.

Women do not fare any better in the world of definitions. What is a woman? According to the mass media, women are thin, have big breasts, and are always ready for sex; they also are more knowledgeable about household cleaners and diapers. Women are seen, for the most part, as submissive to men, protected and saved by men, and more likely to take orders from men. Women are also shown as independent and strong-willed, but this sometimes gets them into trouble.

Women are portrayed as wanting more than a family. The liberated woman wants a career; having children and managing a family are not sufficient in this day and age, mainly because the role of parent is at the bottom of the list of preferred statuses.

This image of a female, however, transfers to the marriage arena a bit more easily than does the image of a male, but not by much. Many males experience marriage as death, the death of the image that portrays them as men. Stag parties for males symbolically represent one last fling (with alcohol and unbridled sex); marriage brings a demise of that image, and there is nothing to put in its place (you certainly do not find one at the stag party).

Bridal showers, on the other hand, symbolically represent nest-building, images that flow from the gifts that usually represent the home. Both males and females are confused about their respective images because the rituals of transition are unclear or nonexistent. In short, husband and wife are not clearly defined; there is no set of instructions.

WHAT IS A "DYSFUNCTIONAL" FAMILY?

As mentioned earlier, the basic concepts wrapped around culture—sharing food (economics), sexual restrictions, and home base (socialization)—also characterize the family. When parental figures are unequally involved in economics (or there is a perception of inequality), there is stress. When there is not enough money for consumer goods and food, there is stress. If there is a lack of sufficient sexual intimacy between the couple (as defined by the individual), there is stress. If there is extramarital sex, there is stress. If there is molestation of children, that indicates stress. If there is insufficient time for socializing the children, the children could interpret this as rejection, which equals stress. Without sufficient socialization, of a specific quality and quantity, there can be social dysfunction in general; this is what we are currently experiencing in North American society.

Usually, though, dysfunctional families are determined by the outcome of the children. If they get into drugs or have problems at school or with the law, it is assumed that the family is dysfunctional. However, this is not a very useful way to define "dysfunctional," for many wonderful, healthy, and socially productive people emerge from very negative and brutal family environments. In fact, it is impossible to speak of dysfunctional families at all, because there is no clear definition of "family." We can speak of dysfunctional wheelbarrows, cars, or bicycles because we understand the characteristics of these things. But once you have no clear definition of something, you cannot know what it does. So here is the big question: What is a family? What is a family in terms of behavior? What are the general rules that define family functioning? Here is a large problem in our society—we do not have a definition that we will clearly state in public. There is no definition that the government will clearly endorse.

The family is the main socializing system in this and all cultures, and when it disintegrates, society loses its main social control mechanism. When the family disintegrates, you no longer have a clear definition of male and female; when the family disintegrates, you no longer have clear definitions of husband, wife, and parent. And, of course, when the family disintegrates, you no longer have a definition for family. This is one of the reasons that homosexuals are pushing for homosexual marriages. Such marriages have little to do with a more liberal attitude toward gender, and perhaps creating a third gender, but are related more closely to a breakdown in the family and the definitions of the people within it. Although homosexual practices probably exist in varying degrees in all cultures, I am not aware of any culture on the face of the earth that legally recognizes homosexual marriages. A cry for homosexual marriages, instead of being a simple lack of understanding of social codes and/or rules of behavior, must be grounded in some other component. The reason is fundamental— sex and marriage are *not* synonymous; marriage, at least traditionally, is an aligning of two groups for political and economic reasons (a breakdown in the family unit represents a breakdown in this alignment), and a marriage is the unit of socialization that requires both a male and female.

One further comment on this last issue. In order to develop a balance for purposes of relating to males and females, the child needs the unique communication and signal attributes of both males and females. These include sight, sound, touch, smell, and so on. The child needs to benefit from the different styles that males and females acquire as they grow up, as well as the genetically given biological signals that one sex alone cannot provide.

Homosexuality is, for the most part, a sexual preference and not, in most cases, an innate biological drive to have sex with a same-sex partner. These sexual preferences evolve through role confusion and as a means of stress reduction and inability to relate (because of reasons of socialization) to the opposite sex. Although this is not politically correct and high-risk to some, it is my point of view. Harris (1989:250) mentions lesbianism as a reaction to male domination, but this reaction does not require any homosexual gene. Harris (1989:315) has also suggested that homosexuality might serve as a population-control device. However, when lesbian couples want one member to be artificially inseminated and to raise children within this union, this defeats the population-control issue.

More recently the concept of homosexual marriage has been wrapped around the social/economic issue of recognizing the same-sex partner for insurance purposes, hospital visits, and so on. A very well known computer chip company recently included homosexual partners in their workers' benefit packages, but did not include heterosexual partners who were living with employees but were unmarried. By legislating homosexuality as approved behavior, you relieve a lot of guilt and help to justify behavior. The homosexual issue, however, tells us more about definitions and male-female antagonisms, antagonisms that are culturally based and that need to be better understood.

WHY INDIVIDUALS COME TO COUNSELING

Why people do anything is subject to debate. In fact, most people are hard pressed to really explain why they do things. This leads us to unconscious motives and depth psychology, which is great intellectual stuff, but I question its usefulness. There are basically five reasons why couples come to counseling. First, one drags the other in and expects you to "fix" this person because "I'm fine; he (or she) has the problem." This type of thinking has to be eliminated immediately. It takes two to create a social or communication problem, and both helped to create the rules in that system, whether these rules involve drug abuse, physical abuse, a lack of positives, and so on. In short, *both* have the problem.

Second, one wants out of the relationship and the other does not. So your job is to "break it gently" to the other. When it becomes obvious that you have been hired as the "hit man," you can go this route or not. I choose not to do this, because the behavior of hiring a hit man is part of the problem. That is, the individual who wants out cannot say "No," or wants permission to leave. You can act as a divorce broker if you like. I choose not to, because my job is to educate, not to break up relationships (although staying in some relationships is physically dangerous, and I will point this out to couples).

A third reason that couples come to you is that one (or both) wants to be able to tell friends or relatives that "I tried everything, even counseling. Nothing worked." These individuals show up for one, perhaps two, sessions, and then get a divorce. They blame you for the failure.

A fourth reason is to use the therapist as a threat. Many of these individuals make appointments but never show up. I know that while I am speaking to the wife (or husband) on the phone, the other is in the background, squirming and turning inside out at the thought of being presented to a stranger as "a failure" or as a drug user, or a spouse beater, or a lazy slug who will not keep a job, and so on. After the caller hangs up, there is begging and pleading: "I'll be good, I'll be good. I've learned my lesson." These people sometimes call and cancel, but usually they just do not show up. However, they invariably call in a couple of months to set another appointment. I usually schedule them at a weird time so that I'm not further inconvenienced. If they show up, that increases the probability that you can work with them.

A fifth reason that couples come in is that they sincerely want to know what happened. It is not that they are necessarily going to stay together, but they do not want to duplicate their problems in another system. The probability for success with these individuals is very high.

So how do you handle individuals who are there to blame or threaten their mate, or who want out of the system? Sometime during the first session you tell them the reasons that most people come to counseling, accentuating the fact that you feel more comfortable working with people who want to know what happened, not that it is your job to put anything back together. In some cases I tell the couple that they are better off working things out, "Because once the lawyers get hold of you, they will want to create more and more conflict; there is no money in mediation." If there are child custody issues involved, "You will probably have to go to Family Court Services, where some overworked bureaucrat will make some decision and you will lose control over your life. Or worse, you will be directed to a clinical psychologist who will perform a divination procedure in order to help the judge make a decision. In any event, when it is over, you will be experiencing financial and emotional ruin. You will not experience anything more violent than the courts. The courts are not interested in who is right or wrong. They are interested in who controls information and presents it most effectively to the court. This means that you cannot possibly tell the truth; you will have to structure information to win. You two will be enemies, and your children are the ones who will really suffer."

When I tell this to clients, I lean forward slightly, look them straight in the eye, and lower my voice and almost growl at them. Do everything in your power to keep them out of court. If you cannot keep them out of court, have contacts with lawyers in whom you have some trust, who know your philosophy, who know that you will send them business if they work toward mediation (see Rush 1996:118, 125 note 16, and 206).

As you become an expert communicator, you will add more and more relationship counseling to your practice. Why? Because it is part of the overall health program that you offer, and holistic health demands that you pay attention to the emotional needs of your clients. Emotional problems will interfere with healing, and they are a priority item. Dealing with emotional and family issues, however, is not your specialty; you are not an MFCC, LCSW, or psychologist. You are a health practitioner, and how people relate and communicate is part and parcel of overall health.

REVIEWING HRMs

As mentioned in Chapter 3, when individuals communicate, they sometimes purposely, but usually inadvertently, tap into HRMs. Over time, the barbs fester as more and more trust is lost, and then individuals do not enjoy being around one another. One of the first steps in marriage or relationship counseling is to uncover each individual's HRMs. It is important not to blame the clients for using negative bits while communicating over the years. I usually ask if either one is a malicious person; there will be a denial of this. I then add that I agree. Next I say, "If neither of you is malicious, then you didn't start off the relationship with the goal of making each other miserable, did you? No, of course not. So this means that you were communicating and simply didn't know what was happening, correct? Then, if you want stress to come down in the relationship, you are willing to communicate in a different way, is this correct?" (This is a "yes" set.)

You ask the couple to identify their HRMs and use this as a homework assignment. They will have plenty of opportunity to discover their HRMs because they cannot change their communication patterns overnight. You give them permission to continue communicating the way they have, in order to uncover HRMs. "How can you uncover HRMs if you don't continue doing what you have been doing, for the next few days at least? Whenever you notice your stress going up while communicating with each other, make note of what was said. Write these down so that they can be dissected in the next session. Remember that you agreed that there is no maliciousness here, just your automatic styles of communicating, is that correct?"

I also add, "Now, if you get into a big tiff, one of two things will happen. First, you will call me, not as a sign of weakness, but simply to do something different. Or, second, you will imagine me, this bald guy with a beard, standing there, taking notes." (This is future pacing.)

There are time limits to counseling. You let the couple know that if things are not better in about three weeks (more future pacing), "then either I'm not doing my job or you are not doing your job, or both." The therapist must take some responsibility for what happens in these sessions.

Once you have introduced them to HRMs, it is important to introduce them to implied rules, for once they understand these, you can avoid a great deal of blame and move toward giving them new tools for enhancing the relationship.

IMPLIED RULES

The only criterion for marriage, as that institution currently exists for most of North American society, is love—or, more to the point, lust. We spend very little time discussing relationships between males and females while growing up in the family, and even less time in our schools. No time is spent teaching low-risk communication tools.

The couple in love identifies with idyllic images presented by novels and television programs. They usually never see their parents in the friendship-dating phase, and thus they usually resort to these other outside-the-family models. While dating, they are creating rules of relating or relationship rules, but in most cases, they are unaware of these rules—love is legally blind and does not hear very well! The rules that evolve are called implied rules. Divorce, in fact, begins with dating. Let me paint a picture about the development of some of these rules.

Sue and Fred are in love. They met at a party. She likes the way he talks and pays attention to her looks; he likes the way she looks. They remind each other of things they like and that, in some measure, is culturally conditioned, and in other ways genetically inspired; there is not an obvious logic in their preferences.

They spend some time talking. Fred is the silver-tongued fox, sending messages of seduction. Sue is receptive to this information, perhaps because of some deep urge to build a nest. They talk about things of mutual interest, friends they have in common, places they would like to visit, and so on.

They begin to date. Sue likes to spend Sunday afternoon with her parents, which is okay because Fred likes to watch the football game with his friends and drink beer. They usually get together a couple of nights during the week and on the weekend (except Sunday), and sometimes on Saturday during the day. Saturday is when Fred likes to hang around with his buddies, play basketball, talk about sports and work, and have a few beers. Sue likes to go shopping with her girlfriends.

When they do get together, they usually have dinner, and flirt with each other, with the promised land in mind.

During their first month together, Fred introduces Sue to his mother—his father lives in another state, and his parents have been divorced for ten years. Sue introduces Fred to her mother. Sue's father works late at the office, so Fred does not get to meet him for several weeks.

They spend a lot of spare time with each other as the bond grows closer and closer. Sue does not like the fact that Fred spends his Sundays drinking beer with his friends. She would rather have him at her house. She does not reveal to Fred that she has concerns about his beer-drinking and his relationship with his buddies.

When she visits Fred's apartment, she notices that he is fairly neat—not a lot of stuff lying around. Fred's visits to Sue's house, however, reveal that Sue does not seem to pick up after herself, nor does her mother. They are not exactly slobs, but....

As time goes on, Sue decides, one Friday afternoon, that she will call Fred at work and offer to come over to his place and cook dinner "rather than going out to the crowded restaurant." Fred says, "Good idea. What should we have?" Sue says she will come up with something wonderful.

At 6 P.M., Sue shows up at Fred's place with all the fixings to make lasagna, garlic bread, and salad—and, of course, a six-pack of beer. Fred ushers her into the kitchen, asking if he can help. Sue replies, "No, no. Here's a beer; you go watch the game."

So Fred sits in the living room, smelling the wonderful food, drinking his beer, and thinking of sex. Sue comes into the living room at intervals, gives him a kiss, promising all kinds of orgiastic delights.

Time for dinner. They sit down by candlelight and have a wonderful meal. At the conclusion, Fred asks if he can help clean up, and Sue says,

"No, I'll take care of it later." They have an exciting evening—so exciting, in fact, that they decide to do it again next week, and the next week, and so on, until they decide to get married.

After the marriage Sue moves in with Fred, and there are many rules in place, rules that they never negotiated. Sue is messy; Fred finds that his organized world is turning into chaos. On Sundays, Sue expects Fred to go to her parents' house, but Fred continues to drink beer with his buddies and watch the ball game. Sue is not as sexually attentive to Fred; Fred wonders about this. Stress is increasing.

One Friday evening, about six months into the marriage, Fred is in the living room drinking a beer, and Sue is in the kitchen cooking, wondering why Fred does not ask her out to dinner the way he did before they got married. Fred wonders why Sue does not come into the living room for a little grab and feel the way she did before they got married. Stress is increasing.

The following Sunday morning, just before noon and the arrival of Fred's buddies, Sue says, "I'm sick and tired of you drinking beer and spending all this time with your drunken friends!"

Fred replies, "What's your problem? This is what I did before you married me. The guys told me you'd try and change me. Why don't you just go to your mother's and stay there? You probably like her messy company better anyway!"

What happened here and in so many other marriages? There are many sets of converging rules in operation in any human system. First, there is no consistency in child-rearing in our culture; one family will rear children in one way, another in another way, and so on. Because there is no set definition for male or female or husband or wife, there is little consistency in these roles as well. Individuals entering the marriage arena, then, can have very different expectations as to the behavior of the other.

Second, during the dating phase of the relationship there are many behaviors that are allowed but are not really acceptable. For example, Sue did not like Fred's drinking, although she allowed it and even contributed to it while dating. Fred did not like Sue's messiness, but said little about it.

Third, the rules of friend and lover are very different from those of husband and wife, and so there is some confusion during the transition. In fact, when moving from friend and lover to husband and wife, individuals often develop amnesia for very useful behaviors. Both Fred and Sue developed amnesia for seduction and talking about life.

One of the first questions that I ask couples is "What are the rules of your relationship?" I am usually met with blank stares or responses like "Well, we are supposed to be loyal to one another," and so on. Each new marriage has to start with an agreed-upon set of rules, explicit rules. In our scenario above, the system was clouded with overlapping sets of implied rules, which I will break down into three general types. First, the expectation rules that you learn in your family of origin; second, the rules constructed while dating; and third, the rules constructed while married and in the roles of husband and wife. Again, all three overlap, but most are implied.

There are two problems with implied rules. One, they are not as amenable to change as situations change, demanding new rules, and, two, they are difficult to identify. Implied rules, in reality, run the system. This is why it is naive to believe that there are really "power plays" and a "need to control" as consciously driven goals in marriages. To my way of thinking, such behavior is best understood as implied rules of expectation or methods of altering old implied rules to fit new circumstances. In any event, as soon as you accuse one or the other of a power play and a need to control, you build resentment and decrease the probability of altering rules in the system. The most effective way of playing it is to say that the person is simply trying to solve a problem and reduce stress in the system. Get the clients to agree with this, and let them know that they are really trying to improve things, but they are not sure how to do so. Then let them know that you will show and describe other ways to reduce stress.

Here is how implied rules become established. I do something, and you let me. I do it again, and now it is expected. We do not have to negotiate anything; we simply do things and they are allowed (or not allowed—see Rush 1996). By the time the couple is several years into the marriage, there are many, many rules in place. Some of these rules are wonderful and others are deadly. Both husband and wife help to create implied rules. Some are constructed out of love, and all hold the potential for stress enhancement in the system.

BUILDING EXPLICIT RULES

There are two general types of rules that need to be negotiated if human systems are to proceed with a minimum of stress: rules of division of labor and relationship rules. These are the basic rule types found in all cultures. Negotiating these rules in a marriage, however, implies equality of the sexes and a democratic approach to things, and thus the following approach is not applicable to all cultures.

Ideally, it would be best for a couple to negotiate both division of labor and relationship rules prior to marriage. In fact, one of the most important questions to ask on a first date is "How do you like to be listened to?" instead of "Your place or mine?" This question is rarely asked during dating, during marriage, or during any relationship.

By asking the couple about their rules for division of labor, you can uncover the models brought from the family of origin; the couple will usually agree that there are inequities in the system. Division of labor is a matter of who, what, when, and for how long, and a rule that says, "All rules for division of labor are renegotiable." If one or the other is tired of cooking, this should be renegotiated. If one or the other is tired of mowing the lawn, this should be renegotiated. If one or the other is tired of washing clothes, this should be renegotiated. There can be no goldbricks in a marriage; each person has to contribute in a mutually agreed-upon manner. If a person thinks that the world owes him or her a living, he or she should not get married. Marriage and family life is hard work, it is complicated work, and it is the most important thing you will ever do. Making a buck at the office or removing an appendix is important. But neither is as important as maintaining a marriage and raising/socializing children. Anyone who will put a career first and family second is a fool.

There are essentially four relationship rules, and if a couple has these rules in place and follows them, then the family will emerge as a safe and sane place to live and come home to. First, you need a set of rules for building trust. You lose trust by tapping into HRMs. You build trust by knowing when you have tapped into a HRM and then taking steps to remove the negative-intrusive symbols. Your first step to removing these symbols is to listen. Listening, then, is the second part of a trust-building tool. Moreover, you teach your clients the very same tool that you are using to collect data. Therapeutic listening techniques were explained in Chapter 3; this is what you teach.

Most couples duel. They need to understand the concept of compressed data and that they can never really know what someone means. Then you teach them when it would be appropriate to listen. Simply ask, "When would it be appropriate to listen to one another in the manner I just described?" They will tell you, and all you have to do is agree in order to set the explicit rule of when to listen.

The next rule involves putting positives into the system. The only way I know to build a positive system is to put positives into it. Here, however, we encounter two large problems. First, we have a nervous system that is designed to pick out the negative in the field. Why is this? Well, there is more survival value in doing so. Our ancient protoancestors did not spend much time sitting around smelling the roses or looking at sunsets. They kept their senses open for negatives, for predators that would eat them, and other potential dangers. Their behavior would have appeared quite paranoid. This is the nervous system that we have inherited. The husband comes home from work, and instead of seeing his beautiful children and a loving wife, he sees the mess on the living room floor. So you have to force the issue, and just as love is very blind to negatives during the courting phase, we have to be a little blind to the negatives during the marriage phase. Moreover, as the couple learns to negotiate division of labor, and as they get the children involved in this, messy living rooms will be less of a problem.

The other issue with positives is that each person has a different reality with respect to what is positive. Some people like to hear positives, that is, caring words, encouragement, and so on. Some people would rather feel positives, that is, a back rub, hug, and so on. Some people would rather see positives, that is, a clean house or a spouse who presents a pleasing image. I have on many occasions had a couple come in and the wife's complaint is that the husband does not give her enough verbal positives. On the other hand, since being married, the wife has gained 100 pounds. Somehow, it is all right for her to gain weight but not all right for the husband to stop giving verbal positives. And then there is the statement "If you really loved me, my weight wouldn't be an issue." The husband could say a similar thing, "If you really loved me, you would ignore that I don't give you positives." I heard a wife say, "Once you get the job, you shouldn't have to keep auditioning." That type of thinking leads to stress and personnel turnover.

In any event, during a session it is important to steer the couple in the direction of giving positives that will be received. If the husband, as in the case above, desires the wife to lose weight, and if she has the sincere desire, you, as the health practitioner, will help and encourage her through this. The husband has to be part of the process. She gained that weight over a period of time, and in some way he helped her.

As an aside, the only way I know of to successfully lose weight and keep it off is to change one's lifestyle, which includes sequencing foods, adding more fiber to the diet, drinking sufficient water, exercise, and making sure there is adequate intake of vitamins and minerals. Obese people have difficulty losing weight because their bodies have adapted to years of a lifestyle that leads to the accumulation of fat and compromised health. It is not that they have a fat gene as such. Most of us have the propensity to gain fat, and this is an adaptation to a particular environment, including climate. Losing weight means adapting to another lifestyle, and this will take perhaps a year or so. We have been conditioned to want instant gratification in this culture, and many look for the magic elixir for instant weight loss. The medical community sees that a buck is to be made in this, and so they engage in some very bizarre and dangerous rituals: liposuction, stapling the stomach, and giving people drugs to shut off signals in the brain that are like the amphetamines used in years past. Fenfluramine hydrochloride, which was taken out of the marketplace, is a very dangerous drug, and like most currently prescribed pharmaceuticals, is not fit for human consumption—at a certain undetermined dose it will cause brain damage. There is no research regarding the long-term effects of most Western pharmaceuticals, yet the majority of the top-selling drugs are prescribed on a long-term basis.

Getting back to positives, if the wife needs verbal positives, the husband should be encouraged to give them. Then you warn them about this. You could say, "Now, let me warn you that sending positives causes the home to be more comfortable, more free time, and causes your creativity to increase." (This is a combination of incongruency and future pacing.)

Both need positives, but on different channels. Once this is recognized, you can use future pacing, tell stories of success, and so on, in order to increase the probability that positives will enter the system.

Sometimes, however, one spouse puts the other in a double bind. The wife, for example, might say to the husband who is now giving positives, "You're only doing this because Dr. Rush told you to!" If he neglects to give positives, he is being inattentive, and if he gives positives, they are not taken as sincere. Sometimes it is useful to warn the couple that initially the positives may not seem sincere, but in time, "it might take two weeks, three, but certainly within four weeks, the positives will be sincere." (This is future pacing and illusion of choice.)

The third set of relationship rules involves shutting off unwanted behavior without creating resentments and wars. This is where you teach the couple all the direct and indirect tools mentioned in Chapter 3. You can probably cover a majority of the tools in one session; have some paper handy, and have the couple write them down.

Now, let us consider what we are doing. After teaching them the skills, each will probably know when the other is using a tool. Although this is not necessarily the case, using the tools will represent a different style of communication, one they are not accustomed to, and it has a tendency to pull the receiver off autopilot. But there is another, very important element in this. The term for it is *sensitivity*. The use of the tools indicates that communication with the other is important. Use of the tools equals sensitivity. Tell your clients, "Now, when one or the other is using these tools, in order to inform you that a behavior is unacceptable, that indicates a great deal of sensitivity to you, right? Because more risky approaches could be used instead, right? So even though you know what is going on, that a tool is being used, at least this means sensitivity toward you, right?" (Another "yes" set.)

The fourth relationship tool is negotiation. Most people negotiate according to what they want, not in terms of what they need. For example, a need is transportation; a want is a Mercedes. By having the clients make a list of needs—food, air, acceptance, sex, companionship, low stress, and so on—they begin to see that they have similar needs, which allows more synchronicity in terms of meeting those needs. Wants are ego- or "I"-centered; needs are group- or "we"-centered. When you go from male and female to husband and wife, you also go from "I" and "me" to "us" and "we."

Sometimes when negotiating or attempting to shut off unwanted behavior, we run into value clashes. I have discussed values at great length elsewhere (see Rush 1976). Briefly stated, the value clashes that generate the most stress are not, in large measure, the social values you acquire when growing into a group. When there are large differences in these values as occurs between cultures, it is very foolish to consider marriage. I am referring to the individual values and idiosyncrasies usually gained in the family of origin. These I label *value behaviors* because they do not have a tangible effect on someone else (although we often attempt to force these intangibles on others). Value behaviors, for example, include sleeping in the nude, how towels are folded, believing in God, one's preference for tea, and so on.

Tangible behaviors, on the other hand, do have a direct effect on others. Tangible behaviors would include rape, murder, gambling or drinking away money that is necessary to run the household, stealing money from each other, playing music so loud that it interferes with the ability to think or at a level that affects heart rate, and so on.

Let me give you an example of a value behavior. A couple came in, and the wife wanted me to set the husband straight on something. She insisted that I *had* to tell him to fold the bath towels in thirds, because "If you don't, they will not fit in the bathroom cupboard." The husband insisted on folding them in half, stating that they fit equally well. I had no idea how large the bathroom cupboard was, but I assumed that a carpenter, no matter how anal retentive, would not construct a cupboard that would accommodate only bath towels folded in thirds. To the wife's astonishment, I told them to go home and fold the towels in quarters, thirds, halves, whatever, and return tomorrow to let me know the results.

When they returned the next day, the wife was somewhat subdued, but still quite angry. Indeed, the towels fit no matter how they were folded. The wife then said, "Everyone folds towels in thirds; that's the way you do things!" So the reason for folding towels in thirds had no practical base to it, until I questioned further. I asked how her mother folded towels. There were three children in the household, and their towels were hung in the bathroom on a rack. The three towels just fit neatly on the rack, with no spaces in between. Her mother folded towels this way because they would not fit on the rack otherwise. The daughter had taken this as her value for folding towels and transposed it to her new home.

We take numerous values like this into marriage, and many do not create a problem. Others, like folding towels, not hanging up one's clothes, showering at night instead of in the morning, leaving the cap off of the toothpaste tube, and so on, can generate a great deal of heat. When dealing with value clashes, make sure that you are dealing with a value behavior rather than a tangible behavior.

One final remark about negotiation. Early in a relationship, preferably in the dating phase, it is very useful to pose the following question: "If you are doing something that is unacceptable to me, how should I communicate this to you?" Often the receiver will say, "Am I doing something wrong?" You simply say, "No, and if you *were* doing something I didn't like, you would want me to tell you, right?"

This usually leads to a discussion of what both do not want to happen, which often reveals more HRMs. One of the interesting features about the "do nots" is that they all point to being respected. In other words, using sarcasm, threats, warnings, loud voice tones, grabbing or hitting, and so on are high on the list when informing about unwanted behavior, and suggest a lack of respect and an inequality in the relationship. In most cases, the agreement revolves around not criticizing in front of others, being brief and to the point, and dealing with only one issue at a time. After the message is delivered, the sender is to shut up and listen. I have even suggested that this procedure be written on a file card and hung in the kitchen as a reminder. This may seem rather juvenile in this day and age. However, it takes very powerful symbols, that are ever present, to alter lifestyle. Essentially you are altering the arguing ritual, ritual behavior that in many cases has been in place for many years. You need all the props and incantations you can muster.

PARENTING

Parenting is the most important job that any male and female can perform. Parenting means living intimately and cooperating, with the goal of raising healthy children who can leave the family and make their way in the world with confidence and communication skills. Parents, then, are personnel managers, and as such they have to be equipped with numerous tools for teaching rules—division of labor rules and relationship rules. As a counselor or therapist, you educate couples about HRMs, rules, and roles; they then use this information to educate their children. Parents need to interact with their children, and if they have the skills taught in this book, they will be reasonably effective parents. Also, parents are the best therapists for their children. Keep children away from therapists; they may learn that something is wrong with them.

The communication styles that parents use with one another end up being the tools they use with their children; give them lots of tools. Empathize with their frustrations; tell them stories of hardship and success. Teach the tools by using the tools. Also, instruct the parents that the most important relationship is between the parents, the husband and wife. If their relationship is in good shape so will be their relationships with the children.

ADDITIONS AND REVIEW

Although it is not politically correct, males and females do have different reproductive agendas; these differences are relative and not absolute.

For most North Americans there is a great deal of confusion as to the behaviors of males and females, and husbands and wives. Males are not necessarily husbands; females are not necessarily wives. A male can be any way you desire to define him; the same is true for a female. However, there has to be some compatibility of these definitions with those of husband and wife.

Husbands and wives, on the other hand, are economic and political roles. Husbands and wives are responsible for managing the system that they create. Husbands do not spend excessive money and time running with their pals and complaining about their wives to friends and parents. They do not drink outside of ritual occasions; they do not chase women (you can look but you cannot touch). Wives do not spend excessive time with their girlfriends or parents, and they do not complain about their mates to their girlfriends or, especially, their parents.

The roles of husbands and wives are not necessarily the roles of friends and lovers, although husbands and wives need to have access to those roles. The roles of husband and wife have to do with making sure that the system does not become economically compromised; they have to establish a budget and stick to it. And, unlike the federal government, you cannot exist long on debt and overuse of credit cards. Simply put, you cannot have everything you want without risking bankruptcy and divorce. You can, however, have everything you need.

Always keep the roles of friend and lover sacred and separate from husband and wife; these are your bonding roles—husband and wife are your business roles. Whenever you are in an argument, ask yourself what role you are in. You will discover that you are either in your parent role or your husband or wife role.

Husbands and wives are also political roles. Here is the bridge with their parent roles. As husbands and wives, they are personnel managers of the external system (parents are personnel managers of the internal system), and they are the first line of defense against unwanted or intrusive elements. Some of these unwanted intruders include, I'm sorry to say, relatives and "friends," as well as salespersons and government agencies; stay out of debt, abide by the law, and avoid litigation.

Managing children is the parent role. Here is where you exercise all the communication tools at your disposal. And, like all the roles you play, it involves knowing what is happening as you communicate. Parents are the rule setters for the children; they are the socializers. Both parents need to be involved in raising the children. Parents need to teach their children communication tools through example (modeling), and more explicitly or directly when the time comes.

As soon as possible, the children need to be actively involved in the division of labor and the problem-solving process where it is appropriate, that is, decisions on where to go on vacations, how they will spend a Sunday afternoon, and so on.

At least once a week family meetings need to be held wherein the children can speak their minds and be listened to. These meetings act as a pressure valve and an environment where rules can be clarified and/or renegotiated. These meetings are not a time for the parents to criticize and emotionally beat up the children or each other. The children may say things that parents do not want to hear; parents are to shut up and listen. Parents need to stay away from physical violence; it only creates more violence.

When it comes to stepparenting, husband and wife (or partners acting in the roles of husband and wife) need to follow the same information outlined above. Stepparents have to be expert communicators; they need a lot of patience. They have to be able to listen, build trust, and send positives. It is also important that stepparents, by consent, are involved in child discipline. If the stepparent is not part of the discipline, he or she is effectively an outsider and will be treated as such by the children. The children will use this to drive a wedge between the couple. The children will, in many cases (depending on age and how much fighting the biological parents have gone through), consider the stepparent an outsider taking up time that they want to spend with the biological parent. Stepparents overcome this by interacting with the children, listening, and being patient. My own research and that of others (see Brown 1991:118–129) suggests that the more contact stepparents have with the children, the lower the probability of molestation and abuse in general. Children are to be treated with respect, and not emotionally or physically brutalized by biological parents or stepparents. People who brutalize others end up in hell. And a stepparent should never, ever get involved in the fighting between the two biological parents; remain neutral. Make this a rule before getting too involved in the system. In my opinion, a marriage is an economic and political union between a male and a female for the purposes of creating a system for the birth and rearing/socializing of children. Marriage is a way of combining sharing of food, sexual restrictions, and home base, with home base being more than a place to hang your hat—it is the geographical locus of primary socialization.

When you consider the relationship rules outlined above, you can see that they exist on an inverted pyramid (see Figure 4.1).

At the apex of the pyramid is emotional responsibility, without which you cannot listen. Next comes the trust-building skill of listening. After that are the relationship-building skills, or adding positives to the system on a day-to-day basis. Dealing with unwanted behavior comes next, which involves all the direct and indirect tools mentioned in Chapter 3. Finally, there is negotiation.

Figure 4.1
The Pyramid of Relationship Rules

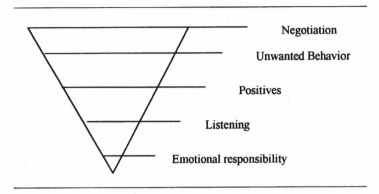

Negotiation

Unwanted Behavior

Positives

Listening

Emotional responsibility

If stress goes up at any point during the communication process, you always back up to emotional responsibility and listening. This will prevent an interaction from escalating out of control. Share this pyramid with your clients.

Chapter 5

Special Issues and Therapies

Chapters 1 through 4 contain most of the information needed to be an effective counselor or therapist with respect to most problems in social living, as well as insights into cross-cultural issues. As you learn the skills, you will combine the information in your own special way and develop new tools. Counseling is a matter of having communication tools, understanding communication processes, and experience. There is no research that I am aware of that says psychiatrists, psychologists, MFCCs, or LCSWs are any better at counseling or therapy than the lay public. In fact, many of these professionals, especially the psychiatrists and psychologists, are so fettered by theories, divination procedures, and naming that being therapeutic seems to be a secondary concern. Again, counseling and therapy are educational endeavors.

You will, however, encounter special circumstances that appear to involve special methods; this is an illusion. What is needed, instead, is more information, which the reader can obtain from books and, over time, through experience. In this chapter, I will briefly discuss some of these special circumstances.

NUTRITION AND BEHAVIOR

Most people die of nutritional deficiencies and/or cellular toxicosis. The rest die from accidents in the home, car crashes, contact with Western biomedical practitioners (these are called iatrogenic illnesses—see Rush 1996: 124, 192), or drowning or being shot or stabbed. In fact, the greatest threat to your health is not gang violence or handguns but nutritional problems, which are in large measure ignored by Western biomedicine (which includes the Food and Drug Administration [FDA] and the American Dietetic Association—see Blumberg 1997). There is absolutely no money in health, and if the citizenry is healthy, the medical establishment loses its research base and its ability to experiment with deadly drugs and procedures.

What you eat literally becomes food for thought and behavior, and many behavioral problems can be directly related to family socialization problems conjoined with inadequate nutrition. Our physiological needs for health maintenance, which includes the nervous system, evolved millions of years ago in response to what nature provided (see Rush 1996: 177–183).

Moreover, different groups have grown up and further adapted to the plants and chemicals within very different environments; this process has occurred over many thousands of years. In short, our physiology and nutrient needs have, in general, been in place for approximately 4–5 million years. And there are more specific adaptations that occurred as our ancestors moved out of ecological niches in Africa into new circumstances in the Near East, Southeast Asia, and Asia somewhere around 1.8 million years ago. Around 10,000 years ago some of our kind, especially in the Middle East, began a process of domesticating grains and animal husbandry; our health has gone downhill ever since (see Larsen 1995). As all groups are different in their physiological and social needs regarding health—as, indeed, all individuals are different—this dispels the idea that there can be a noncultural medicine. Health has to be geared to the needs of the culture and the individuals within that culture. As a health practitioner keep this in mind: You have to tailor your program to each individual and his or her circumstances.

The nervous system needs certain nutrients—amino acids, fatty acids, complex carbohydrates, specific monosaccharides, vitamins, and minerals, and soluble and insoluble fiber—if the individual is to function within some balance (see Rush 1996: xiii for an illustration of "balance"). We live in a culture with some of the poorest eating habits in the world even though we have ample food supplies. We fractionate and literally cook the nutrients out of foods, then put a few of the nutrients back and call the foods "enriched." The United States Department of Agriculture (USDA) and the American Dietetic Association tell consumers to eat a balanced diet of protein, carbohydrates, and fats at the same meal, resulting in digestive problems. (This is also standard teaching to students taking nutrition courses in high schools, colleges, and universities.) Consumers eat at fast food establishments, assuming that this balanced diet is a healthy diet.

Nutrition and behavior are closely intertwined, but the medical establishment only reluctantly suggests that there "might" be a connection in "some" cases. It is more economically sound to think learning disabilities and/or ADD (attention deficit disorder) and ADHD (attention deficit/

hyperactive disorder) are genetic issues. That way you can prescribe very powerful drugs and appear to be engaging in the medical model.

I am very interested in the fact that boys seem to be more frequently diagnosed with learning problems and ADD and ADHD. Why is this? Do boys suffer from more genetic defects than girls? Is the school environment designed more for passive, submissive individuals? Do boys learn differently than girls? What types of learners do best in our school system?

It is a fact that learning disabilities and/or ADD and ADHD are over-diagnosed. My wife and all of my children were tested at community college testing centers, and all of them tested as having learning disabilities. My wife is currently vice principal at a high school, and all my children are in college and doing very well. I have no idea what these psychologists tested, but none of my family members have, in fact, learning disabilities. They sometimes choose not to learn; sometimes they are uninterested in what teachers have to say; or the teachers are basically incompetent and unable to teach to the various learning styles and intelligences (see Gardner 1983). In my opinion, the testing for learning disabilities is an economic concern. In order to justify a special department in a college, manned by licensed individuals, you have to show results. And what are those results? Right, you have to discover (or invent) learning disabilities. Again, the testing involved is a divination procedure—such testing does not represent truth. But because it looks scientific and comes from degreed and licensed individuals, the label "learning disabled" represents a potent negative incantation.

In order to gain insights into the nutritional basis of behavioral problems, I direct the reader to Pfeiffer 1987; Werbach 1991 (an overview of many studies regarding nutrition and behavior); Schoenthaler 1991; Schoenthaler and Amos 1992; and Schauss 1985. At this point, however, I want to review the types of information needed in order to determine if behavioral problems are nutritional, internal looping on HRMs, or both.

First, many parents will bring in children for evaluation; you do not diagnose anything. The term "diagnosis," in fact, is simply our culture's term for divination. There are numerous divination procedures available; refer to them as such. Diagnosing[1] ADD or ADHD is not part of the program. If the child has been diagnosed as ADD or ADHD ask (1) who made the diagnosis; (2) if the child is on medication (Ritalin, etc.); (3) if the medication is having any effect, negative or positive; (4) when the behavioral issues began; (5) whether the behavioral issues are mainly at school; (6) what the relationship is like between the parents—are they getting along, divorced, and so on; (7) how both parents communicate with the child—what is the father's involvement, what is the mother's involvement; (8) what the relationships are between the other children in the family; (9) how much television the child watches and what types of programs; (10) what the child's diet is like—ask for specifics.

With respect to (1), there are some physicians/psychiatrists and psychologists who specialize in learning disabilities and ADD/ADHD. Yes, there are learning disabilities and there are individuals with ADD and ADHD that can be genetically based—*very few*. There is no way that a professional can make a living diagnosing these conditions unless there is overdiagnosis.

If the child is on medication, does that mean there is a deficiency of that drug in the brain? No, that is ridiculous; there has to be some other deficit. There is little research available regarding the long-term effects of using drugs like Ritalin early in life. My experience over the past twenty-five years is that children put on Ritalin tend to become addicted and then move toward amphetamine and cocaine abuse, although I have no statistics to back this up. If the parent states that he or she has "tried everything," get a list. If nothing has worked—nutritional programs (sequencing foods, use of whole foods, avoidance of sugar, addition of fiber, supplements, etc.) that have been followed for at least four or five months, drugs, and so on—then in all probability you are dealing with emotional looping on HRMs. The use of Ritalin, or any other drug, in these cases is at least inappropriate. Many teachers and school psychologists suggest the use of drugs because they are a means of controlling in overcrowded classrooms; because the teacher is tired of dealing with behavioral problems; or because the teacher has a teaching disability—and *not* because there is any real problem with the mental equipment of the child.

Sometimes behavioral problems begin when parents start fighting and threatening divorce. Sometimes behavioral problems begin when a new boyfriend or girlfriend enters the parent's life. Sometimes behavioral problems begin when a new child arrives. Communication skills are necessary in these cases.

Television programming is inadvertently designed for, and probably creates, attention problems. The child learns that life begins and ends on the half-hour. The child learns that life lacks details; television takes you from the idea to the finished product with nothing in between. The child is also exposed to the most psychotic of information-processing, going from a murder story on the news to a happy hamburger commercial or the weather. There is absolutely no connection or logical sequencing in news broadcasts. The structure of television programming has all the elements of attention deficits and disconnected thinking. Finally, television gives the child everything; he or she does not have to engage in critical reasoning. Now, think about it. How does all this translate to the classroom?

The connection between nutrition and behavioral problems is not an easy one to evaluate. However, you will find that if you can get parents to commit to providing good nutrition to their children—which means sequencing foods, adequate fiber, pure water, whole fruits, vegetables, and grains, with a limited amount of meat, and elimination of milk, soda, fractionated foods, candy bars and sugar, and food additives (preservatives, dyes, and so on)—the individual will become healthier, and many behavioral and physical problems will simply go away. Often they go away because the parent is now paying more attention to the child.

Parents sometimes say, "I'll do this, but I *know* my child won't eat what I prepare." The fact remains that the child will eat what is available. Moreover, the child will eat what the parents eat, and many parents are unwilling to alter *their* eating habits. When you come across these cases, utilize future pacing. "I know that this means changing the way you eat. And it might not be today, tomorrow, or even Thursday of next week. But I would say that within two weeks, three days, and ten and one-half hours, you will understand the necessity of proper nutrition, and then it might take a day or two to put it into effect."

DRUG ABUSE

Drug users, especially those who consume alcohol, amphetamines, and cocaine—and, of course, many of the drugs prescribed by Western biomedicine—experience digestive problems and malabsorption of nutrients. (If you look at the *Physician's Desk Reference* [PDR], you will notice that a large majority of the drugs have side effects involving the digestive system.) Many of the behavioral problems associated with alcohol are not simply the result of altered consciousness but include nutritional problems that affect behavior.

Counseling and therapy with drug users and abusers is a problem. According to Peele (1989), there is no one therapy in America that is superior to another when dealing with drug problems. Why is this? First of all, drug issues are treated as a singular problem, or a problem on the shoulders of the individual. Yes, there is theoretical lip service to family dynamics and so on, but when it comes right down to therapy, it is up to the individual to change. Drug abuse, according to my theory, is a method of stress reduction through withdrawal. And what is the individual attempting to withdraw from? Right, rejection. And where does this rejection come from? From the individual's interpretation of the information coming from others. Since individuals are parts of social groupings, drug abuse has to be a social problem and not simply the weakness of the individual. But, of course, we worship individualism and freedom of choice, and we confuse these beliefs with the fact that we are group animals.

There is another factor that is generally ignored. There is drug abuse only because we *say* there is. The types of problems encountered with marijuana, amphetamine, or cocaine use in this country are very different from the problems created after repressive laws were enacted. Such laws were politically created under the guise of "protecting the public," but the reasons for political involvement seem to be less than noble. In fact, the repressive attitude toward marijuana in the 1960s was designed to facilitate arrests of dissidents speaking out against the Vietnam war (see Ott 1993). And now, with all these agencies involved—the DEA, the FDA, local and state law enforcement, and so on—you cannot *un*create the laws without putting a lot of people out of work. That is why the citizens of the state of California can vote for the medical use of marijuana only to find that special-interest groups (the politicians, the CIA), in conjunction with the Justice Department and the DEA, threaten to enforce the law even though the citizens have had their say. Face it, we do not live in a country "of, by, and for the people." At some point, in the not so distant future, we may, indeed, have to grab our pitchforks and march to city hall. It is becoming painfully obvious that the leaders of this country, once in power, operate on their own agendas, their own best interests, and not in the interests of the public they serve.

Taking this a step further, getting people off drugs does not just mean getting people off street drugs and alcohol. The vast majority of your clients are addicted to *legal* drugs prescribed by their doctor, but this is not considered an addiction. It is legal, simply because of the power of the AMA, the pharmaceutical companies, and the FDA to legislate legal addictions. Therefore these types of problems are of no concern to the DEA and other agencies. Such hypocrisy does nothing to promote a health-oriented society.

One of the most effective methods of getting people off drugs and maintaining abstinence is through group or social support. The more people who are involved in the problem, the easier it is to maintain compliance. This is why religious groups are so successful in keeping people clean and sober, though there is also an economic incentive (converts help to maintain the church). AA (Alcoholics Anonymous) is likewise a useful program as long as the individual continues to go to meetings and is monitored, but AA is not for everyone, nor is religious conversion.

One of the most effective approaches I have found for dealing with drug problems came by way of a man calling me, not because he wanted to quit drinking but because he wanted some nutritional information so that he could protect himself from the toxic effects. When he came in, I gave him a formula. The interesting thing about this was that as he more consistently used the information, he drank less and less. The standard counsel I give to individuals with alcohol, prescription, or street drug problems is to tell them how to protect themselves. You will have the best results with people over the age of thirty.

AIDS/HIV

AIDS (acquired immune deficiency syndrome) is considered by Western biomedicine to be caused by HIV (human immunodeficiency virus). The fact that some individuals can test positive for HIV and not have AIDS suggests that it is not a simple case of a virus attacking the immune system, but has to do with nutrition and genetics as well. Stress and mental attitude likewise play a part.

Counseling HIV-positive clients, with or without AIDS, involves the same skills and procedures used with any client. You may have nothing more to offer than an empathic ear. (A useful therapeutic approach for the AIDS patient is hypnotherapy, both for stress reduction and for enhancing the immune system—see Chapter 6.) AIDS, like drug abuse, is not an individual moral issue; it is a social issue and affects all of us. We may, in fact, be witnessing the beginning of future plagues (see Garrett 1994; Lappe 1994).

As you listen without passing judgment, you help to reduce stress. Stress suppresses the immune system. After you listen, and only when your counsel is asked for, do you emphasize stress reduction, nutrition, and the removal of toxins from the body. It is important that the client realize that he or she has to remove all obstacles to the healing process. An AIDS client, like any client, needs to take charge; there is nothing worse than being sick and feeling helpless and dependent. The AIDS client, like all clients, has to become an active participant in his or her health.

DEALING WITH DIVERSE CULTURAL GROUPS

There are many books available that discuss counseling individuals from a culture different from that of the therapist. One of the most recent (Foster et al. 1996) suggests that a Western, psychoanalytic perspective is useful in other cultural groups. I question this. It is most appropriate to know healers within the diverse groups in your community and to refer emotional and physical issues to them. If that is not possible, the following information can be considered with caution. The bibliography contains numerous references to cross-cultural issues, mainly by psychologists. The reader will find that they are high on theory and low on technique (in most cases).

When dealing with diverse groups, one must be careful to determine the client's frame of reference. Usually we tend to categorize cultural groups by country of origin, language spoken, facial characteristics, and skin color. Using facial features and skin color is obviously prejudicial, as these genotypic considerations have nothing to do with behavior. Even determining a person's level of acculturation, as suggested by some authors (see Mendoza 1989; Helms 1986; Chung 1992; Paniagua 1994), is problematical. As Paniagua (1994) points out, there can be different levels of acculturation within the same family. Figure 5.1, another divination procedure, is a simplified method of determining acculturation.

In order to simplify matters, keep in mind the concepts of HRMs and

Figure 5.1
Acculturation Index

Instructions: Please check only one item from the group of generation items, language-preferred items, and the social activity items.

My generation is:

First (1)	Second (2)	Third (3)	Fourth (4)	Fifth (5)

The language I prefer to use is:

Mine Only (1)	Mostly Mine (2)	Both Mine and English (3)	Mostly English (4)	Only English (5)

I prefer to engage in social activities with:

Only Within Cultural Group (1)	Mostly Within Cultural Group (2)	With/Between a Different Cultural Group (3)	Mostly With a Different Cultural Group (4)	Only With a Different Cultural Group (5)

Total Score:
Number of Items Checked:
Acculturation Score (Total Score Divided by Number of Items Checked):

The level of acculturation is: Low (1-1.75); Medium (1.76-3.25); High (3.26-5)

Source: Adapted from Paniagua 1994:11.

rejection; most of the problems you will encounter will involve rejection, regardless of whether you are dealing with a Mexican American, a Hmong, or the couple from a middle-class, suburban neighborhood. The problem involves reframing or retranslating the information with which the individual is distressed. Each culture has its own way of doing this, and to use techniques from another culture (using psychoanalysis with the Hmong, for example) is not only inappropriate, but also will not work. Moreover, certain analytic statements among Asian peoples, especially regarding sex and/or mental problems, will usually alienate the therapist from the client.

The following involve generalizations. Keep in mind that in the most effective counseling, you deal with what the person (couple, family) brings you. In order to do this, you must have an understanding of the culture, which usually means knowing the language. It is important, however, to understand certain factors that can inhibit building trust and rapport, and hinder the delivery of information for retranslating HRMs.

African Americans

Us vs. them attitudes are very much alive in North American culture. Historical precedents make it prudent to discuss how an African American feels about dealing with a therapist of a different ethnic background. Be direct, open, and up-front about this. Many African Americans have what Ho (1992) calls a "healthy cultural paranoia" regarding treatment by those in power or perceived as in power.

There tends to be role flexibility in African American families; at times, and depending on circumstances, the mother may assume the father or head-of-the-family role. Other times, an older child, a grandparent, or an aunt or uncle may take on the parent or family-head role.

Church, especially for women, often plays a significant role in family life. Involvement of specific church members in therapy is a possibility.

Although racism and prejudice are important factors, they must be kept in perspective. For some clients a great deal of blame for current circumstances will be placed on racism and prejudice; the client who remains a victim will have difficulty moving into the future. Although you will not have much impact on the racial attitudes of others, these concerns of the clients need to be listened to.

Family problems are often exacerbated by the way family members communicate. When it comes to interpersonal and family communication, there is no blame; parents are not to blame for anything. There are only implied rules that do not fit, and limited choices or tools for communicating with one another. Moreover, some communicative behaviors (being loud and interrupting) should not, in most cases, be seen as pathological. Instead, they are reactions to being ignored, wanting to deal with issues as they come up, and a questioning about how the therapist feels or thinks about a point.

Although some writers suggest that you avoid "causal explanations of problems" (see Paniagua 1994:27), my experience is that causal explanations are very appropriate *as long as blame is left out of the equation.* If the client asks for your opinion, give him or her your opinion, emphasizing that it is *your* opinion and that you do not speak for others.

Always screen or question for drug abuse, as you would for any client. Drug use or abuse is a mechanism of stress reduction.

Do not recommend medications, herbs, vitamins, and so on; this is seen as an impersonal approach to "obviously" personal problems. You are a holistic health practitioner, so let the clients ask you. Do not jump right into changing food habits; you have to hint at health and the consequences of eating certain foods, and the connection to emotional and behavioral problems.

If the client was referred to you by a school or social welfare agency, this may be seen as a threat to autonomy and free choice. Discuss your client's attitude about this.

Many families with whom you deal (regardless of cultural identity) will have secrets. Such secrets need to be revealed by the client—do not "dig into" these during the first or second session. For example, if a grandparent brings in a child, do not ask where the mother is. As trust is built, this will be revealed. Do not emphasize weaknesses. Fortunately, reframing emphasizes strengths.

If you are teaching assertiveness techniques, make sure you teach responsible assertiveness and not blaming, ordering, threatening, and so on.

African American clients often look to the therapist for a quick fix. Scheduling tasks after the first session is, in most cases, necessary or they will not return.

In family therapy situations, where a discussion of emotional problems or a communication of weaknesses is seen as a threat to ego (especially to the male), see the male client separately. Do not allow mudslinging between husband and wife to go on very long. Although interesting and informative about communicative style, it may end in the "loser" of the duel abandoning therapy. (See Alcena 1994 and Overfield 1995 for African American health problems.)

Mexican Americans

Being "politically correct" is important. Some clients will prefer to be referred to as Hispanic Americans, or persons of Spanish origin born in the United States. Mexican Americans are of Mexican origin but born in the United States. Latino implies that the person is from a country in Latin America.

Machismo equals, among other things, respect, with being respectful an indication of education (not necessarily formal). Thus, if this is a low acculturation situation, then conducting a brief, first interview with the father (or husband) would be expected.

Although women are considered equal to men, they are different. Women are spiritually superior to men and, at the same time, they are to endure all the suffering created by men. The term for this is *maranismo*.

Mexican Americans prefer a more personal approach to counseling. Do not answer your telephone or allow interruptions during therapy; this will be seen as impersonal and disrespectful (unless it is an emergency, do not take telephone calls during counseling sessions with any clients). Attempt to be as formal as possible during a first session. Avoid first names and the familiar *tú* (you). Small talk during subsequent sessions is often very important. It is important that the therapist share things (not too intimate) about his or her life: music you like, food preferences, entertainment, children's names, and so on.

Time is considered less important in Latin cultures; do not ask the reason for showing up late (or early) for an appointment.

Mexican American clients can be very fatalistic, which can sabotage therapy. In other words, why try something different if things will only turn out in a bad way regardless? Here is where your skills in reframing will come in, as well as future pacing. Profound intellectual insights are also useful.

You can expect, in many families, different levels of acculturation—that is, children will be more acculturated than parents, which can lead to behaviors that parents interpret as disrespectful. This needs to be discussed and reinterpreted.

If emotional problems are thought to be brought about by *brujos* or *brujas* (witches, male and female), *mal de ojo* (the evil eye), *susto* (soul loss), *mollera caída* (fallen fontanelle), and so on, do not attempt to talk clients into Western explanations. All of these represent, are analogous to, or are metaphorical of interpersonal and social relationships in general, and relationships with nature. Your goal is to reduce stress, and if seeing a *curandero(a)* is called for, make the suggestion.

Discussion of medication is usually expected. There are many herbal remedies in use. Most grocery stores that cater to Mexican American clients stock numerous herbs (see Clark 1970 for an overview of beliefs and practices among Mexican Americans, and Overfield 1995 for other insights into health problems).

Asians, Southeast Asians, and Asian Americans

The more intact the extended family, the less the likelihood of seeing Asians in counseling sessions. A breakdown in the extended family, because of war situations and relocation (refugee status), disrupts the power structure and sometimes leads to problems with controlling and disciplining children.

Parents, especially females and shamed males, tend to become encapsulated, and acculturation is slow. "Encapsulation" means that the individuals stay within a certain geographical area and associate mainly with others speaking the same language. Such behavior is a means of avoiding stress but limits acculturation. "Acculturation" means the learning of the rules of the dominant society after migration. "Enculturation" is the learning of the social rules of the society into which you are born. Encapsulation is often the case among the Hmong, Lao, and Cambodians. The children, either arriving in the United States in the 1970s or born here, tend to be more acculturated or enculturated; this creates intergenerational problems. Acculturated or enculturated children tend to "buy into" individualism and free choice, and break away from the collective, elder-male-dominated traditional system. If the power base is missing, the children are difficult to control.

As the children have a foot in each culture, they accept individualism and free choice, but the concept of personal responsibility is sometimes lacking. In collectivistic cultures, controls come from outside; directives are given, and the individual does what he or she is told. In Western culture, controls are instilled within, that is, individualism equals taking responsibility for one's actions, and so on. This has led to the concepts of guilt (Western, inner controls) and shame (Asians control by comparison, that is, one's behavior is a reflection on the group). Hmong, Vietnamese, and Lao youth, when arrested and placed in juvenile hall, are very compliant because they recognize and go along with the perceived authority, authority that is lacking in the family. (This offers a potential solution in the counseling situation, that is, developing community methods for bolstering the authority in the family.) Do not recommend that children need to be independent from their families (parents).

There is a public suppression of problems because of fear of law enforcement and the shame it brings on the family. Because of this, the family is usually in an intense, long-standing problem or crisis for months or years before seeking counseling. Usually the counseling is court-ordered, and the counseling with which most of us are familiar is not a feature of Asian society.

Silence is a sign of respect and a desire to continue the conversation after making a point. Prolonged eye contact is a sign of disrespect.

Asians expect counseling to proceed in a formal manner. It is often useful to send a letter or, if reading or speaking English is a problem have a translator inform clients what is expected in counseling before the first session. Expectations build a sense of security.

It is important to show expertise and authority without being condescending. Having diplomas visible or lots of books on shelves is important. Having a sterile, white-walled office with one or two pictures on the walls does not project expertise and authority, only transience.

Asians tend to express emotional problems in somatic terms. These are analogous to interpersonal problems and, sometimes, CIS (critical incident stress) or PTS (posttrauma stress). Do not attempt to undermine the analogy by saying, "It is all emotional conversion." These analogies are socially and emotionally protective. Do not attempt to "dig into" these traumatic events, because you may retraumatize the client; you cannot use a psychoanalytic process with Asian clients. In fact, to suggest that an individual has emotional problems will shame the individual and the family.

Many Southeast Asian groups (e.g., Hmong, Iu Mien) will resort to herbs to cure behavioral problems, or they may call in a shaman to "shake" and commune with spirits. I feel that these approaches to curing are appropriate to recommend because they serve not only to reframe a situation and to cure, but also tend to bring the family back together (reintegration). They are just as scientific, and certainly more effective, than anything that Western culture has to offer.

Do not attempt to collect a "life history" during the first session. Asians and Southeast Asians are not that disclosing to strangers, and you could destroy trust. Let the clients disclose when they are ready. It is important to listen to and give directives regarding the problems the client(s) bring you on the first encounter.

Do not overuse translators; this will undercut your authority. If the language barrier is too great, refer the individual or couple to someone who speaks the language.

Because you are seen in an authority position, you are expected to give directives during the first session. Give concrete advice, such as "I want you to write down when and the number of times you had a stomachache (headache, etc.). When you return next week, we will discuss some of the causes and herbs to use." Or "Make note of the times you weren't able to sleep through the night, and we will discuss this next time." Do not promise anything you cannot deliver. Check your phone book for social agencies for purposes of referral (Asian Community Service Center, Pacific/Asian Preventive Program, Asian American Drug Abuse Program, Asian Counseling and Treatment Center, Korean American Mental Health Service Center, Center for Southeast Asian Refugee Resettlement, and so on). See Overfield (1995) for insights into health problems.

BICULTURAL ISSUES

Bicultural adolescents and adults bring to the counseling session a cluster of issues that are not easy to disentangle. This is because they have to negotiate their own bicultural identities as well as integrate their perceived social status within their peer group, develop a sexual/gender identity, and make commitments to cultural ideals of work and school. This is not an individual issue. Those with understanding and supportive families and peer networks seem to experience the least stress. Stress and subsequent behavioral "packages" appear to result from the following (keep in mind that these represent generalizations).

1. Benson, in his 1981 study of mixed (black and white) families in London, found that nearly all children/adolescents, between the ages of three and sixteen rejected their black identity.

2. Teicher (1968) found that children hold a stronger reference toward the parent considered less socially discounted. In fact, there seems to be an over-identification with the parent perceived as "most similar" (see Gibbs 1987: 268). If the female child identifies strongly with the male parent, this can lead to a very masculine identity. Conversely, if the male child identifies strongly with the female parent, more effeminate traits can manifest themselves. Further, teens who overidentify with their white cultural heritage often conceptualize sex as more " 'repulsive or disgusting,' and [can] be highly invested in a puritanical moral code, as if they were reacting against those same stereotypes of black sexuality" (Gibbs 1987:270).

3. Negative sexual identity increases if the same-sex parent is markedly different physically (Teicher 1968).

4. Negative sexual identity increases if the child discounts the same-sex parent; this is even more dramatic if the opposite-sex parent criticizes the child's or same-sex parent's physical characteristics.

5. The greater the child's confusion as to cultural identity, the greater the negative sexual identity.

6. When a child is raised in a community with many mixed marriages, identity seems to be less of a problem. The opposite follows if the child is raised in a community with few mixed marriages.

7. Bicultural youths tend to be victimized more often than other cultural groups.

8. Parents with poor identities exacerbate the child's identity problems (see Faulkner 1985; Faulkner and Kich 1983; Lyle et al. 1985).

9. Mixed cultural identities are pictured as socially "on the fringes."

10. At some periods in the child's life, he or she can have a close network of peers. Upon entering higher levels of education, with a modification of peer groups or attitudes of existing peer groups, social problems manifest themselves. Females seem to experience more anxiety, especially if they are excluded from certain social activities (slumber parties, boy-girl parties, and so on). Such rejection can be felt by both majority and minority groups (Gibbs 1987:269).

11. Biethnic teens are sometimes overprotected by parents; children become overly dependent. This can result in rebellion (e.g., risk-taking, confrontation with authority figures such as teachers, police, etc.) against parents, especially in

single-parent families, or withdrawal from society, using the home as a refuge. Age regression is also a possibility.

12. Biethnic teens who overidentify with their reality of "black ghetto culture" often "express anti-achievement values and fear rejection by their black peers if they are perceived as 'bookworms' or 'nerds.' In reverse, a strong identity toward Anglo heritage can lead to a need to excel in academic achievement" (Gibbs 1987:271–272).

13. Defensive and coping strategies, designed to reduce stress (although they may be stress-enhancing in the long run), include

    a. Denial of mixed racial heritage

    b. Reaction formation or rationalizations: "They segregate themselves, and I'd rather choose from a broader network of friends" or "There is no point in achieving at school because I wouldn't get a job anyway"

    c. Overidentification: "I'd rather go to white parties"

    d. Withdrawal

    e. Repression, sublimation, or substitution, when sexual identity is in conflict

    f. Sexual acting out, for reasons including being accepted (especially for females) or as a statement about manhood.

14. Generalizations on Biethnic issues

    a. Those with negative group identities and who identify with the most devalued stereotypes, usually resort to acting out and dishonest rebellions, and employ coping mechanisms that are maladaptive and socially dysfunctional. Conversely, those with negative identities *and* who identify with the white stereotypes tend to be overachievers and emotionally and sexually inhibited.

    b. Adopted children shoulder the extra burden of being abandoned by *both* ethnic groups.

    c. According to Gibbs (1987:274), assessment of biethnic adolescents involves taking into consideration

       1. "Age-appropriate development and concerns"

       2. "identify[ing] development and issues (undersocialized and over-socialized)"

       3. "Parental and family attitudes toward their biracial identity"

       4. "Peer relationships."

What is readily apparent is how potent information is in shaping attitude. Consider how powerful many silent incantations (nonverbal messages) are in developing negative identities and stereotypes. But also keep in mind that these attitudes and identities are constructed realities (how the individual interprets information in his or her world); your incantations can be a powerful force in reconstructing identity, beliefs, and behaviors.

The main issues to keep in mind are (1) build trust with the client (avoid

"I know how you feel" and any guilt on your own part); (2) be forth-right—if you are asked an opinion, give your opinion; and (3) move to-ward altering the meaning of events in the client's reality—blaming others and remaining a victim are less than therapeutic.

Remember that the world is how you perceive it. Yes, there is injustice and conflict at every corner, but this seems to be the way social systems work. Develop ways to work with or around the conflict in yourself and others. Most of the conflict in social living centers on rejection and accep-tance.

DEATH AND DYING

Life is a series of births, deaths, and rebirths. It is as if doors are con-tinually opening and closing, with an opening analogous to birth and the closing analogous to death; there are many doors. Figure 5.2 is a variation of the diagram in Chapter 2 (we will encounter it again when I discuss hypnosis in Chapter 6 and social reintegration in Chapter 7).

Life is part of a process, just as disease is part of a process. Most of us in Western culture are frightened of death; I think that Thomas Aquinas and Dante had something to do with this. Figure 5.3 illustrates my more complete thinking about life, illness, and death. As the figure suggests, death and resurrection or rebirth are really the same thing. I do not pre-tend to know the details of this. However, all organic and inorganic forms are part of a larger living system. How can anything really ever die? It can be recycled, yes. But death as an end, no.

I do not mean to imply by this diagram that you are reborn into another person at death; I have no idea what the next part of the process will be.

There is evidence to suggest that what happens when you die is what *you believe* will happen. Let me explain. Time is relative, and seems to be constrained by the speed of light. However, time inside your mind is a totally different thing. During hypnosis, for example, the hypnotist can suggest time alterations; time can be compressed or lengthened. When you dream, a few seconds, as measured by outside-the-body time, can seem like an eternity. Death would appear to be a movement away from exter-nal time to some other dimension. So, *in your mind*, time is endless; you never die. Your thoughts at the time of death, then, may be a represen-tation of your beliefs about an afterlife, and this belief is what you will settle into in the timeless depths of your mind.

When counseling in the area of death and dying, I do not recommend getting into philosophy unless you are asked. Many pastoral counselors use death and dying to save souls; this is not your job. The single most effective activity you can engage in with individuals who have experienced the death of a loved one, or who are going through the process themselves,

Figure 5.2
Life, Death, and Resurrection

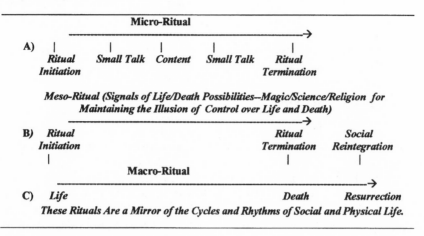

	Micro-Ritual

A)
Ritual | Small Talk | Content | Small Talk | Ritual
Initiation | | | | Termination

Meso-Ritual (Signals of Life/Death Possibilities—Magic/Science/Religion for Maintaining the Illusion of Control over Life and Death)

B) *Ritual*   *Ritual*   *Social*
Initiation   *Termination* *Reintegration*

Macro-Ritual

C) *Life*   *Death*   *Resurrection*
These Rituals Are a Mirror of the Cycles and Rhythms of Social and Physical Life.

Source: Modified from Rush 1996:130.

Figure 5.3
The Balance of Life and Death

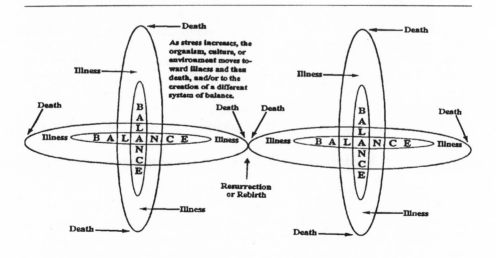

Source: Modified from Rush 1996:xiii.

is to listen and be supportive. Death, like life, is a human activity; there is nothing as empty as having to face death alone.

I recommend the reader review the works of Elizabeth Kübler-Ross (1969, 1974, 1975; she also has written many articles) and the stages (denial, bargaining, anger, depression, grief, acceptance) that individuals go through (in whole or in part) as they come to terms with the death of others or their own personal circumstances. This is especially true with AIDS clients.

CONFLICT MEDIATION

Success in conflict mediation depends, in large measure, on who is in conflict and over what. Usually the conflict is over acceptance, rejection, and/or money, possessions, or territory. Appendix C provides an overview of a basic process of mediation that I developed for a local high school. In that situation, student conflict mediators were trained to deal with the conflicts arising between their peers on campus. Each conflict mediator (ranging in ages from thirteen to eighteen) receives approximately four hours of training before doing mediation. They are trained in emotional responsibility, listening techniques (using the process outlined in this book), isolating HRMs, and basic reframing techniques. The conflict mediators are given a great deal of status, which aids in the therapeutic, stress-reduction process.

The conflict mediators are not counselors, they are not therapists, they are not psychologists. They are very bright students and they are communicators. In fact, they are incredible communicators. Are these unusual and out-of-the-ordinary students? No. They are concerned and motivated, and have a process that works. To give an example, during the school year from September 1995 through June 1996, there were 226 conflicts handled by the student mediators; only twelve had to be referred to the vice principal's office. There are situations that are not dealt with by the mediators, for example, when weapons are encountered. However, the conflict mediation program has significantly reduced that type of potential violence on campus because the conflicts are deescalated before they reach that stage.

The point is that you do not have to be a rocket scientist to be a mediator; mediation is one of the most human of activities. What it takes is a willingness to help and a basic understanding of the communication process.

REVIEW

In this chapter I have covered special circumstances where counseling becomes more specific and may require that the counselor or therapist gain some special knowledge or experience. Nutrition will affect behavior. It is important to understand the effects specific deficits or metabolic imbalances can have on mood, and related reactions to stress, and to educate accordingly.

Drug abuse is a social issue, although the responsibility for drug abuse is, for the most part, heaped on the shoulders of the individual. The more individuals involved in the therapeutic process, the greater the success in achieving and maintaining a clean and sober status. Drug abusers usually have nutritional deficits that need attention.

Counseling HIV-positive clients is a special challenge. The most effective approach is listening and being supportive; the same is true with death and dying situations. As a clinical anthropologist you have special knowledge that you can share regarding other therapies, outside of Western biomedicine, that might be useful in individual cases.

Counseling clients from other cultural backgrounds essentially means becoming an applied anthropologist. Keep in mind that you *cannot* utilize Western theories and practices with most of the other cultures on this planet. It is important to become knowledgeable about curers in the community who might be better equipped to deal with specific issues.

NOTE

1. There are numerous words and terms that have been copyrighted by Western biomedicine, and "diagnosis" is one of them. Others include "treat" and "cure." Visual props that are seen as exclusive to the profession are the white jacket and stethoscope and, of course, the staff intertwined with two serpents, the caduceus, also associated with Asclepius, the god of medicine.

Chapter 6

Hypnosis, Light, and Balancing Electromagnetic Fields: Adjuncts to Emotional and Physical Healing

My interest in trance and hypnosis began in the mid-1960s, as I became more and more involved in the study of anthropology. I became a practitioner of the art in 1969 after several months' study with a clinical hypnotherapist in Toronto, Canada. But it was not until 1976 that I began to understand or develop a model of hypnosis, or how the phenomenon comes about from *my* point of view, rather than staying with the prevailing attitudes at the time. One of the first things I discovered is that hypnotherapists are specialists, in the sense that some are better at bringing about certain results (quitting smoking, for example, or enhancing the immune system, etc.) than others. My other discovery is that just about anyone can learn the techniques, and it does not take years to do so. The toughest part is applying the tools, because you have to say and do things that are quite confusing, if not "schizophrenic"—that is, a sentence embedded in another message, for example, that you speak at the same time you talk to a person's less dominant eye. That is pretty crazy stuff. In another context, one can easily be mistaken for someone quite disconnected from reality. This is what we are seeing in the shaman, a person who goes through a near-death experience, or someone who becomes psychotic (is dead in the sense of being outside of society), somehow pulls himself or herself out, and brings along the behavior and chants peculiar to that mental state. He (or she) can then reenact or re-create the thinking and the behavior, creating variations over time. This out-of-the-ordinary behavior is used to bring the patient and the community (the audience) into that psychosis, that crazy land of possible impossibilities, disorientation, and confusions. Illness is a crisis that opens all possibilities, good and bad. The shaman has been there many times and has returned, and the community trusts that he or she will bring out the good. Finally, the shaman leads them out and back to the point where the next ritual will begin, the patient healed.

Using a Western-type model, the technique of hypnosis is to focus the part of the mind that is least judgmental but, at the same time, most open to altering social symbols and physical processes. This part of the mind is often metaphorically referred to as the "subconscious mind." The goal in hypnosis, then, is to focus the awareness of the subconscious mind on the suggestions of the therapist. Keep in mind that there are multiple levels of awareness connected to the subconscious.

As an anthropologist, I had to come to terms with the concept of hypnosis as opposed to trance. Are these the same thing, or is the former a milder rendition of the latter? Both hypnotic and trance phenomena are culturally conditioned. In other words, the actions of a !Kung San of South Africa while in trance are very different from those of a Hmong shaman. Before going further, let me define these terms so that the emotional/stress components will have a more specific frame of reference.

WHAT IS HYPNOSIS?

In a general sense, hypnosis and trance are the same mental phenomenon. The difference lies in the operator. In a trance state, culture is the operator directing the actions of the tranced. In hypnosis, the specific other, the operator (the hypnotherapist or hypnotist), is guiding the trance phenomenon. Among the !Kung San, cultural expectations and the spirits are the controllers, as is the case with the Hmong. Weitzenhoffer (1989: 298) comments:

In light of symptomatology, it may be reasonable to think of hypnosis as *one kind of* trance state. Therefore, we can speak of a *hypnotic trance. One of the features that distinguishes hypnosis as a trance state from other trance states is the existence of a specific hypnotist–subject relationship that plays an essential part in the production, the shaping, and the utilization of the trance as hypnosis.* (emphasis in the original)

In terms of what hypnosis "is," let me first say what it is not. It is not a state of *un*consciousness, it is not a state of sleep, and it is not a state of noncontrol *unless this is a cultural expectation.* Hypnosis appears to be, as Preston (1998:23–25) states, "*a state of awareness dominated by the subconscious mind*," with various "depths of hypnosis, depths of the subconscious mind, just as there are several depths of conscious awareness—that is, perception."

I believe that it is through this idea of awareness levels in both the conscious and the subconscious minds that one can appreciate how useful this healing tool is. Hypnosis involves incantations that are carefully constructed and handed down in training seminars across the land. The purpose of these incantations is usually to create a situation wherein the client can review various interpretations of negative or traumatic events. This moves the individual toward stress reduction and a positive alteration of physiology; for example, stress reduction enhances immune functioning.

Moreover, this tool cannot be restricted from the public domain. The reason for this is that we all use "hypnotic tools" every day, each and every time we interact with one another or in groups. When we present ourselves to each other, we want the other(s) to focus on or away from our symbols. When the blend is right, there is a synchronicity, but when someone is out of step, that is what gets our attention. The news media have expertise in this: the well-chosen words, insinuations, and suggestions, and the commercials are superb. The sitcoms, the movies, the dramas, are all hypnotic and repetitive.

A deeper form of hypnosis, however, lies at the extremes of deep relaxation and shock or stress. At these times, and metaphorically speaking, the mind is more open to internalizing highly illogical and unanalyzed messages. It is as if these extremes act as openings to different possibilities of physiological functioning, thinking, and behaving, possibilities not seriously considered by the conscious mind.

There is another term, however, that opens the same door, and that is confusion, which is also a state of stress. This is what happens when you break up someone's processing (see "Breaking Process" in Chapter 3).

The two main factors that lead toward the hypnotic/trance phenomenon are relaxation and stress/confusion. This may, at first sight, seem to be a contradiction, so let me explain.

For most individuals, information that is unusual or confusing leads to the freezing-up stress reaction discussed in Chapter 3. The brain literally stops processing and waits for further instructions—this will happen with anyone, given the right information. Stress alters or displaces conscious awareness and tends to activate varying levels of the subconscious and information necessary for automatic responses. It is automatic, you do not have to think about it, and it accounts for the fact that trance states, especially during healing, are so common throughout the world. Figure 6.1, another divination process, illustrates how the hypnotic state can occur from stress. Some individuals who have a basic stress reaction of either emotional conversion or freezing (especially the latter) are very susceptible to trance during everyday situations. These individuals appear to benefit most from structured hypnosis. Those individuals who are prone to verbal or physical fighting under stress, or who engage in sexual behavior as a primary means of stress reduction, may not benefit as quickly, and in the case of sex offenders, not at all.

Trance/hypnosis can also occur during deep relaxation, although there are always elements of confusion during the process of deepening the

Figure 6.1
Stress Leading to Trance/Hypnotic Phenomenon

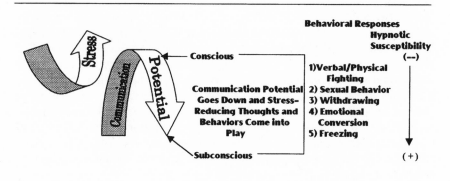

relaxation. Theoretically, the more relaxed you become, the further the separation between the conscious and subconscious minds. As I refer to "conscious" and "subconscious," I am speaking metaphorically, as it is unclear what these "things" are. For my purposes the subconscious mind is a primary program that runs in back of secondary programs, much as DOS is the program that runs in the background of Windows, and of the word processor, as I type these words and phrases. With my word processor, I can consciously type any combination of words, phrases, and sentences. My word processor has a "spell checker" that is probably society (the superego) telling me that I should not spell words in certain ways. However, I can override society and spell in any manner I desire. But there are certain limitations. I cannot press a "b" and expect a "t" to come up on the screen. If there are too many files running, the main program will tell me to close things down. I cannot run my word processor without Windows. In other words, I am locked into the constraints of DOS and Windows. On the other hand, if I know the DOS program, I can make some alterations. In a similar way (and I realize that this metaphor has its limitations) the subconscious mind can be reprogrammed.

We can consider this reprogramming in terms of filters. The conscious mind has several filters that allow information to enter for consideration and storage. One filter is what I call the paradigm filter. In other words, if information fits your current belief structure, it will be accepted. This does not mean that information is correct or true, only that it is believable according to one's current opinions (see Kuhn 1967).

Another filter of the conscious mind is your true or believable filter. Your true filter responds to authority. In other words, you read something in a book written by an expert, and, although it contradicts previous beliefs, you are inclined to accept it because "It is in print, it is written by an expert, and therefore it must be true." This is not logical, but logic has its limitations, especially when it comes to creativity and change—we are not designed always to be logical.

A third filter is your important or useful filter. Ideas, actions, and behaviors that are immediately important or useful to you will override your paradigm filter. For example, a teenager believes that drugs are bad and experts, including his parents, have reinforced this belief. One evening he is with his friends, and at that moment, he is moving away from the influence of his parents and it is important that he belong to his peer group. So he smokes some marijuana because it is *more* important or useful to belong, and thus blasts through his paradigm and true filters. There are other filters, but they seem to be analogues to the true and important filters.

The subconscious mind, on the other hand, apparently has only two filters—self-preservation and stress reduction, which are really parts of the same filter. The subconscious mind does not seem to be too concerned about truth or believability, but it has its own paradigms, some of which are hardwired in much the same way as the hardware in the computer I'm currently using. These paradigms involve self-preservation and "automatic" functioning of the body. In its attempts to protect itself, the subconscious mind will produce symptoms that you and I experience as illness. These symptoms are the body's best attempt to deal with information either produced within or coming from outside the system that pushes the body past a balance point (see diagram in Rush 1996:xiii). It would appear, then, that the subconscious mind is programmed and reprogrammed, in much the same way as a DOS program, by means of information that enters through the conscious mind or during times of stress and/or relaxation. Such information can even alter seemingly hardwired automatic functioning like heart rate, blood pressure, skin temperature, metabolic rate, immune system functioning, and so on. A term for altering immune functioning is *psychoneuroimmunology* (see Rossi and Cheek 1988; Rossi 1993; Lieberman 1991).

The phase prior to the hypnotic or trance state can involve a focusing on repetitive and exhaustive movement (for example, dance) and drumming, leading to mental confusion and then trance through social expectation (as with the !Kung San). It can simply be chanting and the focusing on the particular chanting sounds, again with the social expectation of trance. Or, as commonly utilized in Western hypnotic procedures, it can be a relaxation process, especially of the head, arms, and hands, and then, with the use of language, creation of a sense of confusion that tends to suspend the conscious mind through a process of looping. This looping behavior shuts off the several filters that appear to be operative in the conscious but not the subconscious mind. These filters include social and conditioned truths and information that is considered to be important from a person/social perspective. The subconscious mind, as mentioned, only has one filter—self-preservation—and it would appear that any message that enters the subconscious mind, once the conscious mind is bypassed, is considered true. This is the process, during hypnosis, by which individuals can develop amnesia or anesthesia, hallucinate, develop tremendous strength, or mobilize general self-healing.

Hypnotic states, however, can be brought about under the stress of performing day-to-day activities that can lead to phobic reactions and a disregulation of metabolic activities. For example, a child is playing and the parent walks up, yells at the child, and then calls him stupid or some other name. During the stress phase there is a stop of mental functioning; the conscious mind is put on hold. Because the brain does not like being in limbo (recall the tool of breaking process in Chapter 3), it will often grab the next message presented in order to activate the thinking process. Result: "Stupid" enters into the subconscious mind. Because parents have a style of setting rules, such messages are reinforced over and over. Teachers do the same thing, as do our friends and the mass media. This is especially true when emotionally disturbed, special effects people shock the audience with blood, guts, and gore. The next message presented is often internalized, and these next messages are usually telling the individual to be fearful of something. Sometimes this creates phobias in a way similar to how seeing blood when you were a child, under stressful circumstances (a car accident, for example), creates a phobia for blood or even riding in cars.

Formal Hypnotic Process

Hypnosis can be broken down into several distinct phases. The first phase is induction. This is the process of closing one's eyes, and is part of the initiation ritual as diagrammed in Figure 6.2. The hypnotic process fits within all three portions of the figure, depending on the goals of the operator (culture and/or therapist).

The second phase of hypnosis, which is still within the initiation ritual, involves a process of deep relaxation, beginning with the head and going all the way down to the toes.

The next phase is small talk. This is where you talk about some seemingly meaningless topic, or have the client engage in some simple symbolic task in his or her mind, and then use language to confuse and disorient the individual. This is designed to "shut off" or "shut down" the conscious mind so that the subconscious mind is directly accessed.

The fourth phase, or content phase, is to talk to the subconscious mind, to give directives with respect to eliminating stress, enhancing the immune system, or whatever the goal. I have found that it is not usually necessary

Figure 6.2
Hypnotic Process

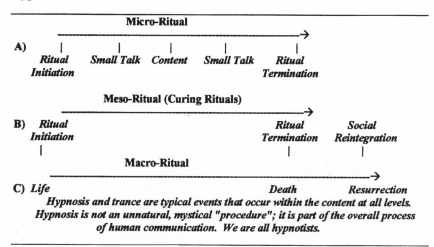

Source: Modified from Rush 1996:130.

to bring up deep dark secrets or to have clients remember traumatic events in order to retranslate them. In fact, during the content stage I often tell clients stories that represent general traumatic events and then allow the subconscious mind to place its own meaning on them. Other times, I am more specific and direct.

Phase five involves more small talk, that is, letting the client rest after all the work, enjoying the rest and relaxation. During the small talk, I reinforce directives and suggestions given in the content phase.

The sixth phase involves a ritual termination, that is, "In a moment I will count to three and you will open your eyelids. And when you open your eyelids, you will remain calm and relaxed, not tired, but calm, relaxed, and comfortable. Here we go. One, two, three."

Ritual termination also signals death of a former belief, habit, or health problem. The individual has changed. This requires social reintegration. How is this accomplished? Although I will suggest a number of methods for accomplishing this in Chapter 7, in hypnosis it is accomplished both during the content phase, as you are giving suggestions for social living (after stress is reduced, emotional and physical balance is achieved, and so on), *and* during the second small talk phase, as you are reinforcing the directives given during the content phase. Sometimes this is as simple as saying, "Exiting from your trauma and understanding its positive effect in your life is easy. That's because you are altering the meaning of the trauma; you alter the meaning of your history every day, is that correct? Now, as the trauma has a new and important and stress-reducing meaning for you *causes you to think about the future, causes you to think about how you will look, how you will sound, and how you will feel tomorrow, the next day, next week. And this causes you to participate in positive relationships with others, is that correct?"*

You always move toward social reintegration, and *not* a neurotic preoccupation with self, personal assertiveness, and independence. You promote *positive* codependence, cooperation, and patience. Again, you want the individual to move toward stress reduction.

Hypnosis and trance are part of the natural healing potential of the body. Hypnosis, then, is a potentially powerful therapeutic tool. Research in hypnosis tells us that awareness is not suspendable, but one's reaction to the outer- as well as inner-generated information is suspendable, and thus subject to alteration. In other words, hypnosis is an altered state of *awareness* of the information available to the senses; and emotions, feelings, and sensations that lead to social and individual stereotypical (emotional pains and pleasures) and automatic reactions (a pinprick) are suspendable and moldable. This accounts for the suggestibility of individuals under hypnosis; the metasystem, that is, emotions, are suspended and incoming data are now neutral to the subconscious mind unless they are life-threatening.

The information stored in a person's head represents a reality constructed of information input through the various senses and judged for storage by emotions. This constructed reality is in a continual state of reinterpretation, and it is this constructed reality that enters the equation of good or poor health. Moreover, because of physical abuse to our bodies over time, because of our socially directed eating habits, the body's physiology has to adapt (it is plastic to a point) to what it is presented. Symptoms of illness are signals that lifestyle is interfering with efficient and balanced body/mind functioning, just as the intrusion of a virus is a signal of information intrusion on that level.

Hypnosis, then, can be a very effective adjunct to nutritional and emotional counseling and therapy. It still fits within the realm of education; it is simply a more specific communication technique or tool. Keep in mind that hypnosis is an art form and it means beginning with understanding one's own style of communicating.

Many states now have laws licensing the art form of hypnosis, but I do not believe that these laws can prevent you from leading people through guided imagery; movies and television programs are guided imagery. Your purpose when using guided imagery is stress reduction, not curing or healing. The body heals itself. If there are laws in your state, then get certification or *do not* call yourself a hypnotherapist. Do not set yourself up for litigation. Circumvent the law or take steps to change the law. Hypnosis, like all therapeutic techniques, is an art form, and licensing an art form is ludicrous.

In terms of works in hypnosis, I recommend that you read everything that Milton Erickson ever wrote or to which he contributed (Bandler and Grinder 1975a; Grinder et al. 1977; Haley 1967, 1973, 1985; Rossi 1980; Rosen 1982; Rossi et al. 1983; Rossi and Ryan 1985, 1986; Zeig 1985).

LIGHT THERAPY

Syntonics, a form of light therapy, was developed in the 1920s, as a method to "treat" numerous health conditions. More recently, Szent-Gyorgyi (1960, 1968), the discoverer of vitamin C, has suggested that biological functioning is altered by sunlight. We know, for example, that when light hits and passes through the epidermis and dermis of the skin, and into the subcutaneous fatty tissue, a number of biochemical changes occur, including an increase in melanin, thus darkening the skin (a protection against too much light exposure), and the conversion of cholesterol to the vitamin D necessary for the absorption of calcium.

We also know that there is a gland in the brain, the pineal gland (often referred to as the "third eye"), that is sensitive to electromagnetic radiation, that is, sunlight. When the body is exposed to sunlight, this gland *does not* produce melatonin, one of the body's very powerful antioxidants and regulator of many of the body's functions (e.g., reproductive functions, blood pressure, immune system functioning, mood, etc.). Melatonin is produced at night while you sleep; that is why it is unwise to use an electric blanket or have the television or other significant light sources on while you sleep—the pineal gland reads these electromagnetic sources as if the sun were out.

Connected to melatonin is the fact that many individuals, especially here in the Sacramento Valley, become depressed during the winter because of a blanket of fog that settles into the low-lying areas and often remains for days or weeks. Not only is this fog dangerous to drive in, it also shuts out the sun and interferes with the body's natural rhythms. The results are depression and lethargy. I have noticed that there is more alcohol consumption during extended periods of fog, an increase in suicide rates, and an increase in absenteeism from work.

Our kind, and our ancient ancestors, developed in relationship to many environmental factors, including sunlight, and it is therefore not surprising that sunlight, and all the fractions of sunlight not blocked by the atmosphere, will have an effect on human physiology. If the reader has ever raised fish, you know that they thrive, as does the plant life you put in the tank, when you use full spectrum lights. The same is true with plants grown indoors.

As this is not a book on light therapy per se, I direct the reader to Lieberman (1991), as I feel that this is an important adjunct to any holistic approach to healing. There is another issue, when engaged in light therapy, that will quickly reveal itself, and that is the affect (emotions) that flows during light therapy. Everything—mind, body, those close to you, the air, the wind, the light—is interconnected. When utilizing light therapy for physical healing, it is not uncommon for emotional issues, in some way stored with the physical problem, to come to the surface. What do you do? Listen and help the person to retranslate the meaning of the emotional pain. The release and retranslation of emotional content, although usually the beginning phase of healing, many times occurs as physical healing proceeds. Emotional healing crises are a signal that healing is in process and, in my opinion, should not be suppressed.

TOUCHLESS THERAPEUTIC MASSAGE

In the late 1980s, Wirth (1990) set up a quite fascinating experiment. A number of college students volunteered to submit to "full thickness dermal wounds" on their arms, and then they were instructed to place their arms through a hole in a wall. None of the students could see what was happening on the other side. At random, some of the arms were subjected to what is called "therapeutic touch," wherein the arms were *not* physically touched but, instead, were passed over by the hands of one skilled in this art form. No therapeutic touching was administered to the remainder. The results are fascinating. The wounds of those who received the therapeutic touch healed faster than those that did not. Moreover, the results have been duplicated.

Developed by Kunz and Krieger (see Krieger 1979) in the mid-1970s, this appears to be a method of manipulating and balancing the electromagnetic energies that surround the human body. And because these waves emanate *from* the human body, it is not necessary to have actual contact, as in the case of traditional massage and acupressure (see Brennan 1987 for another perspective on theory and practice). Reports have suggested that magnets may serve the same function as acupuncture and touchless therapy. Vyse (1997:207) refers to this as "quack therapy" and equates it with magical thinking and the placebo effect, but I do not believe that we can so swiftly dismiss the value of this behavior, if only for its placebo effect.

In some ways therapeutic touch fits in with light therapy, in that both are dealing with, most probably, electromagnetic waves, the former being involved with waves emanating from the body, the latter coming to the body from outside sources. Moreover, there is documented proof of the healing potential of this approach. And, as a bonus, I doubt that anyone can enact legislation to license the practice, since there is no actual touching during the procedure.

REVIEW

There are numerous healing traditions: some old, some new. Holistic health does not necessarily mean that you should become expert in all of them, nor is this possible. However, it is absolutely imperative that you be a therapeutic communicator. Above and beyond the perspectives and tools presented in chapters 1–5, this chapter has offered additional skills and directions: hypnosis, light therapy, and therapeutic touch. All three are more specialized methods of altering information in and around the human body for the purpose of emotional and physical balance.

Chapter 7

Creating a Future and Process in Social Reintegration

Living is essentially a symbolic act accompanied by numerous rituals that tie the symbols together. Since our ancestors were able to discern a rhythm in the universe—the rising and setting of the sun, the phases of the moon, the changes in the seasons, and so on—they conceptualized rhythms in terms of ritual. Through analogous thinking, when formal ritual is not engaged, the natural rhythms are likely to be halted. Although this may seem like magical thinking, observe the rhythms around you. You get up in the morning and you engage in your toilet rituals (urinate, brush your teeth, take a shower, etc.). You get so conditioned to the habit of these daily cycles that any disturbance can lead to stress. For example, you get up late and you cannot have your coffee—or worse yet, you cannot shower or fix your hair. Your whole day is likely to be topsy-turvy; you would like to start all over again. This is precisely what happens when you take a shower and you start to daydream and forget at what point you are at in the scrubbing-down process. What do you do? Right, you start over. Profane rituals allow you to engage your world automatically.

When thrust into the ritual processes of others, we do not immediately discern the rhythms. This can be the case with unfamiliar religious rituals; it can also be the case with hospital rituals. The rhythm of a hospital depends on the enactment of numerous complementary rituals from the moment a patient is admitted right up to the moment of discharge. Patients often get the impression that a hospital stay is all scientific, and that rituals belong in a church, but this is not so. Ritual behavior is all round us.

As illustrated in Figure 7.1, we can see our everyday rituals (A), our healing rituals and religious rituals (B), and our life process rituals (C) involve the same processes but have different purposes and content. From

Figure 7.1
Ritual Is Life

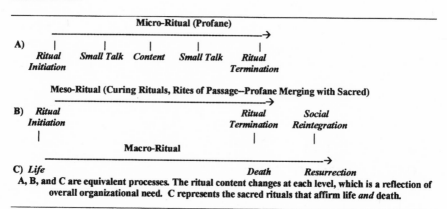

A, B, and C are equivalent processes. The ritual content changes at each level, which is a reflection of
overall organizational need. C represents the sacred rituals that affirm life *and* death.

Source: Modified from Rush 1996:130.

the moment we are born until the day we die, we enact rituals; after death
we return to the rituals or rhythms of the universe, a common theme in
world mythologies.

Referring to healing rituals (B), when someone becomes ill, daily rituals
are interrupted and, in some cases, suspended. Moreover, the disruption
of the rituals of one person can have a ripple effect on family, friends, and
workmates. When you oversleep and disjoint your morning rituals, this
can affect your family and friends. How? Your mood and the behaviors
that flow from the "dis-order" are picked up by others. It is the "Someone
got up on the wrong side of the bed" phenomenon. All behavior is information, and how others interpret that information will affect moods, decisions, and behaviors. We are all interconnected.

Here is the problem. Rituals are sets of rules. When ritual is disrupted,
social events and expectations are disrupted; a door opens, and chaos
threatens (see Rush 1996:92). In order to reinstall order, the rituals have
to be reenacted or new rituals invented. Many times the reenactment of
ritual is automatic, as in the showering example above. Stress and confusion move individuals and groups toward rituals designed to stop or start,
avoid or attract, move forward or go back. For ritual to work, it has to be
completed, with the completion a signal of, for example, cure.

Illness, however, is a metaphor representing the individual within a
larger sphere of existence (see Helman 1994:239–245); this is not just a
small-scale society issue. Since we are social animals with illness as a metaphor of social functioning, healing is not just something that is signaled
by the body. In order for healing to be fully realized, in order for cure to
happen, there needs to be a *social* recognition. Without a social recogni-

tion, there is no reinstallation of social ritual(s). Without social recognition that cure has happened, there can be no cure. In a medical system that is economically based (Western biomedicine), there is no incentive to signal cure. For example—and you think about this—how long does it take to "cure" emotional problems? A week, a month, six months, a year, three years, how long? Psychologists and psychiatrists will tell you that they do not know. Well, I will tell you how long. The cure of emotional problems occurs when the therapist or shaman *says* you are cured (or when insurance runs out!). The message of cure comes through with the termination ritual, the ritual that reinstalls the old rituals or installs a new ritual process. The second half of this is the reintegration of the individual into his or her social unit or a new social unit. Without the termination ritual and the reintegration, there can be no cure in a social sense. This is why you hear of people being in therapy for two or three years; this is why people get sick and stay sick—they have a social "dis-ease" that is not attended to.

THE TERMINATION RITUAL

So how do you enact a termination ritual? What are the elements involved? Well, it is all symbolic. Remember, rituals are sets of symbols enmeshed to form rules. With respect to emotional/social issues, you tell the client, during the first session, how long he or she will be in counseling. When you are instructing husbands, wives, and parents in new communication procedures, your time frame is eight one-hour sessions. (When doing hypnosis, it might be one session.) You instruct the clients that by *that* time they will have the knowledge and skills to "cure" their system. Remember, you do not cure anything; individuals cure themselves and heal or cure the social circumstances that are dis-eased. Occasionally clients will ask me, "How do you know that we will heal our marriage in eight weeks?" I reply, "Well, you can heal the system in eight weeks, at $100.00 per hour, or you can heal the system in twenty-six weeks at $100.00 per hour, or you can heal the system in fifty-two weeks, at $100.00 per hour. Take your choice." When do you think the system will be healed? Right, in eight weeks. I also tell my clients that the longer they stay in counseling, the sicker their system will get. Clients have to be motivated!

At the end of eight weeks, you need a ritual that marks the end of therapy, a ritual that indicates that healing has happened. Now, is anything 100 percent healed? No, life is an ongoing adventure. I do not know what 100 percent healing would be. Do not concern yourself with 100 percent. If individuals alter the way they communicate with the world even 10 percent of the time, that will change their lives. There are numerous rituals you can enact; you are limited only by your creativity. There is an import store near where I live that sells nice little bottles with corks in them. At the end of eight weeks I often present a couple (or individual) with a bottle, and have them write their "illness" or "dis-ease" on a piece of paper. They might write "anger," "lack of patience," "being too nega-tive," "constipation," their HRMs, "drug abuse," whatever. I instruct them to put it in the bottle and "put a cork in it" (a polite metaphor telling the individual(s) to grow up).

Next, I suggest that they bury the bottle in the backyard or even put it in the cupboard at home, "just in case you decide you want your problems back." Individuals and couples find some very creative ways of completing the termination ritual. One man said that he was going to take his bottle with him on his next scuba diving trip.

For other clients the use of a bottle might seem rather strange. A ritual they can perform is the removal of a possession from their home that reminds them of a stressed or traumatic time in their life. This could be a piece of clothing, silverware, whatever. One woman decided to get rid of her pots and pans and buy a new set.

After I told one client that conflict was useful because it opens the door to change, he wrote his first name, followed by "conflict," "Fred's con-flict," on a $20 bill and put it in the collection basket at church, stating, "Into every life should come a little conflict." The rituals you suggest (or that the clients suggest) are limited only by your (or their) imagination.

SOCIAL REINTEGRATION

Ideally it would be nice, at the end of therapy, to have one's friends and relatives show up for a party/ritual celebrating the client's return to health. Illness has been stigmatized in this society, and the reasons are economic. People who are ill are not productive; therefore illness is bad. The development of nondrowsy antihistamine/cold medications that re-move many of the cold symptoms was a godsend to business; they keep people working even when the body is saying "rest." It is interesting that colds and flu have a social rhythm to them. Colds and flu seem to be more of a social phenomenon than a clear example of the germ theory of dis-ease. Colds and flu hit when we find ourselves inside and away from direct sunlight (see "Light Therapy" in Chapter 6). Colds and flu hit during the most physically and emotionally stressful time of the year, during the hol-iday season (social rituals). I have often wondered if cold and flu viruses are our synergistic friends, actually helping us to remove toxins from our bodies; instead of appreciating that, we take medications to suppress the symptoms. Now, where do those toxins go? They stay in the body, and the cold or flu lasts longer.

Getting back to social reintegration, because the ideal of friends and relatives showing up to recognize your health is not practical in most cases, we can return to symbols that represent social reintegration. Social reintegration means being with others, hopefully others with whom we are friends or are close to in some way. But that is not always possible and, from my experience, it is not always necessary. Food is used in all cultures in a symbolic, integrating manner. We speak of "breaking bread" together as a gesture of friendship or peace. On occasion, I have made arrangements for couples to dine out on the evening after their last session and for them to pay special attention to the behaviors of the others surrounding them. I also have made arrangements, when appropriate, to have family members meet them at the restaurant.

I have, on occasion, had my clients take food to the local women's center (usually loaves of bread) or simply give a loaf of bread to one or two of the city's many homeless (remember what I said about food sharing and home base?). It is important for your clients to understand social reintegration and get them involved in the ritual process. What is most interesting is that individuals and couples, at some level of awareness, realize the symbolic significance and will invent some ritual reintegration process. For others, I simply tell the following story, which represents social unity.

Once upon a time, there was a King, not your ordinary king who just sat and gave orders, but a thoughtful king who did much for his people—gifts at holidays and other special occasions—and especially when they were in need. Since he was unable to find a suitable queen, he indeed did have more time for his subjects. Of course, there were always a few discontents who made fun of him, but less so since he gained in age and wisdom.

Each year of his long reign, he would always plan to learn something new, something about the heavens and earth, and the people who surrounded his kingdom. When new things would come to his attention—stories and ideas from foreigners or lands far away, he would store them in his castle.

The King had a desire, you might say, an overwhelming compulsion or commitment to add a level, another story, to his castle each year. This was the one thing he decided to do for himself in hope of eventually having a queen by his side. So year after year he would add level after level to his castle. And because the King always enjoyed new and different things, he chose to move his personal living quarters to the new level. As time went on, his castle grew and grew to great heights, and each year he would find himself living higher and higher, with each story giving him a new perspective of the countryside. But with each passing year it became more and more difficult and it took longer and longer to climb up and down the lengthy staircase. Thus, it took more and more effort to be with or pay attention to his people. He even resorted to messengers, but alas, they were getting worn out as well. All the fair maidens who were brought before him were so exhausted from the climb that they shied away, making excuses of one sort or another.

As you can imagine, with each year's new level, the castle at last nestled in the clouds high above the ground. When he looked out of his immense windows, all he could see was the mist. Eventually, it was such a task to descend and ascend the staircase that he ceased to be with his people; he was becoming a mystery.

Time went on and the King became very lonely in his magnificent castle, which could be seen from miles away. Each day, as he looked into the mist high above the ground, his heart would sink a little lower. Travelers, new to the kingdom, would marvel at this structure sticking into the clouds, and the question was asked, "Who lives there?" Many of the younger folks answered, "We don't exactly know. The King used to reside there but no one has seen him for years. And from what we hear, he was a kindly King, but as you can see, his kingdom has fallen to ruin."

One day when the King was observing the mist, a Raven chanced to land on his balcony. As you can imagine this surprised the King, especially when the Raven began to speak to him.

"Is this a raven's nest, and are you a special kind of raven?"

"No," answered the King. "This is my castle and this is where I live."

"Well, are there any more of you around up here?"

"No," answered the King. "I am here all alone."

"Well, then, you probably wouldn't mind if I came in and looked around."

The King, not having company for so long, was glad to show the bird around the large living quarters, his magnificent fireplace, the beautiful chandeliers, the warmth of the carpets, and all the beautiful things.

"And what is on the other levels of your magnificent nest . . . I mean castle?"

"Oh, more of the same, more of the same," sighed the King.

"Yes, indeed, you have a wonderfully comfortable home," praised the Raven. The Raven had a sense of humor and amused the King so much that the King asked, "Are there others like you that fly so high?" And, of course, the Raven replied, "Oh, yes, I have lots and lots of friends and relatives."

Then the Raven spoke seriously to the King. "I will grant you three wishes if you allow me to make your castle my home. It seems that we can get along just fine. You have plenty of space, and it is very comfortable here."

Well, the King was quite curious about wishes and the possible powers of this bird, and out of curiosity, he agreed. "Now," the Raven warned, "once you make a wish, so it will be: I can't take back a wish."

The King sat and thought, and finally spoke, "Well, Mr. Raven, I am lonely and wish to be closer to my subjects." In a flash, ravens of all ages and sizes swooped in through the balcony window. In shock the King said, "Who are all these birds?"

"They are my friends and relatives and they have come to live here too. You didn't think that I was going to live alone did you?"

"Well, where am I going to live? There isn't enough room here for all of us."

"You can take up residence on the floor beneath, so that you can be closer to your subjects."

Well, a deal is a deal. So the King moved down to the next floor, and as the Raven promised, he was closer to his subjects. But the King realized that he had better be more specific with the two remaining wishes.

"Now, Mr. Raven, I won't be tricked: I want to be really close to my subjects, not just one story." All of a sudden birds came from miles and miles away and occupied every room in the castle except for the ground floor. "You have tricked me Mr. Raven, and have stolen my castle that took me so many years to build."

"You did want to be near your people, didn't you? That *is* where you should be."

The King had to agree. So he moved his quarters to the main floor, where the light, the countryside, and his beautiful subjects could be seen again. "Well, Mr. Raven, I have one last wish and that is to have a queen by my side."

"Your majesty, all you need do is walk out your door and take your pick. You can do that on your own and I will save your last wish for a later date. Now that you have come down out of the clouds, and out of the mist, I am sure that you can see all that is necessary to realize your most wonderful dreams. But take your time, and make the right choice."

So the King strolled from his castle for the first time in many years, and his subjects, not knowing who he was thought that he was a stranger in the land. As he walked around, looked, and listened, he took note of all that needed to be done. The King was embarrassed that his kingdom was in such disrepair, but he realized what he had to do and was quite eager to get started. He also noticed how pretty the young maidens were and he saw them differently now that he had come down from the clouds. He remembered the Raven's advice, to make the right choice. When his neighbors realized who he was, they gathered around him remembering his kindness from years past. The local priest came before him and asked, "Why have you come down from your castle to renew your life with your people?" To this the King replied, "My castle is for the birds."

Chapter 8

Conclusion

There is a great deal in the preceding pages for the reader to think about; this has been a journey for the reader. Be critical, think things through, and spend some time observing and listening to the communication patterns of others. You will be able to identify HRMs, keeping in mind that my model is a metaphor, my thinking about human relationship, stress, and illness from an anthropological perspective.

HRMs are activated by negative bits, a form of information intrusion. Information intrusion can come in many forms—viruses, bullets, and so on—and not all intrusive information results in negative emotional/physical stress (see Rush 1996:110–116 for other types of informational categories involved in illness). One of the first phases of therapy is the isolation and reinterpretation of HRMs; this is the case in either individual or family counseling, or when examining *any* human system (business, government, anthropology department, etc.).

Human systems are governed by rules, many of which are implied. Implied rules are a major factor in the self-assembly of human systems. When systems are prone to rapid change, as is the case in North American society, implied rules cease to fit the new circumstances; stress increases as the system attempts to adapt. By making certain types of rules explicit (division of labor and relationship rules), the system, and the personnel within, can move toward stress reduction. Cast within the division of labor are the roles we play and the masks we wear. The more specifically defined the roles and rules, the more rigid and conservative the culture, and adaptation to new and unique social circumstances is accomplished only within a field of great stress. Contrariwise, low role specificity creates a great deal of confusion and/or miscommunication within, pushing the system toward more clearly defined roles. When there is low role specificity, the rules of relating (relationship rules) have to be more clearly defined (it all has to do with rules at both the physical and the social levels).

An individual's power is based *not* on physical strength, guns, or knives, but on his or her ability to communicate and solve problems with others. This means that an individual needs a variety of communication tools along with a basic understanding of what is happening when people are talking and listening. The clinical anthropologist needs to understand the concept of compressed data, Miller's Number, and emotional responsibility, as well as to be responsible for the messages he or she sends and for the interpretation of incoming data.

During the therapeutic process, the clinical anthropologist is essentially an educator. He or she has to know how to listen and to utilize the power of words, sentences, and phrases, powerful incantations for delivering knowledge to others.

There are numerous therapies available to the health practitioner: hypnosis, light therapy, therapeutic touch, and so on. There are also situations wherein special tools or information will be required. The main ingredient, however, is the symbol, the word, the most powerful invention of our kind. Reviewing one's journey is designed to change the way one sees, hears, and interprets these experiences and reduce both individual and group stress.

Finally, health is a metaphor for many things, including the status of a society, for example, our nation or society. Healing, then, is a metaphor for moving the person's status (different, idiosyncratic, crazy, diseased, bewitched, malnourished, etc.) from a position of ill or incomplete to that of whole and synchronized with others. Healing is a metaphor for reuniting the individual, regardless of the label of difference, with his or her group or other analogous community. Any medical system that does not move toward reintegration is not practicing health, but illness maintenance. Any medical system that keeps people alive but sick is parasitic. We could use a uniting metaphor in this country, but such a metaphor is far away and in conflict with our economic-based systems.

Appendix A

Communication Rules

1. Social rules are followable, prescriptive, and contextual, pertain to human behavior, and are analogues to genetic coding.

2. All human interactions proceed according to rules—rules are explicit and implicit.

3. All systems change through time by altering the division of labor and relationship rules.

4. Understanding the rules of the system allows for the possibility of negotiation and increased interpersonal and group effectiveness; such knowledge can also be used in the reverse.

5. As individuals learn the rules, they also learn who they are in the group. Self-worth, self-esteem, and group worth are by-products of learning the rules and who you are in the group.

6. All humans develop a "cluster" of high-risk messages as they learn who they are in the group. High-risk messages, then, are a normal part of maturation; they are the person's pain, and pain motivates.

7. When high-risk messages are "tapped into" through negative bits, the individual's stress increases and his/her communication potential decreases.

8. As we make contact with others through our emotions, the safest interpretation of any message is the perceived emotion in the message. Different cultures have different rules for displaying emotions; individuals within a culture likewise have their own personalized rules for emotional expression.

9. All human communication, verbal and nonverbal, is subject to interpretation. It represents "compressed data" and the special reality of the sender. The receiver uses his/her reality to "unzip" or "uncompress" the data. Therefore, there is no way of positively knowing how a person will take a message, only probabilities. Feedback, and paying attention to that feedback, represents 50 percent of the communication process.

10. All communication is goal-oriented, consciously and unconsciously.

11. All communication represents an action/reaction potential. Information is stored in the mind in generalities, which determine action and reaction from past situations. Actions and reactions are not always appropriate for solving current problems in social living.

12. There is no way that a person can NOT communicate when in the presence of another.

13. People and systems tend to go toward stress reduction (entropy). Understanding the HRMs of any system places one on a path to manipulate that system in a stress-reducing *or* stress-enhancing manner.

14. Most humans prefer messages of agreement over messages of disagreement.

15. Rules of politeness take precedence over rules of conversation. In short, and in most situations, if you cannot say anything nice, be polite.

16. Ritual communication (micro-ritual) represents one of the first sets of rules one learns.

17. Ritual communication allows for an encounter to begin, continue, and end.

18. Those who do not follow rituals are considered outsiders, ignorant, or stupid, and generally are placed in a negative light.

19. Another set of rules, learned alongside micro-rules of ritual interaction, is the relationship rules, that is, naming who is who. Over time the child connects behaviors and expectations to these names.

20. If engaged in a casual conversation, one should not question the meaning of every utterance.

21. Going off a topic without proper lead-in implies disinterest, impoliteness, special and extenuating circumstances, or a disturbed communication pattern.

22. In most cases, there is an obligation on the receiver of a question to answer that question.

23. People act on what they believe, not according to whether the belief is correct.

24. People act on what they believe to be their best choice at the time.

25. As we generalize, delete, and distort information, ultimate meaning or "real" understanding is almost impossible to achieve. Instead, we generate conflict and creativity.

26. Our receptor preferences determine, to a large extent, what messages we will process and/or internalize.

27. Individuals who feel accepted within a group are less likely to defect from that group. Conversely, social defection increases as the individual feels less and less a part of the group; this is accomplished through activation of the individual's HRMs.

28. The larger the system, the greater the difficulty in understanding how it "works." Further, it is difficult, in large systems, to predict what effect any change will have on the total system.

Appendix B

Maps

Map 1
Nuaulu, South-Central Seram

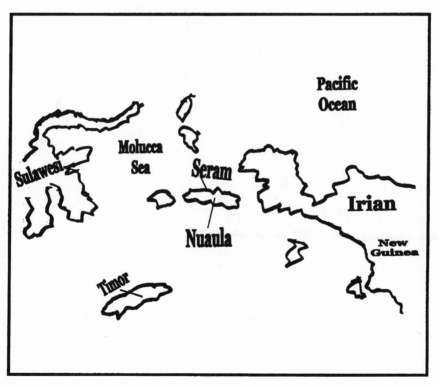

Map 2
Approximate Area of the Navaho Territory, 1980s

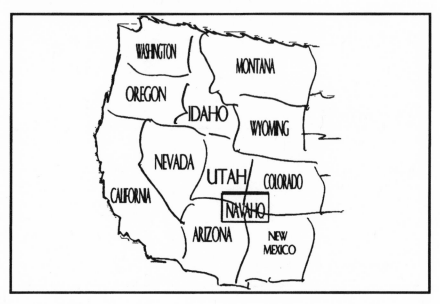

Map 3
St. Lawrence Island

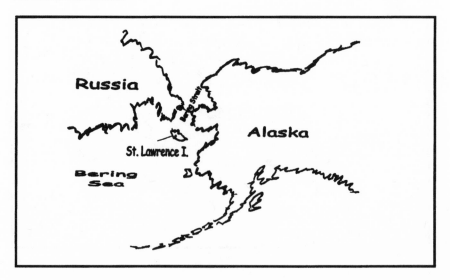

Appendix C

Process in Conflict Mediation

Conflict mediation has three interaction stages.

The first step is to bring together those involved in the conflict. During this phase, it is important to instill the idea that conflict leads to mediation. (The police and television/movie model is that conflict leads to more conflict.) The environment established for conflict resolution has to be perceived as safe and one in which the mediator will not take sides. How you establish a territory that enhances communication is important; as stress goes up, personal space increases between those in conflict, for example.

The mediator must clearly state and stick to his or her role. That role is maintaining a safe environment, collecting data, managing that data, and aiding in the negotiation process.

Once those in conflict are brought together, mediation begins by stating the rules.

1. Each person will have the opportunity to tell his or her story uninterrupted— both will be listened to in an attentive, nonjudgmental manner by the mediator.
2. There will be no name-calling, sarcasm, threats, warnings, orders, or physical violence.

MAKE SURE THAT YOU OBTAIN VERBAL AGREEMENT THAT BOTH UNDERSTAND THE RULES.

3. You can ask who would like to talk first, or you can flip a coin.

A prime task of the mediator is to not only collect data, in order to build understanding about the nature of the problem, but also to be a model for the participants in how to listen, collect data, and negotiate. Mediation should always include an implied educational element.

Conflict cannot be settled unless the problems are discussed and effectively listened to. Listening, then, serves at least four purposes and initiates the process of negotiation.

1. To collect information
2. To reduce stress and build trust (in the process, the mediator, and, hopefully, one another) as each person is able to express his or her opinion in a safe atmosphere
3. To model the behaviors of listening (and negotiating)
4. To negotiate the issues

Negotiation. There are numerous approaches to "negotiation," including forcing solutions on people, avoidance of the problem, and role-playing (often designed to get people to step in the shoes of others), and so on. These are relatively ineffective for various reasons. Forcing solutions causes a win-lose or lose-lose situation (this often occurs when Family Court Services gets involved in child custody cases). Avoidance can lead to extremely dangerous situations wherein resentful people take very drastic actions. Role-playing can be turned around on you; instead of stepping into someone's shoes, the role-player sabotages or shows how "unreasonable" the other players are.

One of the most effective methods of negotiation is defining the problem in terms of needs, *not wants* (see Rush 1976). In a society that worships individualism and free choice each person has a solution wrapped around his or her *wants*; this leads to a win-lose situation that is essentially a no-win position. However, when you negotiate in terms of needs, it becomes obvious in everyday situations that each person has the same needs relative to a problem. Once this is recognized, the solutions usually fit the needs. Most of the needs encountered with the high school students discussed in Chapter 4 involved being respected by others—not necessarily wanting to show respect or be respectful, but wanting respect.

Also keep in mind that most of the conflict in this culture centers on rejection, messages of nonacceptance from others, and greed (fights over money and property). Once the participants agree that they do not like being disrespected, it is usually easy to negotiate another style of communicating. Avoid blame.

Fights over child custody are a form of emotional abuse (rejection) or the punishment of one parent by the other. Such emotional violence is eagerly engaged in by lawyers, experts (psychologists, etc.), and the courts. (In my opinion many lawyers, psychologists, Family Court Service counselors, and judges/courts of this land should go on trial for child abuse.)

All child custody issues should be considered issues of mediation. As mentioned earlier, most child custody cases simply represent the couple's desire to keep fighting to resolve problems that could not be resolved in the family, problems that are taken to another arena.

Appendix D

Rush Dangerous Behavior Quotient— RUSHDBQ-Juvenile*

Instructions for Use: The following are factors currently used when determining dangerousness in juveniles. After each place a "1" for yes and a "0" for no. If information is unavailable, the outcome for that line is 0. The number at the right is an assigned variable or relative weight of a particular factor. These variables do not stay constant, and reflect information available as of January 1995. Consult author for updated information. Add all the variables that are preceded by a 1; disregard the variables associated with a 0. If you have checked "Unknown," this indicates data to be collected. Tabulate the total score by adding all the numbers in the "score" column; enter on line A at the end of this Appendix. Next, add all "yes" variables with asterisk and enter on line B. See instructions (at the end of this Appendix) for assessing the dangerous potential quotient.

Factor:	Yes No Unknown	Variable	Score
1) Age:			
7-9		*10	
10-13		9	
14-17		8	
2) Gender:			
Male		7	
Female		2	

3) Behavior in Educational Environment:

Gets Along with Others _____ 3_____

Quiet or Withdrawn_____ 4_____

Poor Grades_____ 5_____

Truant _____ 6_____

Negative Peer Group_____7_____

4) Hospitalization/Medical Conditions:

Head Injury_____ 5_____

Coma Lasting More

Than 30 Minutes_____ 7_____

Major Surgery_____ 6_____

Metabolic Problems

(Diabetes, etc)_____7_____

Exposure to Heavy

Metals/Other Chemicals

(e.g.,MethylEthylKeytone)_____ 9_____

5) Hospitalization/Therapy for Psychological Problems:

Depression_____ 4_____

Manic-Depression_____ 5_____

Schizophrenia_____ 7_____

Paranoid Delusions_____*9_____

6) **Belief Systems (Ask Questions of interviewee):**

"Do People Make

You Angry?"_____ *10_____

Frequent Denial

of Responsibility

for Behavior_____ *9_____

Women Unequal to Men_____8_____

Hate Men/Women_____8_____

Doesn't Need Others_____7_____

Unlikable_____6_____

Often Frustrated_____7_____

Often Angry_____7_____

Often Depressed_____5_____

Frequent Thoughts

of Revenge_____ *9_____

Extroverted_____3_____

Introverted_____6_____

7) **Suicidal Ideation:**

Never_____5_____

Occasionally_____2_____

Often_____8_____

Has Attempted

Suicide:

Once_____ 7_____

Twice or More_____ *10_____

8) Impulsivity:

Has to Have

Things Now_____ *10_____

Usually Can

Wait for Things_____ 2_____

Has to Wait

for Everything_____ 5_____

9) Tattoos/Piercing:

On Face or Neck_____ *9_____

On Hands_____ 7_____

On Buttocks/Groin_____ 3_____

Piercing _____ 2_____

10) Wounds from Violent Encounters:

Face_____ 8_____

Arms_____ 6_____

Abdomen/Back_____ 5_____

Openly Talks

About Wounds_____ 9_____

11) Group Membership

Gang _____ *10 _____

Want-To-Be _____ 5 _____

Occult _____ 4 _____

12) Music Preference:

Rap_____ 7 _____

Heavy Metal_____ 7 _____

Pop_____ 3 _____

Classical_____ 1 _____

13) Previous Dangerous Behavior:

a) Assault

Single Incident_____ 5 _____

Two/Three Incidents_____ 7 _____

Four or More_____ *10 _____

Nature of Injuries on First and Most Recent Occurrence:

1) Fatal_____ *10 _____

2) Fatal_____ *10 _____

1) Injuries:

Hospitalization_____ 8 _____

2) Injuries:

Hospitalization_____ 8 _____

1) Minor Injuries_____ 5 _____

2) Minor Injuries_____ 5 _____

b) Use of Weapon:

    Use of Firearm_____ *10 _____

    Use of Other Weapon_____ 7 _____

    Time Between Current Event and One Prior:

    One Month or Less_____ *10 _____

    One to Six Months_____ 9 _____

    Seven Months to Year_____ 8 _____

    Single Incident_____ 5 _____

c) Burglary:

    Single Incident_____ 5 _____

    Two/Three Incidents_____ 7 _____

    Four or More_____ *10 _____

    Nature of Burglary(ies):

    Forced Entry_____ *9 _____

    Knew Victim_____ 9 _____

    Didn't Know Victim_____ 8 _____

    Use of Weapon_____ *10 _____

    Violence to Victim_____ *10 _____

Time Between Current Event and One Prior:

    One Month or Less_____ *10 _____

    One to Six Months_____ 9 _____

    Seven Months to Year_____ 8 _____

Single Incident_____ 5_____

d) Rape:

Single Incident_____ *8_____

Two/Three Incidents_____ *9_____

Four or More_____ *10_____

Associated with

Drug/Alcohol Use_____ 7_____

Associated with

Other Criminal Acts_____ *10_____

Use of Weapon_____ *10_____

Physical Injury

to Victim_____ *10_____

Time between current event and one prior:

One Month or Less_____ *10_____

One to Six Months_____ 9_____

Seven Months to Year_____ 8_____

Single Incident_____ 5_____

e) Other Dangerous Behavior (DUI, Drug Sales, etc.)

Single Incident_____ 5_____

Two/Three Incidents_____ *10_____

Nature of Behavior:

Weapons Involved_____ 8_____

Violence to Victims_____ *10_____

Time Between Current Event and One Prior:

    One Month or Less_____ *10 _____

    One to Six Months _____ 9 _____

    Seven Months to Year_____8 _____

    Single Incident _____ 5 _____

14) Availability of Weapons:

    None_____ 2 _____

    Ownership_____ 7 _____

    Readily Available_____ 9 _____

15) Jail Time (Multiply Jail Terms by Variable, e.g., 3 x 9):

    Number of Jail Terms_____ 9 _____

    Total time served:

    4-24 Hrs._____ 4 _____

    48 Hrs.-1 Month_____ 6 _____

    2-6 Months_____ 8 _____

    7-12 Months_____ 9 _____

    13-36 Months+_____ *10 _____

16) Childhood Issues:

    Cruelty to Animals_____ 7 _____

    Fire-setting_____ 8 _____

    Enuresis_____ 3 _____

17) Dysfunctional/Abusive Family of Origin:

    Emotional Abuse_____ 6 _____

Physical Abuse_____ 7_____

Sexual Abuse_____ *9_____

Parents Divorced_____ 5_____

Recent Death of Abusive

Family Member_____6_____

Age at Time of Divorce:

0-6_____ 2_____

7-10_____ 4_____

11-16_____ 9_____

17-21_____ 6_____

Parents Remarried_____ 3_____

Single Parent Family_____ 5_____

Indifferent Father_____ 6_____

Rapid Turnover of

Mother's Live-in

Boyfriends_____ 5_____

Children Set

the Rules_____ 4_____

Parent(s) on Welfare_____ 4_____

Parent(s) Using or

Abusing Alcohol/Drugs_____ 7_____

18) Abuse of Drugs:

Alcohol_____ *9_____

Cocaine/Amphetamines_____ *9_____

Designer Drugs_____ 8_____

Heroin_____ 6_____

Marijuana_____ 3_____

LSD_____ 3_____

Polydrug Use_____ *9_____

19) Use of Prescribed Psychotropic Medications:

Abuse_____ 8_____

Discontinuous_____ 5_____

Appropriate_____ 2_____

20) Employment:

Held Job for at

Least Six Months_____ 2_____

Frequent Job Changes_____ 8_____

21) Base Rates (Rate of Crime in Population/Group to Which Individual Would Return):

High_____ *10_____

Normal_____ 6_____

Low_____ 2_____

No Data_____ 1_____

22) Availability of Victims:

Unlimited_____ 5_____

Situational_____ 9_____

23) Probable Near-Future Stressors:

Pending Court Case_____ 9_____

Financial Problems_____ 8_____

Breakup of Important

Relationship_____ 9_____

Group Pressure

to Engage in

Unlawful acts_____ *10_____

24) Social Resources (*complete a, b, or c*):

a) Halfway House_____ 2_____

Counseling_____ 2_____

Strong Family

Structure_____ 2_____

Other_____ 2_____

b) All or Combination

of Above_____ 1_____

c) None or Limited_____ *8_____

25) Ability to Realistically monitor Individual's Behavior:

None_____ *10_____

Moderate_____ 6_____

Good_____ 3_____

Excellent_____ 2_____

Day-to-Day Ability_____ 1_____

Once a Week_____3_____

Bimonthly_____ 5_____

Monthly_____7_____

26) Time Since Major Natural or Social Disaster (Earthquake, Flood, Bombing, Mass

Murder etc.):

Within 6 Months_____5_____

7 Months to Year_____4_____

13 Months to 2 Years_____3_____

Over 2 Years_____2_____

27) Time Since Major International/Social Conflict (e.g., War):

Within 6 Months_____5_____

7 Months to Year_____4_____

13 Months to 2 Years_____3_____

25 Months to 3 Years_____2_____

3 Years or More_____1_____

29) Current Economic Conditions of Society:

Economic Growth_____2_____

Stable_____3_____

Recession_____ 6_____

TOTALS: Line A _____ Line B (Asterisk)_____

Interpretation Line A: Interpretation Line B:

<u>38 - 250</u> = Low Probability   <u>0 -70</u>   = Low Probability

<u>251 - 549</u> = Moderate   <u>71 - 150</u> = Moderate

<u>550 - 727</u> ⁺ = High Probability   <u>151 - 348</u> = High Probability

The more closely the scores cross-correlate, the better the predictive ability, e.g., if total from

Line A is 106 and total from Line B is 35, then that is a good cross-correlation.

Bibliography

Adler, A. 1964. *Superiority and Social Interest*. Ed. H. Ansbacher and R. Ansbacher. Evanston, IL: Northwestern University Press.

Alcena, V. 1994. *The African American Health Book*. New York: Carol Publishing.

American Psychiatric Association. 1994. *Diagnostic and Statistical Manual of Mental Disorders (DSM-IV)*. Washington, DC: American Psychiatric Association.

Andreas, S., and Andreas, C. 1987. *Change Your Mind, and Keep the Change*. Moab, UT: Real People Press.

Bandler, R., and Grinder, J. 1975a. *Patterns of the Hypnotic Techniques of Milton H. Erickson, M. D.* Cupertino, CA: Meta Publications.

———. 1975b. *The Structure of Magic*. Palo Alto, CA: Science and Behavior Books.

Bates, D. 1996. *Cultural Anthropology*. Boston: Allyn and Bacon.

Bateson, G., Jackson, D., Haley, J., and Weakland, J. 1972. "Toward a Theory of Schizophrenia." In *Steps to an Ecology of Mind*. Ed. G. Bateson, 201–227. New York: Ballantine.

Bayer, R. 1987. *Homosexuality and American Psychiatry: The Politics of Diagnosis*. Princeton, NJ: Princeton University Press.

Benson, S. 1981. *Ambiguous Ethnicity*. London: Cambridge University Press.

Berne, E. 1961. *Transactional Analysis in Psychotherapy*. New York: Grove Press.

———. 1964. *Games People Play*. New York: Grove Press.

Bettelheim, B. 1962. *Symbolic Wounds: Puberty Rites and the Envious Male*. New York: Collier Books.

Bickerton, D. 1990. *Language and Species*. Chicago: University of Chicago Press.

Bieber, I. 1967. "Sexual Deviation. II: Homosexuality." In *Comprehensive Textbook of Psychiatry*. Ed. A. Freedman and H. Kaplan, 963–976. Baltimore: Williams & Wilkins.

Birdwhistle, R. 1970. *Kinesis and Context*. Philadelphia: University of Pennsylvania Press.

Blumberg, J. 1997. "Public Health Implications of Preventive Nutrition." In *Preventive Nutrition: The Comprehensive Guide for Health Professionals*. Ed. A. Bendich and R. Deckelbaum, 1–15. Totowa, NJ: Humana Press.

Bly, R. 1990. *Iron John: A Book About Men*. Reading, MA: Addison-Wesley.

Bonner, J. 1980. *The Evolution of Culture in Animals*. Princeton, NJ: Princeton University Press.

Bower, B. 1996. "New Pitch for Placebo Power." *Science News* 150, no. 8:123.

———. 1997. "Uncovering Traits of Effective Therapists." *Science News* 151, no. 2:21.

Brennan, B. 1987. *Hands of Light: A Guide to Healing Through the Human Energy Field*. New York: Bantam Books.

Brown, D. 1991. *Human Universals*. Philadelphia: Temple University Press.

Buckley, T., and Gottlieb, A., eds. 1988. *Blood Magic: The Anthropology of Menstruation*. Berkeley: University of California Press.

Byrne, D., Griffitt, W., and Stefaniak, B. 1971. "The Ubiquitous Relationship: Attitude Similarity and Attraction—a Cross-Cultural Study." *Human Relations* 24:201–207.

Campbell, Joseph. 1988. *The Power of Myth*. New York: Doubleday.

———. 1989. *The World of Joseph Campbell: Transformation of Myth Through Time*. Vol. 3. St. Paul, MN: HighBridge Productions. (Audiotapes).

———. 1990. *The Transformation of Myth Through Time*. New York: Harper & Row.

Chessick, R. 1992. *The Technique & Practice of Listening in Intensive Psychotherapy*. Northvale, NJ: Jason Aronson.

Chomsky, N. 1957. *Syntactic Structures*. The Hague: Mouton.

———. 1968. *Language and Mind*. New York: Harcourt, Brace and World.

Chrousos, G., and Gold, P. 1992. "The Concept of Stress and Stress System Disorders: Overview of Physical and Behavioral Homeostasis." *Journal of the American Medical Association* 267, no. 9 (March 4): 1244–1252.

Chung, D. 1992. "Asian Cultural Commonalties: A Comparison with Mainstream American Culture." In *Social Work Practice with Asian Americans*. Ed. S. Furuto. Newbury Park, CA: Sage.

Clark, M. 1970. *Health in the Mexican American Culture*. Berkeley: University of California Press.

Colby, B. 1958. "Behavioral Redundancy." *Behavioral Science* 3:317–322.

Corcoran, K., and Fischer, J. 1987. *Measures for Clinical Practice: A Sourcebook*. New York: Free Press.

Das, A. 1987. "Indigenous Models of Therapy in Traditional Asian Societies." *Journal of Multi-cultural Counseling and Development* (January):25–37.

Dilts, R., Grinder, J., Bandler, R., Bandler, L., and Delozier, J. 1980. *Neuro-Linguistic Programming*. Vol. 1, *The Study of the Structure of Subjective Experience*. Cupertino, CA: Meta Publications.

Dobkin de Rios, M. 1990. *Hallucinogens: Cross-Cultural Perspectives*. Bridport, UK: Prism Press.

Dorpat, T. 1996. *Gaslighting, the Double Whammy, Interrogation, and Other Methods of Covert Control in Psychotherapy & Analysis*. Northvale, NJ: Jason Aronson.

Douglas, M. 1991a. "A Distinctive Anthropological Perspective." In *Constructive*

Drinking: Perspectives on Drink from Anthropology. Ed. M. Douglas, 3–15. New York: Cambridge University Press.

———, ed. 1991b. *Constructive Drinking: Perspectives on Drink from Anthropology.* New York: Cambridge University Press.

Dunnigan, T. 1982. "Segmentary Kinship in an Urban Society: The Hmong of St. Paul-Minneapolis." *Anthropological Quarterly* 55, no. 3:126–134.

Eliade, M. 1972. *Shamanism: Archaic Techniques of Ecstasy.* Princeton, NJ: Princeton University Press.

Ellen, R., 1993. "Anger, Anxiety, and Sorcery: An Analysis of Some Nuaulu Case Material from Seram, Eastern Indonesia." In *Understanding Witchcraft and Sorcery in Southeast Asia.* Ed. C. Watson and R. Ellen, 81–97. Honolulu: University of Hawaii Press.

Epstein, S. 1959. "A Sociological Analysis of Witch Beliefs in a Mysore Village." *The Eastern Anthropologist* 12:234–251.

Erickson, M. 1980. *The Collected Papers of Milton H. Erickson on Hypnosis.* Ed. E. Rossi. 4 vols. New York: Irvington.

Erickson, M., and Rossi, E. 1979. *Hypnotherapy: An Exploratory Casebook.* New York: Irvington.

Estes, C. 1992. *Women Who Run with the Wolves: Myths and Stories of the Wild Woman Archetype.* New York: Ballantine Books.

Evans-Pritchard, E. 1937. *Witchcraft, Oracles, and Magic Among the Azande.* Oxford: Oxford University Press.

———. 1940. *The Nuer: A Description of the Modes of Livelihood and Political Institutions of a Nilotic People.* Oxford: Oxford University Press.

Fabrega, H. 1997. *Evolution of Sickness and Healing.* Berkeley: University of California Press.

Fagan, B. 1995. *People of the Earth: An Introduction to World Prehistory.* New York: HarperCollins.

Faulkner, J. 1985. "Women in Interracial Relationships." In *Women Changing Therapy.* Ed. R. Robbins and B. Siegel. New York: Harrington Park Press.

Faulkner, J., and Kich, G. 1983. "Assessment and Engagement Stages in Therapy with the Interracial Family." *Family Therapy Collective* 6:78–90.

Fernandez, J., ed. 1991. *Metaphor: The Theory of Tropes in Anthropology.* Stanford, CA: Stanford University Press.

Fessler, D. 1996. "The Next Frontier: Anthropology and Evolutionary Psychology." *Anthropology Newsletter* 37, no. 9:7.

Fortune, R. 1932. *Sorcerers of Dobu.* New York: E. P. Dutton.

Foster, R., Moskowitz, M., and Javier, R., eds. 1996. *Reaching Across Boundaries of Culture and Class: Widening the Scope of Psychotherapy.* Northvale, NJ: Jason Aronson.

Fowles, D. 1992. "Schizophrenia: Diathesis-Stress Revisited." *Annual Review of Psychology* 43:303–326.

Freud, S. 1946 (orig. 1918). *Totem and Taboo.* New York: Vintage Press.

Gadpaille, W. 1989. "Homosexuality." In *Comprehensive Textbook of Psychiatry.* 5th ed. Ed. H. Kaplan and B. Sadock. Vol. 1, 1086–1096. Baltimore: Williams & Wilkins.

Gardner, H. 1983. *Frames of Mind.* New York: Basic Books.

Garrett, L. 1994. *The Coming Plague.* New York: Farrar, Straus, and Giroux.

204

Bibliography

Gediman, H., and Lieberman, J. 1996. *The Many Faces of Deceit: Omissions, Lies, and Disguise in Psychotherapy*. Northvale, NJ: Jason Aronson.
Gibbs, J. 1987. "Identity and Marginality: Issues in the Treatment of Biracial Adolescents." *American Journal of Orthopsychiatry* 52, no. 2: 265–278.
Gordon, D. 1978. *Therapeutic Metaphors: Helping Others Through the Looking Glass*. Cupertino, CA: Meta Publications.
Gordon, J., ed. 1994. *Managing Multiculturalism in Substance Abuse Services*. Thousand Oaks, CA: Sage.
Grinder, J., and Bandler, R. 1976. *The Structure of Magic II*. Palo Alto, CA: Science and Behavior Books.
Grinder, J., DeLozier, J., and Bandler, R. 1977. *Patterns of the Hypnotic Techniques of Milton H. Erickson, M.D.* Vol. 2. Cupertino, CA: Meta Publications.
Haley, J. 1973. *Uncommon Therapy: The Psychiatric Techniques of Milton H. Erickson*. New York: W. W. Norton.
———. 1985. *Conversations with Milton H. Erickson, M.D.* 3 vols. New York: Triangle Press.
———, ed. 1967. *Advanced Techniques of Hypnosis and Therapy: Selected Papers of Milton Erickson, M.D.* New York: Grune and Stratton.
Hall, E. 1959. *The Silent Language*. New York: Doubleday.
Hamilton, W., Axelrod, R., and Tanese, R. 1990. "Sexual Reproduction as an Adaptation to Resist Parasites: A Review." *Proceedings of the National Academy of Sciences* 87: 3566–3573.
Hammond, D., ed. 1990. *Handbook of Hypnotic Suggestions and Metaphors*. New York: W. W. Norton.
Hampden-Turner, C. 1981. *Maps of the Mind*. New York: Macmillan.
Harley, G. 1970. *Native African Medicine*. London: Frank Cass.
Harner, M. 1982. *The Way of the Shaman: A Guide to Power and Healing*. New York: Bantam Books.
———. 1984. *The Jivaro: People of the Sacred Waterfalls*. Berkeley: University of California Press.
Harris, M. 1989. *Our Kind*. New York: Harper Perennial.
Hart, D. 1978. "Disease Etiologies of Samaran Filipino Peasants." In *Culture and Curing: Anthropological Perspectives on Traditional Medical Beliefs and Practices*. Ed. P. Morley and R. Wallis, 57–98. Pittsburgh: University of Pittsburgh Press.
Harvey, P., and Gow, P., eds. 1994. *Sex and Violence: Issues in Representation and Experience*. New York: Routledge.
Havens, R., and Walters, C. 1989. *Hypnotherapy Scripts: A Neo-Ericksonian Approach to Persuasive Healing*. New York: Brunner/Mazel.
Heath, D. 1991. "A Decade of Development in the Anthropological Study of Alcohol Use: 1970–1980." In *Constructive Drinking: Perspectives on Drink from Anthropology*. Ed. M. Douglas, 16–69. New York: Cambridge University Press.
Helman, C. 1994. *Culture, Health and Illness*. Oxford: Butterworth-Heinemann.
Helms, J. 1986. "Expanding Racial Identity Theory to Cover the Counseling Process." *Journal of Counseling Psychology* 33: 62–64.

———. 1989. "Considering Some Methodological Issues in Racial Identity Counseling Research." *The Counseling Psychologist* 17, no. 2: 227–252.

Herman, E., and Chomsky, N. 1988. *Manufacturing Consent: The Political Economy of the Mass Media*. New York: Pantheon.

Hinde, R., and Groebel, J., eds. 1991. *Cooperation and Prosocial Behavior*. New York: Cambridge University Press.

Ho, M. 1992. *Minority Children and Adolescents in Therapy*. Newbury Park, CA: Sage.

———. 1993. *Family Therapy with Ethnic Minorities*. Newbury Park, CA: Sage.

Hsu, F. 1955. *Americans and Chinese*. London: Cresset Press.

Hughes, C. 1993. "Culture in Clinical Psychology." In *Culture, Ethnicity, and Mental Illness*. Ed. A. Gaw. Washington, DC: American Psychiatric Association Press.

Iwu, M. 1993. *Handbook of African Medicinal Plants*. Boca Raton, FL: CRC Press.

Jenkins, A. 1985. "Attending to Self-Activity in the Afro-American Client." *Psychotherapy* 22, no. 2: 335–341.

Jenkins, Y. 1985. "The Integration of Psychotherapy-Vocational Interventions: Relevance for Black Women." *Psychotherapy* 22, no. 2: 394–397.

Jones, A. 1985. "Psychological Functioning in Black Americans: A Conceptual Guide for Use in Psychotherapy." *Psychotherapy* 22, no. 2: 363–369.

Jones, D., ed. 1994. *African American Males: A Critical Link in the African American Family*. New Brunswick, NJ: Transaction.

Kiev, A., ed. 1964. *Magic, Faith, and Healing*. New York: Free Press.

Kim, S. 1985. "Family Therapy for Asian Americans: A Strategic Structural Framework." *Psychotherapy* 22, no. 2: 342–348.

Kim, U., and Berry, J., eds. 1993. *Indigenous Psychologies: Research and Experience in Cultural Context*. Newbury Park, CA: Sage.

Kinzie, J., Fredrickson, R., Ben, R., Fleck, J., and Karls, W. 1984. "Posttraumatic Stress Disorder Among Survivors of Cambodian Concentration Camps." *American Journal of Psychiatry* 141, no. 5: 645–650.

Kleinman, A., and Good, B., eds. 1985. *Culture and Depression: Studies in the Anthropology and Cross-Cultural Psychiatry of Affect and Disorder*. Berkeley: University of California Press.

Kline, P. 1981. *Fact and Fantasy in Freudian Theory*. New York: Methuen.

Knight, C. 1991. *Blood Relations: Menstruation and the Origins of Culture*. New Haven: Yale University Press.

Kochman, T. 1983. *Black and White Styles in Conflict*. Chicago: University of Chicago Press.

Krieger, D. 1979. *The Therapeutic Touch*. Englewood Cliffs, NJ: Prentice-Hall.

Kübler-Ross, E. 1969. *On Death and Dying*. New York: Macmillan.

———. 1974. *Questions and Answers on Death and Dying*. New York: Macmillan.

———. 1975. *Death: The Final Stage of Growth*. Englewood Cliffs, NJ: Prentice-Hall.

Kuhn, T. 1967. *The Structure of Scientific Revolutions*. Chicago: University of Chicago Press.

Labov, T. 1990. "Ideological Themes in Reports of Interracial Conflict." In *Conflict Talk: Sociolinguistic Investigations of Arguments in Conversations*. Ed. A. Grimshaw. Cambridge: Cambridge University Press.

Lakoff, G., and Johnson, M. 1980. *Metaphors We Live By*. Chicago: University of Chicago Press.

Lappe, M. 1994. *Evolutionary Medicine: Rethinking the Origins of Disease*. San Francisco: Sierra.

Larick, R., and Ciochon, R. 1996. "The African Emergence of Early Asian Dispersals of the Genus *Homo.*" *American Scientist* 84, no. 6: 538–551.

Larsen, C. 1995. "Biological Changes in Human Populations with Agriculture." *Annual Review of Anthropology* 24: 185–236.

Leak, G., and Christopher, S. 1982. "Freudian Psychoanalysis and Sociobiology." *American Psychologist* 37, no. 3: 387–395.

Lehmann, A., and Myers, J. 1993. *Magic, Witchcraft, and Religion: An Anthropological Study of the Supernatural*. Mountain View, CA: Mayfield.

Lieberman, J. 1991. *Light: Medicine of the Future*. Sante Fe, NM: Bear & Company.

Lin, E., et al. 1985. "An Exploration of Somatization Among Asian Refugees and Immigrants in Primary Care." *American Journal of Public Health* 75, no. 9: 1080–1084.

Lopez, S. 1989. "Development of Culturally Sensitive Psychotherapists." *Professional Psychotherapy: Research and Practice* 20, no. 6: 369–376.

Loriedo, C., and Vella, G. 1992. *Paradox and the Family System*. New York: Brunner/Mazel.

Lyles, M., Yancey, A., Grace, C., and Carter, J. 1985. "Racial Identity and Self-esteem: Problems Peculiar to Bi-racial Children." *Journal of American Academy of Child Psychiatry* 24: 150–153.

Macrone, M. 1992. *By Jove!* New York: Cader Books.

Majors, R., and Billson, J. 1992. *Cool Pose: The Dilemmas of Black Manhood*. New York: Touchstone.

Malgady, R., Rogler, L., and Costantino, G. 1987. "Ethnocultural and Linguistic Bias in Mental Health Evaluation of Hispanics." *American Psychologist* 42, no. 3: 228–234.

Malinowski, B. 1948. *Magic, Science, and Religion*. New York: Free Press.

Maltz, M. 1969. *Psycho-Cybernetics*. New York: Pocket Books.

Margolis, R., and Rungta, S. 1986. "Training Counselors for Work with Special Populations: A Second Look." *Journal of Counseling and Development* 64: 642–644.

Marsella, A., Sartorius, N., Jablensky, A., and Fenton, F. 1985. "Cross-Cultural Studies of Depressive Disorders: An Overview." In *Culture and Depression: Studies in the Anthropology and Cross-Cultural Psychiatry of Affect and Disorder*. Ed. A. Kleinman and B. Good. Berkeley: University of California Press.

Marwick, M. 1970. *Witchcraft and Sorcery*. Baltimore: Penguin Books.

Maslow, A. 1954. *Motivation and Human Personality*. New York: Harper & Row.

Matthews, J., ed. 1992. *The World Atlas of Divination*. Boston: Little, Brown.

Mays, V. 1985. "The Black American and Psychotherapy: The Dilemma." *Psychotherapy* 22, no. 2: 379–388.

McGue, M., Pickens, R., and Svikis, D. 1992. "Sex and Age Effects on the Inheritance of Alcohol Problems: A Twin Study." *Journal of Abnormal Psychology* 101, no. 1: 3–17.

McLennan, J. 1865. *Primitive Marriage*. London: Black.

Mendoza, R. 1989. "An Empirical Scale to Measure Type and Degree of Acculturation in Mexican-American Adolescents and Adults." *Journal of Cross-Cultural Psychology* 20: 372–385.

Middleton, J. 1967. *Magic, Witchcraft, and Curing.* Garden City, NY: The Natural History Press.

Miller, G. 1956. "The Magical Number Seven, Plus or Minus Two: Some Limits on Our Capacity for Processing Information." *Psychological Review* 63:81–97.

Mills, J., and Crowley, R. 1986. *Therapeutic Metaphors for Children and the Child Within.* New York: Brunner/Mazel.

Milton, G., Petrila, J., Poythress, N., and Slobogin, C. 1987. *Psychological Evaluations for the Courts.* New York: Guilford.

Min, P. G., ed. 1994. *Asian Americans.* Thousand Oaks, CA: Sage.

Mollica, R., Wyshak, G., and Lavelle, J. 1987. "The Psychosocial Impact of War Trauma and Torture on Southeast Asian Refugees." *American Journal of Psychiatry* 144, no. 12: 1567–1572.

Moore-Howard, P. 1982. *The Hmong—Yesterday and Today.* Lansing, MI: PAJ NTAUB/PLIA YANG.

———. 1989. *The Iu Mien: Tradition and Change.* Sacramento, CA: Board of Education, Sacramento City Unified School District.

———. 1992. *The Ethnic Lao—Who Are They?* Sacramento, CA: Board of Education, Sacramento City Unified School District.

Morgan, E. 1990. *The Scars of Evolution: What Our Bodies Tell Us About Human Origins.* New York: Oxford University Press.

Morgan, W. 1931. "Navaho Treatment of Sickness: Diagnosticians." *American Anthropologist* 33:390–402.

Morley, P., and Wallis, R., eds. 1978. *Culture and Curing: Anthropological Perspectives on Traditional Medical Beliefs and Practices.* Pittsburgh: University of Pittsburgh Press.

Murphy, J. 1964. "Psychotherapeutic Aspects of Shamanism on St. Lawrence Island, Alaska." In *Magic, Faith, and Healing.* Ed. A. Kiev, 53–83. New York: Free Press.

Neff, J. 1993. "Race/Ethnicity, Acculturation, and Psychological Distress: Fatalism and Religiosity as Cultural Resources." *Journal of Counseling Psychology* 21:3–20.

Newcomb, T. 1978. "The Acquaintance Process: Looking Mainly Backward." *Journal of Personality and Social Psychology* 36:1075–1083.

Nikelly, A. 1992. "Can *DSM-III-R* Be Used in the Diagnosis of Non-Western Patients?" *International Journal of Mental Health* 21, no. 1: 3–22.

Oler, C. 1989. "Psychotherapy with Black Clients: Racial Identity and Locus of Control." *Psychotherapy* 26, no. 2: 233–241.

Orbach, M., and Beckwith, J. 1982. "Indochinese Adaptation and Local Government Policy: An Example from Monterey." *Anthropological Quarterly* 55, no. 3: 135–145.

Ortiz, A., ed. 1983. *Handbook of North American Indians.* Vol. 10, *Southwest.* Washington, DC: Smithsonian Institution Press.

Ott, J. 1993. *Pharmacotheon: Entheogenic Drugs, Their Plant Sources and History.* Kennewick, WA: Natural Products Co.

Overfield, T. 1995. *Biologic Variation in Health and Illness: Race, Age, and Sex Differences*. Boca Raton, FL: CRC Press.

Paniagua, F. 1994. *Assessing and Treating Culturally Diverse Clients*. Thousand Oaks, CA: Sage.

Papez, J. 1937. "A Proposed Mechanism of Emotions." *Archives of Neurological Psychiatry* 38:725–743.

Parham, T., and McDavis, R. 1987. "Black Men, an Endangered Species: Who's Really Pulling the Trigger?" *Journal of Counseling and Development* 66: 24–27.

Paster, V. 1985. "Adapting Psychotherapy for the Depressed, Unacculturated, Acting-Out, Black Male Adolescent." *Psychotherapy* 22, no. 2: 408–417.

Pavkov, T., and Lyons, J. 1989. "Psychiatric Diagnosis and Racial Bias: An Empirical Investigation." *Professional Psychology: Research and Practice* 20, no. 6:364–368.

Pedersen, P. 1987. "Ten Frequent Assumptions of Cultural Bias in Counseling." *Journal of Multi-cultural Counseling and Development* 16:16–24.

Peele, S. 1989. *Diseasing of America: Addiction Treatment out of Control*. Lexington, MA: Lexington Books.

Perls, F. 1951. *Gestalt Therapy: Excitement and Growth in the Human Personality*. New York: Delta Press.

———. 1973. *The Gestalt Approach & Eyewitness to Therapy*. New York: Bantam Books.

Pfeiffer, C. 1987. *Nutrition and Mental Illness*. Rochester, NY: Healing Arts Press.

Phillips, M., and Frederick, C. 1995. *Healing the Divided Self: Clinical and Ericksonian Hypnotherapy for Post-traumatic and Dissociative Conditions*. New York: W. W. Norton.

Pinker, S. 1994. *The Language Instinct: How the Mind Creates Language*. New York: William Morrow.

PMIC. 1997. *The International Classification of Diseases*. 9th rev., Burr Ridge, IL: Context Software Systems.

Ponterotto, J. 1987. "Counseling Mexican Americans: A Multimodal Approach." *Journal of Counseling and Development* 65:308–312.

Preston, M. 1998. *Hypnosis: Medicine of the Mind*. Mesa, AZ: Blue Bird Publishing.

Ramirez, M. 1984. "Assessing and Understanding Biculturalism-Multiculturalism in Mexican-American Adults." In *Chicano Psychology*. Ed. J. Martinez and R. Mendoza. Orlando, FL: Academic Press.

———. 1991. *Psychotherapy and Counseling with Minorities*. New York: Pergamon Press.

Rasmussen, K. 1908. *The People of the Polar North*. Philadelphia: J. B. Lippincott.

Reed, W., ed. 1993. *Research on the African-American Family: A Holistic Approach*. Westport, CT: Greenwood Press.

Robbins, J. 1996. *Reclaiming Our Health: Exploding the Medical Myth and Embracing the Source of True Healing*. Tiburon, CA: H. J. Kramer.

Roheim, G. 1950. *Psychoanalysis and Anthropology*. New York: International University Press.

Root, M. 1985. "Guidelines for Facilitating Therapy with Asian American Clients." *Psychotherapy* 22, no. 2: 349–356.

Rosen, S., ed. 1982. *My Voice Will Go with You: The Teaching Tales of Milton H. Erickson.* New York: W. W. Norton.

Rosenberg, K., and Trevathan, W. 1995/1996. "Bipedalism and Human Birth: The Obstetrical Dilemma Revisited." *Evolutionary Anthropology* 4, no. 5: 160–168.

Ross, C., and Pam, A. 1995. *Pseudoscience in Biological Psychiatry: Blaming the Body.* New York: John Wiley & Sons.

Rossi, E. 1993. *The Psychobiology of Mind-Body Healing: New Concepts in Therapeutic Hypnosis.* New York: W. W. Norton.

———, ed. 1980. *The Collected Work of Milton H. Erickson.* 4 vols. New York: Irvington.

Rossi, E., and Cheek, D. 1988. *Mind-Body Therapy: Methods of Ideodynamic Healing in Hypnosis.* New York: W. W. Norton.

Rossi, E., and Ryan, M., eds. 1985. *Life Reframing in Hypnosis by Milton H. Erickson: The Seminars, Workshops, and Lectures of Milton H. Erickson.* Vol. 2. New York: Irvington.

———. 1986. *Mind-Body Communication in Hypnosis by Milton H. Erickson: The Seminars, Workshops, and Lectures of Milton H. Erickson.* Vol. 3. New York: Irvington.

Rossi, E., Ryan, M., and Sharp, F., eds. 1983. *Healing in Hypnosis by Milton H. Erickson: The Seminars, Workshops, and Lectures of Milton H. Erickson.* Vol. 1. New York: Irvington.

Rubel, A., O'Nell, C. and Collado-Ardon, R. 1991. *Susto: A Folk Illness.* Berkeley: University of California Press.

Ruesch, J. 1972. *Disturbed Communication.* New York: W. W. Norton.

———. 1973. *Therapeutic Communication: A Descriptive Guide to the Communication Process as the Central Agent in Mental Healing.* New York: W. W. Norton.

Ruesch, J., and Bateson, G. 1968. *Communication: The Social Matrix of Psychiatry.* New York: W. W. Norton.

Rush, J. 1974. *Witchcraft and Sorcery: An Anthropological Perspective of the Occult.* Springfield, IL: Charles C. Thomas.

———. 1976. *The Way We Communicate.* 2nd ed. Shelburne Falls, MA: Humanity Publications.

———. 1978. *Communication Skills Training Manual.* Shelburne Falls, MA: Humanity Publications.

———. 1990 (1st ed. 1988). *Managing Aggressive/Violent Behavior.* Workbook prepared for the California State Board of Corrections, STC Program. Orangevale, CA: Humanity Publications.

———. 1992a (1st ed. 1987). *Evaluation of Dangerous Behavior.* Workbook prepared for the California State Board of Corrections, STC Program. Orangevale, CA: Humanity Publications.

———. 1992b. *Listening: Purpose and Process.* Workbook prepared for the California State Board of Corrections, STC Program. Orangevale, CA: Humanity Publications.

———. 1993a (1st ed. 1987). *Approaches to Stress Management.* Workbook prepared for the California State Board of Corrections, STC Program. Orangevale, CA: Humanity Publications.

————. 1993b. *Techniques in Crisis Counseling*. Workbook prepared for the California State Board of Corrections, STC Program. Orangevale, CA: Humanity Publications.

————. 1994. "Curing and Crisis in an Italian Kindred: The Adaptive Role of the *Fattucchiera*." Ph.D. dissertation, Columbia Pacific University. Ann Arbor: U.M.I. Dissertation Services.

————. 1995a (1st ed. 1990). *Evaluating and Communicating with the Violent Juvenile*. Workbook prepared for the California State Board of Corrections, STC Program. Orangevale, CA: Humanity Publications.

————. 1995b (1st ed. 1992). *Dealing with Lies and Denial*. Workbook prepared for the California State Board of Corrections, STC Program. Orangevale, CA: Humanity Publications.

————. 1995c (1st ed. 1993). *Process in Cultural Sensitivity: An Anthropological Perspective of Cross-Cultural Conflict*. Workbook prepared for the California State Board of Corrections, STC Program. Orangevale, CA: Humanity Publications.

————. 1995d (1st ed. 1987). *Communicating with the Juvenile Offender*. Workbook prepared for the California State Board of Corrections, STC Program. Orangevale, CA: Humanity Publications.

————. 1996. *Clinical Anthropology: An Application of Anthropological Concepts Within Clinical Settings*. Westport, CT: Praeger.

————. (in preparation). *The Holistic Health Practitioner: Clinical Anthropology and the Return to Traditional Medicine*.

Salar, B. 1964. "Nagual, Witch, and Sorcerer in a Quiche Village." *Ethnology* 3: 305–328.

Sapir, E. 1966. *Culture, Language and Personality*. Berkeley: University of California Press.

Schauss, A. 1985. *Nutrition and Behavior*. New Canaan, CT: Keats Publishing.

Schoenthaler, S. 1991. "Applied Nutrition and Behavior." *Journal of Applied Nutrition* 43, no. 1:131–150.

Schoenthaler, S., and Amos, S. 1992. *A Controlled Trial of Vitamin-Mineral Supplementation Within the California Youth Authority: The Effect on Institutional Violence and Antisocial Behavior as Well as Non-verbal Intelligence*. Report Prepared for Senator Robert Presley, the Office of Senate Research, the California Senate Research Oversight Committee, and the California Youth Authority.

Scott, G. 1982. "The Hmong Refugee Community in San Diego: Theoretical and Practical Implications of Its Continuing Ethnic Solidarity." *Anthropological Quarterly* 55, no. 3:146–160.

Selye, H. 1956. *The Stress of Life*. New York: McGraw-Hill.

Sissa, G. 1994. "Interpreting the Implicit: George Devereux and Greek Myths." In *Anthropology and Psychoanalysis: An Encounter Through Culture*. Ed. S. Heald and A. Deluz. New York: Routledge.

Snowden, L., and Cheung, F. 1990. "Use of Inpatient Mental Health Services by Members of Ethnic Minority Groups." *American Psychologist* 45, no. 3:347–355.

Springer, S., and Deutsch, G. 1989. *Left Brain, Right Brain*. San Francisco: W. H. Freeman.

Stanley, S. 1996. *Children of the Ice Age*. New York: Harmony Books.

Stein, H. 1987. *Developmental Time, Cultural Space*. Norman: University of Oklahoma Press.

Stinson, S. 1992. "Nutritional Adaptation." *Annual Review of Anthropology* 21: 143–170.

Sue, D., and Sue, D. 1990. *Counseling the Culturally Different: Theory and Practice*. New York: John Wiley & Sons.

Sulloway, F. 1979. *Freud: Biologist of the Mind*. New York: Basic Books.

Szasz, T. 1972. *The Myth of Mental Illness*. Frogmore St. Albans, UK: Paladin Press.

———. 1977. *The Manufacture of Madness: A Comparative Study of the Inquisition and the Mental Health Movement*. New York: Harper & Row.

———. 1994. *Cruel Compassion: Psychiatric Control of Society's Unwanted*. New York: John Wiley & Sons.

Szent-Gyorgyi, A. 1960. *Introduction to a Submolecular Biology*. New York: Academic Press.

———. 1968. *Bioelectronics*. New York: Academic Press.

Teicher, J. 1968. "Some Observations on Identity Problems in Children of Negro-White Marriages." *Journal of Nervous and Mental Disorders* 146:249–256.

Thomas, M., and Dansby, P. 1985. "Black Clients: Family Structures, Therapeutic Issues, and Strengths." *Psychotherapy* 22, no. 2:398–407.

Tobin, J., and Friedman, M. 1983. "Spirits, Shamans, and Nightmare Death: Survivor Stress in a Hmong Refugee." *American Journal of Orthopsychiatry* 3, no. 3:439–448.

Tracey, T., Leong, F., and Glidden, C. 1986. "Help Seeking and Problem Perception Among Asian Americans." *Journal of Counseling Psychology* 33, no. 3:331–336.

Tsui, A. 1985. "Psychotherapeutic Considerations in Sexual Counseling for Asian Immigrants." *Psychotherapy* 22, no. 2:357–362.

Tsui, P., and Schultz, G. 1985. "Failure of Rapport: Why Psychotherapeutic Engagement Fails in the Treatment of Asian Clients." *American Journal of Orthopsychiatry* 55, no. 4:561–569.

Van der Veer, G. 1992. *Counseling and Therapy with Refugees*. New York: John Wiley & Sons.

Van Praag, H. 1993. *"Make-Believes" in Psychiatry or The Perils of Progress*. New York: Brunner/Mazel.

Vargas, L., and Koss-Chioino, J., eds. 1992. *Working with Culture: Psychotherapeutic Interventions with Ethnic Minority Children, and Adolescents*. San Francisco: Jossey-Boss.

Vyse, S. 1997. *Believing in Magic: The Psychology of Superstition*. New York: Oxford University Press.

Wallas, L. 1985. *Stories for the Third Ear: Using Hypnotic Fables in Psychotherapy*. New York: W. W. Norton.

———. 1991. *Stories That Heal*. New York: W. W. Norton.

Watson, C., and Ellen, R. eds. 1993. *Understanding Witchcraft and Sorcery in Southeast Asia*. Honolulu: University of Hawaii Press.

Watzlawick, P. 1978. *The Language of Change: Elements of Therapeutic Communication*. New York: Basic Books.

————. 1990. *Munchhausen's Pigtail or Psychotherapy & "Reality."* New York: W. W. Norton.

Weitzenhoffer, A. 1989. *The Practice of Hypnotism.* Vol. 1, *Traditional and Semi-Traditional Techniques and Phenomenology.* New York: John Wiley & Sons.

Werbach, M. 1991. *Nutritional Influences on Mental Illness: A Sourcebook of Clinical Research.* Tarzana, CA: Third Line Press.

Westermeyer, J. 1993. "Cross-Cultural Psychiatric Assessment." In *Culture, Ethnicity, and Mental Illness.* Ed. A. Gaw. Washington, DC: American Psychiatric Association Press.

Westermeyer, J., and Zimmerman, R. 1981. "Lao Folk Diagnosis for Mental Disorder: Comparison with Psychiatric Diagnosis and Assessment with Psychiatric Rating Scales." *Medical Anthropology* 5, no. 4:425–443.

Whorf, B. 1967. *Language, Thought & Reality.* Cambridge, MA: M.I.T. Press.

Wirth, D. 1990. "The Effect of Non-Contact Therapeutic Touch on Healing Rate of Full Thickness Dermal Wounds." *Subtle Energies* 1, no. 1:1–5.

Wright, R. 1994. *The Moral Animal.* New York: Pantheon.

Zeig, J., ed. 1985. *Ericksonian Psychotherapy.* 2 vols. New York: Brunner/Mazel.

Index

About the Author

JOHN A. RUSH is Adjunct Professor of Anthropology at Sierra College in Rocklin, California, and is a Clinical Anthropologist Naturopathic Physician and Certified Medical Hynotherapist. He is the author of *Clinical Anthropology* (Praeger, 1996).

ISBN 0-86569-290-4

90000>

EAN

9 780865 692909

HARDCOVER BAR CODE